e-Video

Producing Internet Video as
Broadband Technologies Converge

H. Peter Alesso

ADDISON-WESLEY

Boston • San Francisco • New York • Toronto • Montreal
London • Munich • Paris • Madrid
Cape Town • Sydney • Tokyo • Singapore • Mexico City

Many of the designations used by manufacturers and sellers to distinguish their products are claimed as trademarks. Where those designations appear in this book, and Addison-Wesley was aware of a trademark claim, the designations have been printed with an initial capital letter or in all capitals.

The author and publisher have taken care in the preparation of this book, but make no expressed or implied warranty of any kind and assume no responsibility for errors or omissions. No liability is assumed for incidental or consequential damages in connection with or arising out of the use of the information or programs contained herein.

The publisher offers discounts on this book when ordered in quantity for special sales.
For more information, please contact:

Pearson Education Corporate Sales Division
One Lake Street
Upper Saddle River, NJ 07458
(800) 382-3419
corpsales@pearsontechgroup.com

Visit us on the web: www.awl.com/cseng/

Library of Congress Cataloging-in-Publication Data

Alesso, H. Peter
   e-Video : producing Internet video as broadband technologies converge / H. Peter Alesso.
      p. cm.
   Includes bibliographical references and index.
   ISBN 0-201-70314-9
   1. Internet television. I. Title.

TK5105.887 .A44 2000
006.7'876--dc21   00-038999

ISBN 0-201-70314-9
Text printed on recycled paper.
1 2 3 4 5 6 7 8 9—CRS—04 03 02 01 00
First printing, July 2000

*To my kind and devoted wife Chris for her support
and helpful insights.*

Acknowledgments

Thanks to Theres-Marie Rhyne, Paulo de Andrade, Mitchel Ahern, Michael Callery, and Chuck Fuller for their helpful review comments and suggestions.

Special Thanks to Dr. Craig F. Smith and Doug Vogt for their continuing suggestions, attention to detail, and words of encouragement.

Thanks and appreciation to Mary O'Brien, Mariann Kourafas, and the production team at Addison Wesley for their invaluable editorial support and professionalism.

Contents

List of Acronyms

A

AAL: ATM adaptation layer
ABR: asynchronous bit rate
ADM: add/drop multiplexer
ADSL: asymmetric digital subscriber line
AON: All-Optical Network
AN: access node
ANS: advanced network and services
ANSI: American National Standards Institute
ASF: active streaming format
ASM: adaptive stream management
ATM: asynchronous transfer mode

B

BER: bit rate error
BSS: broadcast satellite service

C

CATV: coaxial cable television or community antenna television
CBDS: constant bit rate data service
CMISE: common management information service elements

COM: Component Object Model
CSMA/CD: carrier sense multiple-access high collision detection

D

DBS: direct broadcast satellite
DCC: data communication channel
DSP: digital signal processors
DTP: data transport protocol
DWDM: dense wave division multiplexing

E

EDFA: Erbium-Doped Fiber Amplifier

F

FDDI: fiber distributed data interface
FDM: frequency division multiplexing
FTP: file transfer protocol
FTTH: fiber to the home

G

GAN: global area network

H

HDSL: high bit-rate digital subscriber line

HDTV: high definition television

HTML: HyperText Markup Language

I

IP: Internet Protocol

ISDN: integrated services digital network

ISO: International Organization for Standardization

ISP: Internet service provider

ITU: International Telecommunications Union

J

JPEG: Joint Photographic Committee Group

L

LAN: local area network

M

MAN: metropolitan area network

MPEG: Motion Picture Experts Group

MIDI: Musical Instrument Digital Interface

MIME: multipurpose Internet mail extensions

N

NMA: Network Monitoring and Analysis

O

OADM: optical add/drop multiplexer

OC: Optical Carrier

OS: operating system

OXC: Optical Cross-Connect

P

PHY: physical layer protocol

PTM: packet transfer mode

Q

QoS: Quality of Service

R

RBOCs: regional Bell operating companies

RMA: RealMedia Architecture

RMFF: RealMedia File Format

RSVP: Real-Time Reservation Protocol

RTP: Real-Time Protocol

RTSP: Real-Time Streaming Protocol

RTP: Real-Time Transport Protocol

RTSP: Real-Time Streaming Protocol

S

SMIL: Synchronized Multimedia Integration Language

SDH: synchronous digital hierarchy

SMDS: Switched Multimegabit Data Service

SONET: Synchronous Optical Network

T

Tbps: Terabit per second (1 trillion bits per second)

TDM: time-division multiplexing

TCP: Transmission Control Protocol

U

URL:	uniform resource locator
UDP:	User Datagram Protocol
UTP:	unshielded twisted pair

V

VDSL:	very high speed digital subscriber line
VOD:	video on demand

W

WAN:	wide area network
WWW:	World Wide Web

X

x-DSL:	x-digital subscriber line
XML:	Extensible Markup Language

List of Figures

List of Tables

Introduction

Overview

If you can recall the special effects from *Star Wars*, then you can already appreciate the impact of video. ▶

S omeday, when you go on-line to make a purchase, you'll see a video demonstration of the product in action. If it needs assembly, instead of piecing it together from a single sheet of indecipherable instructions, you'll go back on-line for step-by-step video instructions. And you'll be able to ask questions and receive answers in real-time.

Someday, you will attend school classes only if you want to because much of your education and training will be available on Web video.

Someday, video will be everywhere. Someday. But not today!

Today the delivery bandwidth just isn't there yet. But, don't be concerned. Broadband technologies are converging at breakneck speed, and higher quality video is on the way. But what will you do in the meantime?

If you knew just how TV, phone, and cable broadband technologies were converging, couldn't you make better multimedia choices? For example, have you ever tried to add a video product demo to your Web site, only to be frustrated by hardware and software incompatibilities? Are you trying to start a video Web-based business, but find yourself thwarted by server and network limitations? Have you found your video application software development plans stymied by the chaos of technology standards?

Good news! This book offers powerful insights into the synergism between producing Internet video and technology convergence. This book will enable you to make the most knowledgeable investments in hardware and software to produce Web video and anticipate future trends. It provides the necessary How-To information for putting video on your business Web site today, without the hazard of imminent obsolescence.

So, if you need to make the best decisions today to prepare for that someday, this book is for you.

▶ Background

When Thomas Alva Edison invented the phonograph in 1877, he gave us the freedom to select and play music in our own home at our own convenience. It took another century until the VCR became widely available and we gained the ability to similarly select and play videos. But Edison's contribution wasn't just the invention of the phonograph, or the lightbulb, or even the 1,093 inventions for which he received a patent. He helped found an industry, the industry of electric power and analog appliances that transformed the twentieth century in both the home and the factory.

Now another industrial transformation is underway, the digital revolution. It can be traced to Tim Berners-Lee's creation of the graphical interface, which allowed the

Internet to become a popular communication tool. As a result, within only six years the Internet had reached 80 million users. This is astonishing compared to past communication media successes.

The Internet had existed for decades mostly for scientific workers and the military. When in 1989, while working at the European Particle Physics Laboratory (CERN) in Geneva, Berners-Lee proposed a global hypertext system he called the *World Wide Web*. It could link more than just text—it could link graphics, sound, and video to create an entire hypermedia system. Instead of a single database, the basis for his World Wide Web would be the Internet, the vast network of networks around the world.

Over the next couple of years, Berners-Lee and his collaborators laid the groundwork for the Web, inventing and refining the HyperText Transfer Protocol (HTTP) for linking Web documents, the Hypertext Markup Language (HTML) for formatting Web documents, and the Universal Resource Locator (URL) system for addressing Web documents. These days, most of us reach the Web through commercial browsers, such as Netscape Navigator or Internet Explorer.

The first contact most Internet users had with streaming data started with Progressive Network's RealAudio releasing its RealAudio Server and client programs. RealAudio started playing as soon as the user chose a selection. It was a cross-platform program that could be played from Windows, Unix, and Mac systems.

The first true streaming videos ran during 1994 over the experimental Mbone (Multicast Backbone) network. This protocol is a form of Internet Protocol (IP) multicasting, which replicates streaming videos to thousands of servers. Access to these events was initially confined to users with high-end Sun workstations. The primary media server distributed its signal to other repeater servers on the network.

Streaming media started with the Internet's first streaming player, RealAudio. In April 1995, it allowed listeners to hear audio as it was being downloaded. The first Internet streaming video player was Xing Technologies' StreamWorks, released in August 1995. It was based upon Motion Picture Expert Group (MPEG) compression and provided jerky "talking heads" images the size of a postage stamp. This was followed shortly by VDOLive from VDOnet Corp. In early 1997 Progressive Networks, renamed RealNetworks, released RealVideo along with an all-in-one audio-video player called RealPlayer.

As the use of streaming media has increased, competition for customers in the streaming media market has intensified. While RealNetworks has emerged as the clear leader as of 1999, rapid changes in compression-decompression (codec) standards offers many new challengers. Increasingly, however, the question is asked, How do Microsoft's Windows Media and other formats stack up against the RealNetworks?

Microsoft entered into the streaming video market in 1997 with its buyout of WebTV Networks and Vxtreme. Microsoft introduced its Active Streaming Format (ASF) in conjunction with the developing MPEG-4 standard. This protocol provides a standard method of synchronizing audio, video, and multimedia. Competition between ASF and RealNetworks' G2 emerged in 1999, as the World Wide Web Consortium (W3C) endorsed Synchronized Multimedia Integration Language (SMIL). SMIL provides a text-based tag markup format for streaming multimedia, freeing developers from proprietary formats and enabling multiple vendors to supply software tools. Other groups developed open standards with Java-based applets that didn't require preinstalled players in order to stream video.

Macromedia's Shockwave and Flash protocols first produced streaming animation. Authoring platforms for real-time delivery of animation during streaming videos have become available. They allow multimedia-style animation and interactive controls to be linked with broadcast-style audio and video.

Regardless of which vendor you choose, the equipment and software used in multimedia production is often on the cutting edge and not as fully developed as products in the more established computer desktop applications. As a result, there are often compatibility issues that must be resolved in making a set of software and hardware choices to complement your production system.

The actual making of the multimedia content involves the following five basic steps:

1. Preparing the content source material

2. Capturing the audio/video using a computer with a video capture card

3. Editing the video and saving the large uncompressed file

4. Compressing the video

5. Delivering the movie content over the Web

Each of these steps can be optimized toward improving the final client video. For example, optimizing computer capture hardware requires a balanced understanding of data-flow versus choke points within the PC capture process. A high speed Pentium III, with 256MB RAM, an 8.4GB (8 millisecond) hard drive, and wide-SCSI-3 bus can demonstrate up to 40Mbps throughput while capturing video. Unfortunately, many low-to-medium-priced capture cards provide a throughput of only 2 to 5Mbps (even after optimal configuration), producing a limiting choke point in your systems.

But even after heroic efforts on your part in optimizing the source video, the hardware and software, and the editing and compression process, there remains a significant barrier to delivering your video over the Web. This is the "last mile" connection to the client.

The Bandwidth Problem

The bandwidth of Internet communications has been steadily increasing due to the overall pressures to improve performance from users. The important point is that the infrastructure provided by the Internet has become widespread and has developed enough performance to allow rapid transmission of large volumes of data. Now it is becoming ready for video.

The problem with video, however, has been trying to push it over digital networks where it clogs and chokes the critical connections. The arrival of data compression has reduced the problem of transmitting video data to more manageable levels. The technology has only recently reached the point where video can be digitized and compressed to levels that allow reasonable quality of appearance following distribution over digital networks.

The Bandwidth Solution

Yogi Berra once said, "Predictions can be tricky, especially when you're talking about the future." And looking forward is certainly more perilous than using hindsight to review history. However, the future of rapidly converging technology is not so complex and uncertain that a few reasonable predictions about certain aspects of streaming video as well as the future of the Internet can't be discerned.

Electronic Video, or "e-Video," includes all audio/video clips that are distributed and played over the Internet, either by direct download or streaming video. And it is streaming video that is the nexus of technology convergence because it is the improvement in bandwidth to deliver video that will prove decisive in reconciling competing technology standards. As this last stumbling block of bandwidth limitation is finally overcome, the television, cable, data, and telecommunication technologies will converge toward a compatible and coherent industry standard based on a one-to-one customized Internet commerce model.

Up to this point, video has involved moving very large files (3–40Mbps), and delivering such large data rates on the Internet seemed prohibitive. Consider that to expand the Internet bandwidth a factor of 10 times its current backbone would cost additional billions of dollars for construction of fiber, copper, or satellite equipment. Now consider the relatively small cost of an equivalent expansion of bandwidth improvement produced by software changes in data compression or by equipment upgrades, such as, optical multiplexing.

The ideal vision for broadband may be an end-to-end optical fiber network with fiber direct to the home. But this expensive and long-term option may be preempted by a combination of a near term breakthrough in compression technology and/or less expensive optical wave division multiplexing. Obviously, the data compression of streaming video compression-decompression (codec) standards will play a critical role in the form of required bandwidth reduction. This in turn will contribute to technology convergence.

In this book, we show that the bandwidth problem is really two interrelated problems. The backbone network problem and the "last mile" problem, each of which will be addressed according to their ability to deliver video.

How This Book Is Organized

The technology revolution sweeping the world today is creating unparalleled opportunity. One area dramatically poised to take advantage of this new technology is video. In Part I of this book, Video Opportunity, we provide the background for the emerging broadband technologies (Chapter 1) and economic opportunities (Chapter 2).

In Chapter 1 we start by asking, Just why are analog technologies for data, voice, and video being replaced by digital technologies? Chapter 1 defines and compares analog and digital communication technologies as they are currently competing and describes the advantages digital has over analog. It includes a big-picture view of the spectrum of bandwidth requirements for video delivery—from low-end broadband (1.5Mbps) to the ultimate HDTV at 38Mbps.

Chapter 2 presents the e-commerce opportunities emerging from streaming video. What does multimedia Internet technology offer to business that makes it attractive? We will illustrate how multimedia e-commerce will lead the business-to-business, business-to-customer, on-line education and entertainment industries and which of these will become the "killer-application" for streaming video that will power technology convergence.

Included with this book is a CD-ROM with an example directory called How To, which contains a sequential series of examples to guide you through the Internet video production process. The production process follows the chapters of the book. An HTML Web page is provided that connects to a general link page. Here the links to various software vendors offering player, editing, compression, and server software are provided.

In Part II, the video preparation and production process is explained. Chapter 3 portrays the video production, editing, and management that bring together the components necessary to develop Web video. This chapter will help you understand the desktop video production cycle and the roles of various software tools for developing differing content. This chapter begins the description of the How To example included on the CD-ROM as it progresses through the various stages described in the book.

In Part III, we present video compression. Data compression algorithms are in their early stage of development. By presenting the basics of how data are compressed in Chapter 4, an appreciation of how much more is yet to come can be obtained. Chapter 4 highlights the key elements of data compression as a form in reduction of bandwidth. It reviews streaming video (codec) standards and state-of-the-art advances. In addition, it sets the stage for understanding codec standards from narrowband to broadband.

Then, in Chapters 5 and 6, narrowband streaming video compression technology is detailed with How To examples. Chapter 5 presents an overview of the RealVideo software tools and player. In this chapter, RealVideo software and SMIL applications are presented and detailed examples are provided. The code and video demos for the examples are available both on the enclosed CD-ROM and on our associated Web site (www.video-software.com). This chapter begins the description of the conversion of the How To example included on the CD-ROM into streaming format.

Then, in Chapter 6, software from Microsoft, Apple, and other formats are presented along with examples. The code and video demos for the examples are available both on the enclosed CD-ROM and on our associated Web site. Chapter 6 presents an overview of Microsoft software tools and player. It concludes with a direct comparison of all media production software technologies.

Chapter 7 moves streaming compression to the next stage, MPEG streaming, which is preparing for low-end broadband (1.5Mbps) delivery within a very few years. The chapter highlights several of the key MPEG software developers and their products.

In Part IV, we present video delivery over the Internet. The networks and servers supporting Internet video are critical in delivering high performance and quality for the viewing experience and are an integral part of the Webcasting production process.

In Chapter 8, the difficult but important aspects of networking connectivity are outlined. When it comes to networks, how fast is fast enough? We conclude that it is always just a little more than anyone ever gets. How is data transmitted and controlled over the Internet? The transition from electronic routers and switches to optical nodes is as powerful a paradigm shift as analog to digital.

Chapter 9, the problems with video servers as related to protocols and the delivery of streaming video to the networks are presented. The innovations in developing network caching and data storage on the Internet are highlighted.

Chapter 10 presents live streaming applications. This presents the convergence of traditional broadband video with the digital-targeted audience approach.

We begin this book by stating that there is video opportunity through technology convergence. In each succeeding chapter, the elements of streaming video are presented along with their particular impact on technology convergence. The goal is to show how to use streaming video as it forms the nexus of technology convergence.

In Chapter 11, we conclude with some basic truths that have already begun to emerge from convergence. Our crystal ball will reveal how transmission of TV quality video over the Internet through improved compression algorithms will prove cost-effective in producing rich media at improved effective bandwidths. Our picture melds the technological issues and standards into a narrowing focus centered on streaming video with the initial impetus provided by product demos in order for e-commerce business to meet customer demands.

In the Appendices, some essential aspects of standards for TV, cable, wireless, telecommunications, Internet, compression, and markup languages are individually summarized.

◄❿ Who Should Read This Book

Web designers and developers with a background in HTML will be primarily attracted to this book. But in general, many Web businesses will find the necessary how-to information and simple examples for providing Web video today, without the hazard of imminent obsolescence.

Entrepreneurs, video hobbyists, and Web site enthusiasts will also find valuable insights and how-to examples to inspire their own video Web business. Business opportunities include video capture, editing, compressing, hosting, Webcasting, custom software, and consulting.

For broadcasters, producers, and content providers interested in preparing to take advantage of broadband, there is information necessary to adapt their skills to Webcasting opportunities.

Computer science educators and students looking for the "big picture" for Web video will find this book a good reference.

◄❿ Associated Resources

In order to get the full value from this book, it is important for readers to see and hear streaming video and the Web for themselves, as well as explore the most advanced research projects in this field. To support this goal we suggest you visit our Web site:

http://www.video-software.com

The Web site provides download links for *free* video players from all the major developers (RealNetworks, Microsoft, Apple, Emblaze, Bitcasting, LZX-MPEG), as well as video encoding tools, editing tools, and server software.

A CD-ROM with example code and streaming video demos is included at the back cover of this book.

Video
Opportunity

The technology revolution sweeping the world today is creating unparalleled opportunity. One area dramatically poised to take advantage of converging broadband technology is video. In Part I of this book, we provide the background for the emerging technology delivering video (Chapter 1) and economic opportunities for exploiting video (Chapter 2).

Bandwidth for Video

Electronic-Video, or "e-Video," includes all audio/video clips that are distributed and played over the Internet, either by direct download or streaming video. The problem with video, however, has been its inability to travel over networks without clogging the lines. If you've ever tried to deliver video, you know that even after heroic efforts on your part (including optimizing the source video, the hardware, the software, the editing, and the compression process), there remains a significant barrier to delivering your video over the Web. That is the "last mile" connection to the client.

So before we explain the details of how to produce, capture, edit, and compress video for the Web, we had better begin by describing the technology innovations overcoming the current bandwidth limitations of delivering video over the Internet. ▶

In this chapter, we will describe how expanding broadband fiber networks will reach out over the last mile to homes and businesses creating opportunities for video delivery. In order to accomplish this, we will start by quantifying three essential concerns:

1. The file size requirements for sending video data over the Internet

2. The network fiber capacity of the Internet in the near future and

3. The progress of narrowband (28.8Kbps) to broadband (1.5 Mbps) capabilities over the last mile

This will provide an understanding of the difficulties being overcome in transforming video from the current limited narrowband streaming video to broadband video delivery.

Transitioning from Analog to Digital Technology

Thomas Alva Edison's contributions to the telegraph, phonograph, telephone, motion pictures, and radio helped transform the twentieth century with analog appliances in the home and the factory. Many of Edison's contributions were based on the continuous electrical analog signal.

Today, Edison's analog appliances are being replaced by digital ones. Why? Let's begin by comparing the basic analog and digital characteristics.

Analog signals move along wires as electromagnetic waves. The signal's frequency refers to the number of times per second that a wave oscillates in a complete cycle. The higher the speed, or frequency, the more cycles of a wave are completed in a given period of time. A baud rate is one analog electric cycle or wave per second. Frequency is also stated in hertz (Hz). (Kilohertz or kHz represents 1000Hz, MHz represents 1,000,000Hz and GHz represents a billionHz).

Analog signals, such as voice, radio, and TV, involve oscillations within specified ranges of frequency. For example:

- Voice has a range of 300Hz to 3300Hz.
- Analog cable TV has a range of 54MHz to 750MHz.
- Analog microwave towers have a range of 2GHz to 12GHz.

Sending a signal along analog wires is similar to sending water through a pipe. The further it travels the more force it loses and the weaker it becomes. It can also pick up vibrations, or noise, which introduces signal errors.

Today, analog technology has become available worldwide through the following transmission media:

1. Copper wire for telephone (one-to-one communication)

2. Broadcast for radio and television (one-to-many communication)

3. Cable for television (one-to-many communication)

Most forms of analog content, from news to entertainment, have been distributed over one or more of these methods. Analog technology prior to 1990 was based primarily on the one-to-many distribution system, as shown in Table 1-1 below, where information was primarily directed toward individuals from a central point.

Prior to 1990, over 99 percent of businesses and homes in the United States had content reach them from any one of the three transmission delivery systems. Only the telephone allowed two-way communication, however. While the other analog systems were reasonably efficient in delivering content, the client could send feedback, or pay bills, through ordinary postal mail only. Obviously, the interactivity level of this system was very low.

The technology used in coaxial cable TV (CATV) is designed for the transport of video signals. It is comprised of three systems: AM, FM, and digital. Since the current CATV system with coaxial analog technology is highly limited in bandwidth, new technology is necessary for applications requiring higher bandwidth. In the digital system, a CATV network will get better performance than AM/FM systems and ease the migration from coaxial to a fiber-based system. Fiber optics in CATV networks will eliminate most bottlenecks and increase channel capacity for high-speed networks.

Analog signals are a continuous variable waveform that are information intensive. They require considerable bandwidth and care in transmission. Analog transmissions over phone lines have some inherent problems when used for sending data. Analog signals lose their strength over long distances and often need to be amplified. Signal processing introduces distortions and become amplified, raising the possibility of errors.

In contrast to the waveform of analog signals, digital signals are transmitted over wire connections by varying the voltage across the line between a high and a low state. Typically, a high voltage level represents a binary digit 1 and a low voltage level represents a binary digit 0. Because they are binary, digital signals are inherently less complex than analog

Table 1-1   **Analog Communication Prior to 1990**

| Content | Type | Analog Delivery | |
		Communication Direction	Number of Participants
Person to person	Copper wire	Two-way	One-to-one
Information and entertainment	Coax Cable (CATV) Broadcast	One-way One-way	One-to-many One-to-many

signals and over long distances they are more reliable. If a digital signal needs to be boosted, the signal is simply regenerated rather than being amplified.

As a result, digital signals have the following advantages over analog:

- Superior quality
- Fewer errors
- Higher transmission speeds
- Less complex equipment

The excitement over converting analog to digital media is, therefore, easy to explain. It is motivated by cost-effective higher quality digital processing for data, voice, and video information.

In transitioning from analog to digital technologies, however, several significant changes are also profoundly altering broadcast radio and television. This transition introduces fundamental changes from one-way broadcast to two-way transmission—and thereby the potential for interactivity—and scheduling of programming to suit the user's needs.

Not only is there an analog to digital shift, but a synchronous to asynchronous shift as well. Television and radio no longer need to be synchronous and simultaneous. Rather the viewer and listener can control the time of performance.

In addition, transmission can be one of three media: copper wire, cable, or wireless. Also, the receiver is transitioning from a dumb device, such as the television, to an intelligent set-top box with significant CPU power. This potentially changes the viewer from a passive to an interactive participant.

Today, both analog and digital video technologies coexist in the production and creative part of the process leading up to the point where video is broadcast.

Currently, businesses and homes can receive content from one to six delivery systems:

analog:
- Copper wire (telephones)
- Coaxial cable (TV cable)
- Broadcast (TV or radio)

digital:
- Copper wire (modem, DSL)
- Ethernet modem
- Wireless (satellite)

At the present time, analog systems still dominate, but digital systems are competing very favorably as infrastructure becomes available. Analog/digital telephone and digital cable allow two-way communication, and these technologies are rapidly growing. The digital systems are far more efficient and allow greater interactivity with the client.

Competing Technologies

The race is on as cable, data, wireless, and telecommunications companies are scrambling to piece together the broadband puzzle and to compete in future markets. The basic infrastructure of copper wire, cable and satellite, as well as the packaged contents are in place to deliver bigger, richer data files and media types.

In special cases, data transmission over the developing computer networks within corporations and between universities already exists. Groups vying to dominate have each brought different technologies and standards to the table. For the logical convergence of hardware, software, and networking technology to occur, the interface of these industries must meet specific interoperational capabilities and must achieve customer expectations for quality of service.

Long distance and local regional Bell operating companies (RBOC) telephone companies started with the phone system designed for point-to-point communication, POTS (plain old telephones) and have evolved into a large switched, distributed network capable of handling millions of simultaneous calls. They track and bill accordingly with an impressive performance record. They have delivered 99.999 percent reliability with high quality audio. Their technology is now evolving toward DSL (digital subscriber line) modems.

AT&T has made significant progress in leading broadband technology development now that it has added the vast cable networks of Tele-Communications Inc. and MediaOne Group to telephone and cellular. Currently, with about 45 percent of the market, AT&T can plug into more U.S. households than any other provider. But other telecommunications companies, such as Sprint and MCI, as well as the regional Bell operating companies, are also capable of integrating broadband technology with their voice services.

Although both routing and architecture of the telephone network has evolved since the AT&T divestiture, the basics remain the same. About 25,000 central offices in the United States connect through 1,200 intermediate switching nodes, called *access tandems*. The switching centers are connected by trunks designed to carry multiple voice frequency circuits using frequency division multiplexing (FDM), synchronous time-division multiplexing (TDM), or wavelength division multiplexing (WDM) for optics.

The cable companies Time Warner, Comcast, Cox Communications, and Charter Communications have 60 million homes wired with coaxial cable, primarily one-way cable, offering one-to-many broadcast service. Their technology competes through the introduction of cable modems and the upgrade of their infrastructure to support two-way communication. The merger between AOL and Time Warner demonstrates how Internet and content companies are finding ways to converge.

Cable television networks currently reach 200 million homes. On the other hand, satellite television can potentially reach 1 billion homes. These will offer nearly complete coverage of the United States. Digital satellite is also competing. DirecTV has DirecPC, which can beam data to a personal computer (PC). Its rival, EchoStar Corp., is working with interactive TV player, TiVo Inc., to deliver video and data service to a set-top box. However, satellite is currently not only a one-way delivery system, but is also the most expensive option in the United States. In regions of the world outside the United States, where the capital investment in copper wires and cable has yet to be made, satellite may have a better competitive opportunity.

The Internet itself doesn't own its own connections. Internet data traffic passes along the copper, fiber, coaxial cable, and wireless transmission of the other industries as a digital alternative to analog transmissions.

The new media is being built to include text, graphics, audio, and video across platforms of television, Internet, cable, and wireless industries (see Figure 1-1). The backbone uses wide-area communications technology, including satellite, fiber, coaxial cable, copper, and wireless. Data servers mix mainframes, workstations, supercomputers, and microcomputers, and a diversity of clients populate the end points of the networks including conventional PCs, palmtops, PDAs, smart phones, set-top boxes, and TVs.

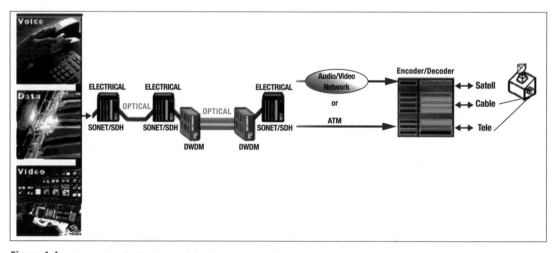

Figure 1-1   Connecting the backbone of the Internet to your home

Web-television hybrids, such as WebTV, provide opportunities for cross-promotion be-tween TV and Internet. Independent developers may take advantage of broadcast-Internet synergy by creating shows to targeted audiences.

Clearly, the future holds a need for interaction between the TV and the Internet. But will it appear as TV-quality video transmitted over the Internet and subsequently displayed on a TV set, or, alternatively, as URL information embedded within existing broadcast TV set pictures? Perhaps both.

◖ Streaming Video

Streaming is the ability to play media, such as audio and video, directly over the Internet without downloading the entire file before play begins. Digital encoding is required to con-vert the analog signal into compressed digital format for transmission and playback. Streaming videos send a constant flow of audio/video information to their audience. While streaming videos may be archived for on-demand viewing, they can also be shown in real-time. Examples include play-by-play sports events, concerts, and corporate board meetings. But a streaming video offers more than a simple digitized signal transmitted over the Inter-net. It offers the ability for interactive audience response and unparalleled form of two-way communication. The interactive streaming video process is referred to as *Webcasting*.

Widespread Webcasting will be impractical, however, until audiences have minimum ac-cess rates of 1.5Mbps or faster. By 2006 the best estimates indicate that 40 million homes will have cable modems and 25 million DSL connections with access rates of 1.5Mbps.

We shall see in Chapters 5, 6, and 7 how the compression codec and software standards will competitively change effective Internet bandwidth and the quality of delivered video.

The resultant video quality at a given bandwidth is highly dependent upon the specific video compressor. The human eye is extremely nonlinear and its capabilities are difficult to quantify. The quality of compression, specific video application, typical content, avail-able bandwidth, and user preferences all must be considered when evaluating compressor options. Some optimize for *talking heads* while other optimize for motion.

To date, the value of streaming video has been primarily the rebroadcast of TV content and redirected audio from radio broadcasts. The success of these services to compete with tra-ditional analog broadcasts will depend upon the ability of streaming video producers to develop and deliver their content using low-cost computers that present a minimal barrier to entry. Small, low-cost independent producers will effectively target audiences previously ignored. Streaming video is steadily moving toward the integration of text, graphics, audio, and video with interactive on-line chat will find new audiences. In Chapter 2, we present business models to address business's video needs.

Despite these promising aspects, streaming video is still a long way from providing a satisfactory audio/video experience in comparison to traditional broadcasts. The low-data transmission rates are a severe limitation on the quality of streaming videos. While a direct broadcast satellite dish receives data at 2Mbps, an analog modem is currently limited to 0.05Mbps. The new cable modems and Asymmetric Digital Subscriber Line (ADSL) are starting to offer speeds competitive with satellite, but they will take time to penetrate globally. Unlike analog radio and television, streaming video requires a dynamic connection between the computer providing the content to the viewer. Current computer technology limits the viewing audience to up to 50,000. While strategies to overcome this with replicating servers may increase audiences, this too will take effort.

The enhancement of data compression reduces the required video data streaming rates to more manageable levels. The technology has only recently reached the point where video can be digitized and compressed to levels that allow reasonable appearance during distribution over digital networks. Advances continue to come, improving look and delivery of video.

◖ Calculating Bandwidth Requirements

So far we have presented the advantages of digital technology. Unfortunately there is one rather large disadvantage—bandwidth limitations. Let's try some simple math that illustrates the difficulties.

Live, or on-demand, streaming video and/or audio is relatively easy to encode. The most difficult part is not encoding the files. It is determining what level of data may be transmitted. Table 1-2 contains information that will help with some basic terms and definitions.

Why the difference between Kbps and KBps? File sizes on a hard drive are measured in Kilobytes (KB). But the data transferred over a modem are measured in kilobits per second (Kbps) because it's comparatively slower than a hard drive.

In the case of a 28.8Kbps modem, the maximum data transfer rate is 2.5KBps, even though the calculated rate is 28.8Kbps/8 bits in a byte = 3.6KBps. This is because there is approximately a 30 percent loss of transmission capabilities due to Internet noise. This is due to traffic congestion on the Web and more than one surfer requesting information on the same server.

Table 1-3 provides information concerning the characteristics of video files. This includes pixels per frame and frames per file (film-size file).

Table 1-2   **Basic Terms and Definitions**

Term	Definition
Bandwidth	Data transmission capacity usually measured in bits per second
bit	Binary value of 0 or 1
Kilobit (Kb)	1,000 bits (approx.)
byte	8 bits (that is, 00101101), sufficient to encode 1 character (that is, "A")
Kilobyte (KB)	1,000 bytes
Megabyte (MB)	1,000,000 bytes
Gigabyte (GB)	1,000,000,000 bytes
Kbps	Kilobits per second (1,000 bits in a second)
KB/sec	Kilobytes per seconds (1,000 bytes in a second)

Table 1-3   **Data Volumes for a Film at Three Resolutions**

	High Resolutions	Medium Resolutions	Low Resolutions
Frame Resolution Size (in pixels)	3000 × 4000	2000 × 3000	1000 × 2000
Data per Frame (in bytes)	48 million	18 million	6 million
Data per Films (in bytes) (with 130,000 frames)	6240 billion	2320 billion	780 billion

We can use the information in Table 1-3 to compare some simple calculations. We will use the following formula to calculate the approximate size in megabytes of a digitized video file.

$$\frac{(\text{pixel width}) \times (\text{pixel height}) \times (\text{color bit depth}) \times (\text{fps}) \times (\text{duration in seconds})}{8,000,000 \ (\text{bits/MB})}$$

For three minutes of video at 15 frames per second with a color bit depth of 24-bit in a window that is 320 × 240 pixels, the digitized source file would be approximately 622 megabytes:

$$(320) \times (240) \times (24) \times (15) \times (180) / 8,000,000 = 622 \text{ megabytes}$$

We will see in Chapter 4 how data compression will significantly reduce this burden.

Now that we have our terms defined, let's take the case of a TV station that wants to broadcast their channel live 24 hours a day for a month over the Web to a target audience of 56Kbps modem users. In this case, a live stream generates 4.25KBps since a 56Kbps file transfers at 4.25KBps. So how much data would be transferred in a 24-hour period if one stream was constantly being used?

ANSWER = 4.25KBps $\times$ (number of seconds in a day) $\times$ 30 days per month
= 11GB/month

Therefore, one stream playing a file encoded for 56Kbps for 24 hours a day will generate 11 gigabytes in a month. How is this figure useful?

This figure becomes important because if you can estimate the average number of viewers in a month, then you can estimate the total amount of data that will be transferred from your process. Ultimately the issue becomes one of the need for sufficient backbone infrastructure to carry many broadcasts to many viewers across the networks.

For HDTV with a screen size of 1080 $\times$ 1920 and 24-bit color, a bandwidth of 51.8Mbps is required. This is a serious amount of data flow to route around the Internet to millions of viewers.

◖◗ Transitioning from Narrowband to Broadband

In telecommunications, bandwidth refers to data capacity of a channel. For an analog service, the bandwidth is defined as the difference between the highest and lowest frequency within which the medium carries traffic. For example, cabling that carries data between 200MHz and 300MHz has a bandwidth of 100MHz.

In addition to analog speeds in hertz (Hz) and digital speeds in bits per second (bps), the carrying rate is sometimes categorized as narrowband and broadband. It is useful to relate this to an analogy in which wider pipes carry more water. TV and cable are carried at broadband speeds. However, most telephone and modem data traffic from the central offices to individual homes and businesses are carried at slower narrowband speeds. This is usually referred to as the "last mile" issue.

The definitions for narrowband and broadband vary within the industries, but are summarized for our purposes as
  ▸ Narrowband refers to rates less than 1.5Mbps.
  ▸ Broadband refers to rates at or beyond 1.5Mbps.

A major bottleneck of analog services exists between cabling of residents and telephone central offices. Digital subscriber line (DSL) and cable modem are gaining in availability.

Cable TV companies are investing heavily in converting their cabling from one-way-only cable TV to two-way systems for cable modems and telephones.

In contrast to the "last mile" for residential areas, telephone companies are laying fiber cables for digital services from their switches to office buildings where the high-density client base justifies the additional expense.

We can appreciate the potential target audience for video by estimating how fast the last mile bandwidth demand is growing. Because installing underground fiber costs more than $20,000 per mile, fiber makes sense only for businesses and network backbones, not for last mile access to homes. Table 1-4 shows the estimated number of users connected at various modem speeds in 1999 and 2006. High-speed consumer connections are now being implemented through cable modems and digital subscriber lines (DSL). Approximately 1.3 million homes had cable modems by the end of 1999 in comparison to 300,000 DSL connections primarily to businesses. By 2006, we project 40 million cable modems and 25 million DSL lines will be in use.

Potentially, data at the rate of greater than one megabit per second could be delivered to over 80 percent of more than 550 million residential telephone lines in the world. Better than one megabit per second can also be delivered over fiber/coax CATV lines configured for two-way transmission to approximately 10 million out of 200 million total users (though these can be upgraded).

Currently, the median bandwidth in the United States is less than 56. This is de facto a narrowband environment.

But worldwide there is virtually limitless demand for communications as presented by the following growth rates.

1. The speed of computer connections is soaring. The number of connections at greater than 1.5Mbps is growing at 45 percent per year in residential areas and at 55 percent per year in business areas.

Table 1-4   **Estimated Number of U.S. Users' Connections**

Medium	Data Rate	1999	2006
Cable	1.5Mbps–10Mbps	1.3 million	40 million
x-DSL	1.5Mbps–6Mbps	0.3 million	25 million
Modem	< 56Kbps	48 million	135 million
		Median ~56Kbps	Avg. 560Kbps

2. Because of improving on-line experience, people will stay connected about 20 percent longer per year.

3. As more remote areas of the world get connected, messages will travel about 15 percent farther a year.

4. The number of people on-line worldwide in 1999 was 150 million, but the peak Internet load was only 10 percent and the actual transmission time that data were being transferred was only 25 percent of that number. With the average access rate of 44Kbps, this indicates an estimate of about 165Gbps at peak load.

In 2006 there will be about 300 million users, and about 65 million of these will have broadband (>1.5Mbps) access. With the addition of increased peak load and increased actual transmission time, this will result in an estimated usage of about 16.5 terabits per second of data processing.

It all adds up to a lot of bits. It leads to a demand for total data communications in 2006 of nearly a 100-fold increase over 1999. With the number of new users connecting to the Internet growing this fast, can the fiber backbone meet this demand? Figure 1-2 answers this question. It shows the growth in local area networks (LANs) from 1980 to 2000 with some projection into the next decade. In addition, it shows the Internet capacity over the last few decades and indicates the potential growth rate into the next decade. The jump up in Internet capacity due to dense wavelength division multiplexing (DWDM) is a projection of the multiplying effect of this new technology. As a result, this figure shows that we can expect a multi-terabit per second performance from the Internet backbone in the years ahead, which will meet the projected growth in demand.

Great! But, what about that last mile of copper, coax, and wireless?

Initially, the last mile will convert to residential broadband not as fiber optics, but as a network overlaid on existing telephone and cable television wiring. One megabit per second can be delivered to over 80 percent or more of 550 million residential telephone lines in the world. It can also be delivered over all fiber/coax CATV lines configured for two-way service. The latter represents a small fraction of the worldwide CATV lines however, requiring only 10 million homes out of 200 million. But upgrade programs will convert the remainder.

The endgame of the upgrade process may be providing fiber directly to the customer's home, but this will not happen for the next decade or two. A fiber signal travels coast to coast in 30 ms and human latency (period to achieve recognition) is about 50 ms. Thus fiber is the only technology to deliver viewable HDTV video. However, due to the cost and manpower involved, we're stuck with the last mile remaining copper, coax, and wireless for a while yet.

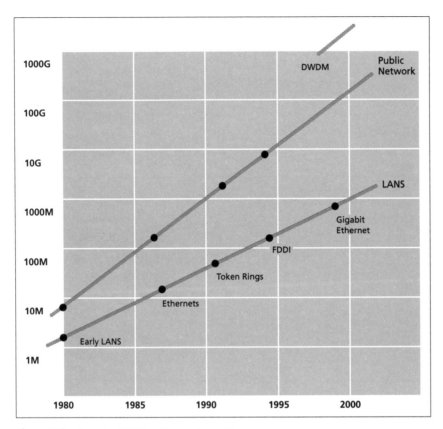

Figure 1-2   Growth of LAN and Internet capacities

Table 1-5 summarizes how the five delivery approaches for analog and digital technologies will coexist for the next few years. In Chapter 8, we will present network background on the technologies and standards and revisit this table in more detail.

Preparing to Converge

To be fully prepared to take advantage of the converging technologies, we must ask and answer the right questions. This is not as easy as it might seem.

We could ask, Which company will dominate the broadband data and telecommunication convergence? But this would be inadequate because the multi-trillion-dollar world e-commerce market is too big for any one company to monopolize.

Table 1-5 **Summary of Broadband Access Today**

	Copper	*Cable*	*FTTC/FTTH**	*Distribution*	*Satellite*
Transmission	Twisted pair	Coaxial fiber	Fiber-twisted	Wireless fiber	Radio signal
Technology	SONET, TDM	MPEG-2, ATM, AM, FM	MPEG-2, ATM	MPEG-2, ATM, AM, FM	MPEG-2, ATM, AM, FM
Advantages	Widely deployed	High bandwidth	High bandwidth	High bandwidth	Global coverage
Disadvantages	Legacy infrastructure	Upgrade to two-way	Cost to deploy	Expensive	One-way

* (FFTH is fiber to the home, FTTC is fiber to the curb, MPEG-2 is a compression standard; see Chapter 4, ATM is Asynchronous Transfer Mode; see Chapter 8, TDM is Time Division Multiplexing; see Chapter 8).

We could ask, Which broadband networks will dominate the Internet backbone? But this would be inadequate because innovative multiplexing and compression advances will make broadband ubiquitous but subservient to the last mile problem.

We could ask, Which transmission means (cable, wireless, or copper) will dominate the last mile? But this would be inadequate because the geographical infrastructure diversity of these technologies throughout the world will dictate different winners in different regions of the world demonstrating this as a local problem.

Individually, these questions address only part of the convergence puzzle. It is e-commerce's demand for economic efficiency that will force us to face the important question of the convergence puzzle.

What are meaningful broadband cross-technology standards? ▶

Without globally accepted standards, hardware and software developers can't create broad solutions for consumer demand.

As a result, we will be concerned throughout this book in pointing out the directions and conflicts that various competing standards are undertaking.

◀▷ Conclusion

In this chapter, we presented the background of analog technology's transition digital technology. This chapter provides a calculation that illustrates why digital video data are such a difficult bandwidth problem. It evaluated the rate of change of conversion from narrowband connections to broadband. This rate establishes a critical perspective on the timeline of the demand for Internet video.

On the basis of this chapter, you should conclude that:

▶ The Internet backbone combination of fiber and optical multiplexing will perform in the multi-terabits per second range and provide plenty of network bandwidth in the next few years.

▶ The last mile connectivity will remain twisted pair, wireless, and coax cable for the next few years, but broadband (1.5Mbps) access through cable modems and x-DSL will grow to 65 million users in just a few years.

▶ Streaming video was identified as the crossroads of technology convergence. It is the bandwidth crisis of delivering video that will prove decisive in setting global standards and down-selecting competing technologies. The success of streaming video in its most cost-effective and customer-satisfying form will define the final technology convergence model of the twenty-first century.

CHAPTER 2

Internet Video Opportunities

Today, Internet video can be used in the most exciting ways. From on-line education and entertainment, to product demos and corporate training, video is already proving to be an essential substitute for the reassuring touch, sight, and feel experience that brick and mortar establishments traditionally offer. But which applications will lead and grow the fastest? And which applications face the most frustrating obstacles? ▶

In this chapter, we will differentiate the growth potential of streaming video in the areas of business, education, and entertainment based on bandwidth and financial resources. We will show that e-commerce bulges with financial resources, that education applications have the advantage of Internet-2 (the new upgrade to the Internet) and budding intellectual talent, and that entertainment suffers from lagging bandwidth for their most prized offerings.

▶ Bandwidth Requirements Differentiate Video Applications

While video applications of all description are being attempted on the Internet their growth rate varies widely. Their success depends largely on bandwidth and financial incentives.

In Table 2-1, we show the different Web bandwidth requirements for some key video applications. The table shows that five applications—video conferencing, video on-line education, video catalogs, virtual malls, and corporate communications—are within the 1.5Mbps last mile bandwidth reach. They are all very attractive business model targets for the near future.

Business has adequate bandwidth for immediate exploitation of streaming video in the area of business-to-business (B-to-B) relationships. Corporate LAN Ethernets are widely deployed at 10Mbps to the wire closet and about 1.5Mbps to the desktop. As video demands drive corporations toward 100Mbps Ethernets to the wire closet, it will take 3 to 5 years to distribute10Mbps to the desktop. Already, corporations have begun deploying the

Table 2-1   **Application Bandwidth Requirements**

Application	Required Bandwidth (Mbps) (after compression)
Video Conferencing	0.384
Video On-Line Education	1.5
Video Catalogs	1.5
• (B-to-B)	
• (B-to-C)	
Virtual Video Mall	1.5
Complex Web pages	1.5
Corporate LAN	1.5
Digital TV	
(MPEG-2 compression)	
• On demand	1.5
• Live	3
• Sports	6
Entertainment Video	
(HDTV 1080 × 1920 × 24-bit color)	19.3 to 38.6
Medical Imagery	20
Digital Professional Photography and Video Studios	20

new 1 Gigabit Ethernets as a corporate backbone to meet even greater delivery demand (see Chapter 8). As homes deploy cable modems, business-to-customer (B-to-C) relationships will rapidly expand.

Business has adequate financial incentives for immediate exploitation of streaming video in the area of B-to-C. A driving economic issue is Internet advertising revenue, which has been rising from $50 million in 1995, to $907 million in 1997. In 1999 Internet advertising revenue reached $6 billion (which is 12 percent of the total TV advertising budget). Certainly the demographics of the Internet users are attracting advertisers. The advent of streaming video will only help to expand these advertising efforts.

On-line education has the advantage of Internet-2 (see Chapter 8) and budding intellectual talent to exploit the available bandwidth, but it may suffer from a constant struggle for adequate funding.

The more demanding applications of entertainment media, such as Digital TV, require 1.5Mbps to 6Mbps per channel. While these applications are a little beyond the last mile broadband 1.5Mbps expectations for the next few years, they are not so far beyond to prohibit some early experimentation. The merger of AOL (with its subsidiary *www.Broadcast.com*) and Time Warner (with its cable and content businesses) demonstrate that large Internet providers and content companies are searching for the key to exploit just this opportunity.

◖ The Explosion of e-Commerce

The amount of wealth creation through high technology is staggering. Regardless of the future course of the Internet, it will continue to be a chaotic marketplace for some time to come. Electronic commerce, or e-commerce, offers business opportunities on the Internet with broad national and international access and a low barrier to entry. The Internet allows new small companies to grow and big companies to grow even bigger and at a faster rate. How e-commerce and consumer behavior are changing influences the possible strategies and tactics businesses will follow. It will put economic pressure on the technology developers to pursue the options directly addressing business and consumer needs.

From a business perspective, e-commerce is an evolution of international trade on a multilevel scale. It involves every aspect of existing business from sales, marketing, production, product development, implementation, merchandising, logistics, and distribution. Electronic commerce is a big-picture phenomenon changing all elements of relationships between suppliers, partners, and clients. The business-to-business segment accounts for 80 percent of all e-commerce.

In 1999, the estimated number of Web sites reached 2.9 million while Web pages totaled 1.2 trillion. This is equivalent to 20 terabytes of information. And it has been estimated that e-commerce will reach $1.3 trillion by 2003. Today, we are still in the early stages of Internet commerce development and only a few business models are becoming successful. It is readily conceded that many business models can be enhanced with electronic-video, or e-video.

The best way to see the big picture of how e-commerce can be significantly enhanced with e-video is to stand back a bit. First, the march toward increasingly open electronic marketplaces is progressing strongly. Second, where traditional marketplaces relied upon known relationships, digital markets rely on "virtual" or unpredictable relationships made up of various new digital values created and re-created between buyers and sellers. Therefore, the future methodology for succeeding in e-commerce will consist of evaluating and understanding business-to-business and business-to-customer virtual relationships and formulating appropriate strategies.

The appropriate strategies to base relationships for e-commerce will consider the customer's new power in controlling the interactive buying process more directly. The result is more than a one-time transaction. It is the establishment of a database for long-term relationships between buyer and seller. This exchange of information and services in an open marketplace produces an interaction between all members. The Internet provides e-commerce with two key concepts that change commerce itself. The first relates to what is being bought in terms of new products and services. The second relates to how things are bought and sold. The conclusion is new efficiencies leading to lower costs.

Why Long Distance Two-Way Communication Needs Internet Video

Is digital convergence overhyped? Perhaps, but here is another dynamic involved: the dynamic of shifting generations. A new generation even larger than the Baby Boomers called *Next-Generation,* or *N-Gen,* or *Generation-X,* is poised with 81.1 million children born between January 1977 and December 1997. The N-Gen is bigger than the 77.2 million strong baby boom generation (1946–1964). The Boomers were the TV generation shaped by a passive one-way relationship with television. The N-Gen is shaped by two-way interactive video games and the Internet. The Internet is the first phenomenon of a two-way marketing medium.

In the past, analog technology and its one-way communication led to a particular business-to-customer relationship. The one-way communication of radio and television broadcast, as well as newspapers and magazine advertisements, offered products for sale directly to consumers. The process was based on one broadcast distributed to many people simultaneously, or a one-to-many distribution through a one-way flow of information from the business to the consumer. A typical distribution channel had several intermediary layers: manufacturer, wholesaler, distributor, retailer, and finally the consumer. Feedback from the consumer back to the business through customer service departments was often designed to provide more pacification of customers than business improvements.

Two-way communication with the customer only happened either through telephone solicitation or by the consumer traveling to a brick and mortar store to browse and select. This process is being changed by the interactive two-way communication nature of e-commerce. The Internet eliminates most of the intermediary layers and allows direct sales from the manufacturer to the consumer, thereby potentially reducing costs while promoting a direct dialogue.

Two-way interactive communication through e-commerce is readily illustrated by the online auction house e-Bay (www.e-bay.com). Consumers can see and read about an item and place a bid. If the bid is successful they receive delivery through the mail. A perfect example of virtual shopping. But will the consumer keep coming back to e-Bay? Will they purchase a wider variety of consumer goods? How will e-Bay manage its customer database of information and its valuable long-term relationship with individuals who use their service?

If the interface between business and consumers is to remain at a distance and yet provide a two-way interaction, then more than just text and graphics will soon be needed. Data-rich media types of audio and video will be required to grow a stable and trusting B-to-C relationship. Let's examine the needs of buyers and sellers to see why this is true.

 ▸ Buyers want access to an unlimited variety of choices with the broadest possible information at the very lowest prices.
 ▸ Sellers want to make profitable sales over and over again.

The Internet offers to meet both of their needs. It offers the buyer the ability to search huge databases of rich media on variously priced products for the buyer. It offers the seller a transaction with minimal overhead and data and a relationship with the customer that will lead to additional sales at another time.

Video essentially offers a substitute for the touch, sight, feel experience that brick and mortar establishments offer.

But it is the buying and selling relationship between business and its customers (either B-to-B or B-to-C) where video can provide its greatest benefit. Product demonstrations during the sales process can augment the consumer's interest. But the role of video doesn't have to stop there.

Video on-line help for product assembly and repair will become an important consumer demand. Consider for a moment the instructions from that bicycle you purchased for your child's birthday present that read, ". . . some assembly required." It would not be cost effective for the manufacturer to provide a video instruction tape with the purchase, though goodness knows the sheets of "insert widget 12b into widget 34d" could be written more clearly. Now, however, that manufacturer can cost effectively put one bicycle assembly help video on his Web site and let every consumer get to bed early the night before with a fully assembled and functioning birthday present.

In 1994, Jeff Bezos saw an opportunity in selling products on-line. He concluded that books had sales potential in this high-tech medium, and Amazon (www.Amazon.com) started business later that year. The on-line bookstore opened its virtual doors in July 1995 with a million books. Customers could buy almost any book in print and have it delivered within a few days at discount prices. The site offered security with encrypted credit card transactions.

Amazon introduced some e-commerce innovations, like incentive programs that encourage other sites to recommend books and then link readers to Amazon. The company has also helped build an Internet community around a commercial site. In 1998, Amazon expanded to CDs, software, and videos. Amazon is now an icon of e-commerce. One can expect other industries to mimic Amazon.

The digital economy holds virtually unlimited possibilities for business. To take advantage of them, employees, partners, and customers all need to operate in an environment that allows a media rich, rapid, and accurate flow of product information.

The user interface between business and its customer will become increasingly more important as the consumer travels less to the brick and mortar establishments and becomes a virtual shopper. The interface must provide a rich and simple access for the consumer and develop a satisfying and long-term relationship with the consumer. Today business is satisfactorily solving the security and database information record keeping for the new business-to-customer relationship. This must be expanded to a visual presence. Customer service needs to have a face even if it is not in person but only over the Internet. And business video conferencing will reduce business travel when it becomes more an individual's choice and convenience rather than a studio production.

Internet Video Business Models

Clearly, as e-commerce expands, it is developing great financial incentives for the application of video on the Internet. Video is already being used to enhance business-to-business and business-to-customer relationships. It provides product demonstrations, on-line help, interactive customer service, advertisements, travel illustrations, real estate walk-throughs, corporate training, CEO and management presentations, conferences, and much more.

Many businesses today do not have their own video production capabilities because of the cost and the expertise barrier to entry. But this may change as Internet video production and delivery becomes easier and more accessible. Businesses will need to be able to produce video routinely at low cost and with greater simplicity. Expertise will be readily required. This proliferation of video everywhere not only will benefit the business-to-customer relationship, but will create new video production–related businesses specializing in Internet delivery. We will illustrate how video e-commerce led by business-to-business and business-to-customer relationships will become the "killer-app" for streaming video.

The relationship between a business and its customer revolves around the following.

▸ Discovering the customer's needs through interaction and feedback. Web site interactivity enables users to learn about the business's organization, products, or services, conducts personalized dialogue with each user, promotes loyalty, and provides information through e-mail announcements, newsletters, and targeted advertisement.

▸ Meeting the customer's needs by customizing product or service. The more convenient and comfortable the marketing experience is for the customer, the more successful the business will be. If customer's can order, learn, ask, do, see, hear, and research from the comfort of their homes or offices versus having to travel, then transactions will be more appealing to the customer and more cost effective as well.

Imagine working at a company that produces its own training videos that are available on the company's servers so employees can view them as their schedule allows, or work group collaborative computing environments that create high-performance health care teams or clinical information systems.

For an example, see Dell (www.Dell.com). Dell Computers has added streaming video computer product demos to its on-line ordering site. These clips include video of the computers fully configured and broken apart to view inside boards and cable configurations. The voice-over explains the features and advantages of the computer configurations. All in all it is an excellent customer purchasing experience. This application of streaming video for Internet business will have important consequences for technology convergence.

◖ Video Service Business Models

Internet video offers many new small start-up business opportunities including video capture, editing, encoding, hosting, and broadcasting, all of which are in the grasp of anticipated technological enhancements.

Before hanging out our sign, however, we need to discover how the needs and demands of these new Internet start-up opportunities are different from traditional small business.

The components of traditional brick and mortar business start-ups include understanding the market, finding a business location, financing, establishing a sole proprietorship, legalities, fictitious name, local business license, state sales tax, federal identification number, federal permits, insurance, initial cash outlays, bookkeeping, hiring help, taxes, and more.

The advantages of an Internet business include market recognition, penetration with exposure to many eyeballs, reduced operating costs, selling overseas, operating 24 hours a day, 7 days a week, competing head-to-head with large corporations, and an inexpensive trail of new ideas.

Now add the requirements of a video Internet business:

1. Content development (see Chapter 3)

2. Software (see Chapters 5 and 6)

3. Hardware for video capture, editing, and administration (see Chapter 3)

4. ISP connectivity (see Chapter 8)

5. Computer video server (see Chapter 9)

6. Expertise and training

Some ideas for Internet video businesses include video capture, editing, and encoding services, video hosting service, video broadcasting service, video network consulting service, customized SMIL code and Web design, video product database development, and video products with URL hotspot links.

Virtual Shopping Malls

The number of users of the Internet will increase from 97 million in 1998 to 500 million by the end of 2003. With the emergence of faster access technologies such as digital subscriber line, cable modem, and wireless, the speed and flexibility with which users are accessing the Internet are also increasing. Because of the increasing capabilities and accessibility of the Internet, companies are building their business models around the Internet and developing mission-critical business applications. These e-businesses rely on the Web to communicate with customers, access and share business information, engage in marketing activities, and conduct e-commerce transactions.

Virtual shopping malls could produce an integrated business system for business-to-customer relationships. Content appropriate to individual customers would offer ads and newsletters to invite customers toward their preferences. Live broadcasts of trade shows and infomercials can target specific audiences. Search engines geared to product video will greatly enhance the experience.

A virtual reality experience on the Web makes the experience more engaging and entertaining. With Virtual Reality Modeling Language (VRML) and 3D scenes, text is enriched with animation, sound, music, and video. The new level of experience enhances interaction with sellers.

Video for On-Line Education

Across the United States efforts are underway to upgrade the network infrastructure. Universities are connecting to the next generation of the Internet, called Internet-2. About 20 corporate partners are currently involved with 154 universities in establishing gigabits per second points of presence nationwide. The payoff will come when this wide bandwidth can produce powerful Web applications.

In late February 1999, Internet-2 went live, with speeds up to 2.4Gbps. Colleges and universities must now upgrade campus networks to fiber optic cabling to take advantage of the Gbps speeds promised by the high-speed network. While video for on-line education has the advantage of Internet-2 and the access to some of the newest, most creative innovative minds available, financing may not be as available as e-commerce financing in general.

The rapidly changing digital world is engendering a myriad of innovations in distance learning. The innovations in learning include scientific visualization, collaboration, and simulation. Technology has advanced to the point where instructors need not leave the classroom to be able to create a multimedia Webcast of their lesson that includes their writing on their classroom whiteboard and audiovisual.

The use of video, both live and prerecorded, has become an important tool in training and education. Use of video enriches the learning experience and brings the power of rich multimedia into the classroom. Some example sites include *www.CollegeLearning.com*, which offers live videoconferencing from classrooms to anywhere in the world supported by the Web. And *www.eCollege.com* is a provider of technology and services enabling colleges to offer an Internet-based environment for distance and on-campus learning. Comprised of educators and technologists, eCollege partners with institutions to design, build, and operate on-line campuses and courses to deliver course content in a highly interactive and engaging educational manner. The faculty members convert courses into presentations designed for delivery over the Internet using an array of course design tools and support services.

Of particular interest to on-line education applications is Synchronized Multimedia Integrated Language (SMIL). SMIL allows integrating a set of independent multimedia objects into a synchronized multimedia presentation. Using SMIL, you can

- Describe the temporal behavior of the presentation
- Describe the layout of the presentation on a screen
- Associate hyperlinks with media objects
- Simultaneously stream text, graphics, audio, and video all in one player

We shall provide details and examples for SMIL in Chapter 5, along with this book's associated CD-ROM.

In addition, Windows PowerPoint 2000 will provide presentation capabilities over the Web that will include audio and video.

Entertainment

Today digital technology can create homogenized, easily delivered content that is instantly convertible into whatever medium or platform the user chooses. The only limit is the bandwidth.

Media can be categorized into three broad types:

- Broadcast media (such as, digital TV)
- Package media (such as, DVD and DVD-ROM) and
- Network media (such as, Internet)

After five years of commercializing the Web, media conglomerates are still trying to figure out how to profit from it. Sure, they use Web sites for promoting shows, print publications, and movies. But the media giants are still on the outside looking in, at least regarding developing a new mass consumer medium comparable to broadcast, print, cable, and radio.

In the early days of television, broadcasters focused on re-creating radio-style programs until they realized that visual and audio programs called for distinctly different presentations. The same factors arise in adapting a passive TV to the interactive medium of the Web. As a result, some media conglomerates—Walt Disney, NBC, USA Networks, and AOL Time Warner—are now approaching the Web through mass-market portals and linked special-interest destinations. Portals lure a broad range of consumers with entertainment and news content, search engines, links, directories, e-commerce, and communities.

The more demanding applications of entertainment media, such as Digital TV, require bandwidth capacity of 1.5Mbps to 6Mbps per channel. While these applications are a little beyond the last mile broadband 1.5Mbps expectations for the next few years, they are not so far beyond to prohibit some early experimentation. The merger of AOL (with its subsidiary *www.Broadcast.com*) and Time Warner (with its cable and content businesses) demonstrates that large Internet providers and content companies are searching for the key to exploit just this opportunity. We will provide more on bandwidth opportunities in Chapter 8.

After all the hype of the 1990s, why are we still overwhelmingly viewing and listening to our news and entertainment through analog television and radio? The quick answer is that digital video delivered today is either too expensive or of poor quality in comparison to the analog video alternative. The streaming video on the Internet is just not a satisfying experience for the entertainment viewer.

The value of streaming video has been primarily the rebroadcast of TV content and redirected radio. The success of these services to compete with traditional analog broadcasts will depend upon:

- *Low cost.* IP multicast networks will allow a single streaming video to be replicated for delivery to thousands of viewers. Small low-cost independent producers will effectively target audiences previously ignored.
- *Niche audiences.* Streaming videos are steadily moving toward the integration of text, graphics, audio, and video with interactive on-line chat.
- *On-demand.* The digital nature of the Internet will create large inventories of selections to be accessed at the client's leisure. Content providers may develop large databases with search engines allowing viewers to find very limited highly focused content.
- *Audience growth.* The number of Internet users is expected to double every two years. The Web is pulling audiences away from traditional media and, as technology improves, the Web experience will continue to grow.
- *Entry level.* Unlike other media that are usually controlled by established conglomerates, the Internet is wide open to new entries.

Web surfers are mainly looking for information, and TV watchers mainly want entertainment. Interactive TV content is carried out by shrinking the video to a portion of the TV screen and filling the rest with program-related Web content.

The ability to stream live broadcasts extends a regional venue audience into global demographics. As streaming videos extend into the domain of broadcast-style productions, they need help from professionals who have experience in this area.

Internet television efforts now include "The People's Court," which provides streaming video live. NCAA games are being broadcast as live sporting events. Original content developers are moving content to the Web, such as tech talk and starstreams (www. starstreams.com).

▶ Conclusion

In this chapter, we differentiated the growth potential of streaming video in the areas of business, education, and entertainment based on bandwidth and financial resources. We showed that education applications have the advantage of Internet-2 and budding intellectual talent, that e-commerce bulges with financial incentives, and that entertainment suffers from inadequate bandwidth for their most prized offerings.

On the basis of this chapter, you should conclude that:

- Corporate and e-business can make excellent use of the 1.5Mbps access customers will soon have by providing video product demos, video instructions, and interactive video customer service.
- That education on-line will develop as a strong application for innovative Internet video.
- That entertainment content will be seeking to exploit available bandwidth as rapidly as possible to reach to the consumer.

PART II

Video Production

Here we focus on the preparation, production, capture, and editing of video for existing narrowband to low-end broadband (1.5Mbps) delivery.

CHAPTER 3

Producing, Capturing, and Editing Video Content

Because of the quality of delivery issues, traditional analog radio and television broadcast will continue to dominate content in the entertainment area for the next few years. However, for B-to-B, B-to-C, and on-line education, product demos, advertising, corporate training, and classroom learning content will greatly expand onto the Web.

But how can you produce, capture, and edit your videos optimally for Web delivery? ▶

This chapter concentrates on audio/video production and how to capture it to your computer. There is a list of manufacturers and hardware devices. We focus on capturing and editing audio/video for the existing narrowband and for the lower-end reaches of broadband (1.5Mbps). The emphasis is on preparing audio/video content that will show well for Web delivery after significant compression.

▶ How to Produce Video Content Optimized for Web Delivery

Today, the quality of analog delivery of audio and video through radio and television is based upon large, clear pictures without noticeable interruption or downtime. While digital video can produce higher quality imagery, it's the delivery of digital that is a problem. In order to deliver digital content, large data files must be compressed and, in so doing the size and quality of the image can suffer. It is therefore important to prepare the content as much as possible to target the best possible video end product.

When planning your video project, start by considering:

- What is the objective of the project?
- Who is the intended audience?
- What is the target bandwidth range?
- What input hardware and software will you use?

The purpose of the project will impose certain requirements on the features that must be delivered by the software, including responsiveness, speed, complexity of interactivity, animation, graphics, and performance of digital video and audio.

The intended audience and target bandwidth will determine, among other things, the minimum hardware requirements of the delivery computers, and this in turn will determine a host of other technical production parameters.

It is important to decide what constitutes acceptable delivery standards. If the limit is a delivery platform for narrowband, you will be accepting severe performance limitations. Conversely, if a higher standard is set, such as residential broadband, you will have more flexibility. Just as any good cook tastes his dishes, you need to test the project on each target platform frequently during development to verify the acceptability of the presentation.

Most multimedia projects require extensive media preparation. Often the time spent in preparing media for use will exceed the time spent in actually assembling the product. In the case of cross-platform development, you may have files on both platforms that require backup, along with files in multiple formats. The basics of project management are important here: establish a reliable and regular backup system and make sure that your files are backed up regularly.

The equipment and software used in multimedia production is often cutting edge and may not be as reliable as products in the more established computer desktop applications. As a result, there are often compatibility problems. Your planning can minimize compatibility issues by starting with a system that will meet your needs for an extended period of time. This will avoid expensive and difficult upgrades.

The actual making of the multimedia content involves five steps:

1. Preparing and developing the source material

2. Capturing the audio/video using a computer with a video capture card

3. Editing the video and saving the large, uncompressed edited file

4. Compressing the content for Web distribution

5. Delivering the final compressed movie content

The following figure (Figure 3-1) illustrates the steps in the process of creating and delivering streaming video on-line.

◗ Step 1: Preparing and Developing the Source Material

In Chapter 2, we presented the contrast of required bandwidth for different target audiences. The characteristics of talking heads for CEO presentations, or the slide show–like on-line help presentations are readily transformed into narrowband video. But the sports action of football, or product demos, requires different handling. It is still possible to show action video, but only as a small image size and only over the best available bandwidth.

Product demos in particular take some careful planning to optimize for the Web. To get across the product's message, you may need audio voice-over, perhaps some music, a variety of configuration images, and clarifying text. While traditional video production houses do a great job for TV and CD-ROM delivery, these high production value videos often drastically disappoint when delivered over the Web. Often the disappointed viewer sees a shrunken image, obscure text, fading audio, jerky motion, and blurry image.

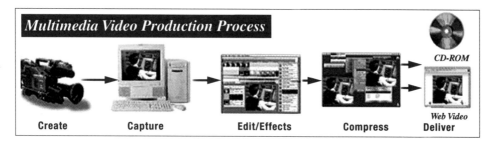

Figure 3-1   Multimedia production process

It doesn't have to be that bad. But it does take some planning. Teaming with a traditional video production company is a great idea, however. Many of them are already adding streaming capabilities to their existing talents (see, for example, ICV (www.icv.com). This video production company includes a state-of-the-art studio with blue screen capability, produces professional video for TV and commercial applications, and has recently acquired streaming capabilities. Digital Reality is a television production, special effects, and computer animation company in Seattle *www.digreality.com*, and also offers a good starting point for a video project.

Here are 10 tips aimed at improving some of the specifics of Web video production.

1. Video production starts by capturing a video source by shooting a scene with a video camera. The higher the quality of the original, the better the final movie.

2. Video capture places a large burden on a computer's Central Processing Unit (CPU) and hard drive. To avoid dropping frames during video capture, use a hard drive specially made for audio and video work. Check the throughput capacity of each of the key hardware elements (CPU, Bus, hard drive, capture card).

3. It's important to consider the video's final frame size to reach Web viewers with 28.8Kbps modems before shooting starts. Important visual elements must be framed well. The image will appear sharper if there are minimal image changes between frames. For example, RealVideo compression technology reuses existing data when frames are similar, so a video with relatively stationary subjects, such as talking heads, will look better than an action video with rapid scene changes and considerable movement. Using a mounted rather than handheld camera also reduces slight frame motions that disrupt efficient compression.

4. It is usually best to capture video at the planned delivery size to a standard file format, such as AVI or QuickTime, in order to get the best resolution. Then editing software can prepare the content before encoding. It is better to work with uncompressed formats. Otherwise, the source is compressed once when you digitize it and again when you encode. This double compression can decrease the image quality and produce "blocky" defects in the final image.

5. Generally speaking, movies that are well lit and don't have a lot of contrast will compress better than very dramatically lit videos. Make sure to use enough light since low-light conditions produce high-grain, which is bad for compression.

6. Every change in the image will make it harder to compress. This applies both to camera movement and subject movement. Use hard cuts instead of pans, avoid zooms, and watch out for scenes in which everything changes. Keep the camera steady by using a tripod at an appropriate distance.

7. Keep the background simple. This will make the image easier to see when it is reduced in size to the small dimensions needed for multimedia production. Keeping the detail to a minimum will also help the image compress better.

8. Bright lighting at a constant exposure keeps the foreground detail crisp. Complex textures and stripes degrade the final image quality with distortion effects.

9. The maximum recommended frame rate for streaming video over a network is 15fps. Higher frame rates may cause playback problems on slower client machines. It is usually best to use 24-bit color since lower color resolution reduces video quality.

10. Shoot tests of the material and run it through to see what the final output will look like before going into production.

The critical elements of production, design, content development, and expertise require central consideration. The production team is responsible for the organizational content and technology, and must develop a strategy that puts all elements together in a timely mosaic.

What are the basic hardware components necessary to produce and stream video for a Web site? In the following paragraphs, the capture cards, camera, and microphones necessary to produce audio/video are reviewed, with particular emphasis toward compatibility and quality of audio/video performance for the final streaming video product.

To stream the video, an Internet connection and video server are also necessary. These issues will be addressed in Chapters 8 and 9, respectively.

Analog and Digital Tape Formats

There are significant differences between digital tape formats and analog tape formats. The primary difference is how the data are stored on the tape. Initially, all of the videotape formats were analog and their data were stored in an essentially uncoded format. In practice, degradation of data is most significant in the lower-end analog formats, where a lot of data is stored on a small amount of low-quality tape. Thus, if you copy your home VHS tape onto another VHS tape, you will likely notice a marked decrease in quality.

The first digital videotape format was D1, introduced by Sony in 1986. For nearly a decade digital videotape was used only at the very high end of videotaping. But starting in 1995 with DVPRO, digital videotape has become a reality at the lower and middle levels of videotaping. In digital tape, the raw data are stored as sets of zeros and ones. With higher quality formats, there are fewer problems with replication, and by the time you get to professional formats, such as Betacam SP, multi-generational copies do not degrade the quality. The following are common videotape formats.

Analog Tape Formats

- VHS (video home system) is the format used in nearly all home VCRs today. This format was introduced by JVC in 1976. The VHS format is still very important in terms of distributing taped programs. The problem with the VHS format is that quality of the image on the tape is not really very good. This becomes a problem when you have what appear to be some great shots taken with a professional format machine and then duplicate them onto VHS.

- S-VHS (Super VHS) is a marked improvement over VHS. The signals from the camera are handled differently from VHS, with color and brightness handled separately resulting in improved color rendition. The tape is similar in size to the VHS tape cassette. S-VHS is a common format for use on nonbroadcast video projects and is sometimes used for broadcast video in smaller stations.

- Hi8 is a marked improvement in picture quality over VHS. Used Hi8 industrial-level camcorders are still readily available, and there are many new, consumer level Hi8 camcorders available.

- ¾ inch U-Matic is an old format introduced in 1971, but it is still used by some videographers who have been using the format for a long time. It can produce good quality video, and ¾ inch decks are still commonly available in duplicating houses.

- Betacam is a Sony product first introduced in 1982. It is currently geared for broadcast use, although there have been some less-expensive models designed more for industrial use. Betacam, MII, and other digital formats use a different way of handling color information than the VHS or S-VHS formats. The color information from the picture is broken into three channels (one each for red, green, and blue information). This type of format is known as *component format* as opposed to *composite formats*. Colors in particular come out looking much more vibrant and objects appear three-dimensional. The difference between Betacam and Betacam SP, introduced in 1986, is in the tape. Betacam SP uses a metal tape and is an improvement over large Betacam cassettes.

- MII, introduced in 1986, is Panasonic's answer to Betacam SP. All MII tape is metal. The 90-minute cassette at 4 by 8 inches (11 cm by 19 cm) is considerably smaller than the 90-minute Betacam SP cassette.

Digital Tape Formats

There is a proliferation of digital tape formats. Often when neophyte videographers think of digital videotape, they are thinking of DV or DVC, the consumer digital videotape format introduced in 1996. In addition there are related digital videotape formats using the same cassette size, such as DVCPRO, DVCPRO50, and DVCAM. Then there are other digital tape formats using larger tape such as Digital S, Betacam SX, DS, Digital Betacam, D1, D2, D3, D6, and DCT.

▸ DV or DVC (digital videocassette), the first consumer digital videotape format, was introduced in 1996. The tape used for this format is quite small: 6.35 mm wide and 8.8 microns thick. A cassette with up to approximately 3.5 hours of playing time is only 3.5 inches by 5 inches (9 cm by 12 cm). Smaller cassettes with shorter playing times are also available. Like Betacam SP and MII, it is a component format with separate channels for red, green, and blue. The data on the tape are compressed at a 5:1 ratio. This means that four-fifths of the data in the original image is thrown away. The quality that can be obtained from this format is close to the quality once expected only in broadcast quality systems.

▸ DVCPRO was introduced in 1995 by Panasonic. It is similar in most respects to DV except that the tape speed is twice that of DV, resulting in reduced error rates. DV equipment cannot read DVCPRO tapes or record on DVCPRO tapes. However, DVCPRO equipment can play back DVCAM and DV format tapes.

▸ DVCAM was introduced in 1996 by Sony and can be considered as Sony's answer to Panasonic's DVCPRO. DVCAM is partly compatible with DV.

Video Cameras

There are several options for selecting an input analog or digital camera. Low-end models connect directly to your computer's parallel port, while high-end cameras connect to video capture cards. VHS and Hi8 cameras are still popular, but despite their higher cost and various formats, digital cameras are the wave of the future.

For a fast, pure digital connection to your computer, DV cameras can use a FireWire (or IEEE 1394) connection. FireWire is a connection for direct transfer of digital video at 100MBps to 1000MBps to your hard drive. Table 3-1 provides a list of digital cameras available.

▣ Step 2: Capturing the Audio/Video

You capture a digital signal in your computer with a capture card, and then store the video on a hard drive. The captured video should be in a format that is not dependent on your capture card. Recording video requires a video camera compatible with the video capture card. Recording audio requires the use of a microphone, sound card, and editor.

The basic hardware components necessary for audio/video production include

▸ Sound card

▸ Microphone

Table 3-1   **Digital Cameras**

Vendor	Name	Comment
Canon *www.usa.canon.com*	GL1	
Hitachi *www.hdal.com*	SK 3000P	Digital multi-standard camera provides no-compromise NTSC and HDTV.
IKEGAMI Electronics *www.ikegami.com*	HL-V77	DVCPRO camera
JVC professional products *jvc.com/pro*	GY-DV500	DV component
NEC America, broadcast equipment dept. *ccgw.nec.com*	DiskCam	MPEG-2
Panasonic Broadcast television system *www.panasonic.com/broadcast*	AJ-D215	DVCPRO
Sony electronics *www.sony.com*	DSR-500WSL	DVCAM

‣ Camera
‣ Video capture card
‣ Computer with SCSI controller and fast hard drive

In the following sections, we will describe these requirements and their hardware and software needs in detail.

▣ Audio Requirements

Internet audio can approach the quality of the best broadcast audio when appropriately prepared. You will need to know the basics about digital audio. When recording audio it is usually saved as raw audio file with the following properties: sampling rate (can range from 8kHz to 48kHz), number of bits per sample (8 to 16), and number of channels (Mono or Stereo). The higher the sample rate, the better the sound quality. Therefore a file that is 48kHz, 16-bit stereo will sound better than 8kHz, 8-bit mono. The 48kHz file, however, will be larger. CD-quality audio is set at 44.1kHz, 16-bit stereo that produces a data rate of 176KBps.

The frequency range defines the highest and lowest pitches sampled during capture. The human hearing is sensitive to sound over a wide range. The dynamic range defines the highest and lowest volume for sound delivered and is measured in decibels (db), a logarithmic unit based upon the minimum sound the human ear can hear. CD-quality audio ranges to 90db.

The timbre character of sound is a fingerprint of primary and harmonic frequencies. The human voice has complex and individualistic capacity to detect timber but can be adequately represented for speech recognition by a small set of frequencies.

The ratio of sound versus silence during a sampling period is called the *sound density*. Low density sound recordings allow streaming to cache more efficiently.

Audio equipment is most likely a mixture of analog and digital devices. Typically, audio signal is captured digitally on the encoding computer and passes through several stages of analog processing. Many audio programs like Windows Sound Recorder allow you to convert files from one sample rate to another or to change bits from 8 to 16. Live audio is captured using microphones to convert sound energy into electric current and/or digital data. Microphone categories include:

- *Condenser microphone.* Works by forming an electric potential between a vibrating membrane and a back plate.
- *Dynamic microphone.* Uses a flat plate, or diaphragm, that transforms sound waves into motion.
- *Ribbon.* Uses a thin metal strip that vibrates directly without a separate membrane. These are used primarily for voice.

Cable connectors used by audio and video systems include

- Mono or stereo jacks identified by a single or double strip, respectively
- RCA plug
- XLR plug
- BNC connector

Speakers provide monitoring and amplification of audio for the audience.

Recording audio is simple. Just connect a microphone to the sound card of your computer. Windows users can record speech using Sound Recorder, the standard Windows audio player and recorder. Just connect the microphone and hit the **Record** button.

Sound editors give better control of your recording sessions and a wide variety of input sources (microphone, CD-ROM, or audio card). The following are leading sound editor software packages that are excellent for most Windows and Mac applications.

SoundEdit 16 by Macromedia (www.macromedia.com) is a powerful Mac sound editor with multitrack editing.

Sound Forge by Sonic Foundary (www.sfoundry.com) is a Windows 32-bit sound editor well suited for the Internet and streaming (see Figure 3-2).

Video Requirements

Video is nothing more than a series of images displayed quickly enough to give the illusion of motion. The basic characteristics of digital video include resolution, color depth, and frame rate.

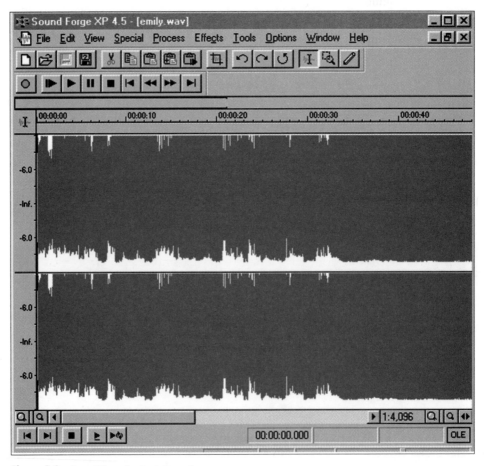

Figure 3-2   **Sound Forge by Sonic Foundary**

Picture resolution is a measure of the number of pixels in a video frame expressed as width and height. Most computer monitors display a wide range of screen sizes, such as 1024 × 768.

Color depth expresses the number of colors used in the video file, such as 8-, 16-, and 24-bit color depths. The 8-bit color depth can produce only 256 colors, while the 24-bit color depth displays 16 million.

Frame rate is the rate at which images are shown on the screen represented in frames per second (fps). Normal television is displayed at approximately 30fps (actual 29.97fps).

Even a short video of 320 × 240 size at 24-bit color depth and a 15fps produces about 207MB for one minute of video. Of course, this is a demanding throughput of video from the camera through the capture card through the SCSI bus and onto the hard drive. For example, optimizing computer capture hardware requires a balanced understanding of data flow choke-points within the PC capture process. A high speed Pentium III, with 256MB RAM, an 8.4GB (8 millisecond) hard drive, and wide-SCSI bus can accomplish up to 40Mbps throughput while capturing video. Unfortunately, many low- to medium-priced capture cards only perform at 2Mbps to 5Mbps throughput (even after being optimally configured).

Most video capture systems use a lossy format (such as JPEG). When the file is saved, there is some loss of quality. Multiple JPEG passes tend to add color noise and blockiness, especially around fine detail areas.

▶ Video Processing Systems

Table 3-2 summarizes the minimum hardware and software requirements for video production.

▶ Video Capture Cards

The capture card takes the analog video signal through an analog-to-digital converter to produce a digital signal, then compresses the signal using special chips on the card, and finally stores the compressed signal on a hard drive. The captured signal may be 1Mbps to 20Mbps. Needless to say, this will fill up a hard drive fast. The greater the capture rate, the faster the drive must be to keep up with it. However, higher capture rates generally yield higher image quality.

Table 3-2   Video Systems

	Preferred System	*Minimal System*
Processor	Pentium III 500MHz or G-4 Power-Mac	Pentium II 300MHz or G-3 Power-Mac
Memory (RAM)	128MB	64MB
Software	Microsoft Windows 2000 or Microsoft Windows NT Server version 4.0 with Service Pack 5 (real-time and scalable encoding of audio and video up to 320 × 240 × 15 frames per second). Windows Media Encoder has been tested on dual-processor systems. These systems provide additional encoding capabilities over a computer with a single processor.	Windows 95 or OS-7
Audio Card	Any sound card compatible with Creative Labs Sound Blaster 16 for Windows	Any sound card compatible with Creative Labs Sound Blaster 16 for Windows
Video Capture Card	A video capture card that supports Video for Windows or QuickTime. See the video capture cards below.	A video capture card that supports Video for Windows or QuickTime. See the video capture cards below.

Like the source, the quality of your capture card or system will affect the quality of your final movie. More expensive systems, such as the Media 100, Avid Media Composer, Digital Origin Telecast, and Truevision Targa 2000 will generally produce good image quality with more features than the less expensive cards such as the Miro Motion DC-20, Truevision Bravado, 8500 AV Macs. Very inexpensive cards, such as the built-in Mac AV cards in the lower end Macs and video display cards that capture video, will work, but often don't produce images that are as high quality, and some produce larger files (because they don't support hardware compression).

There are plenty of video capture cards with a wide variety of features and quality. The most basic and least expensive cards are for input only. It simply captures the data into your computer. The second type has input and output capabilities. These capture video, edit the video, and output the video in analog form, like a VCR. Manufacturers offer a variety of video capture kits with many options. Some things to look for include the following.

▸ Make sure the card can handle the input type you need, such as S-Video or RCA-style plugs.

▸ Ensure the card supports your TV format (NTSC or PAL).

▸ Read the vendor's feature and option lists for capture rate, codecs supported, and maximum resolution.

▸ Color depth from true-color cards is important.

▸ Make sure the card comes with editing software.

▸ Compatibility with your computer's bus (PCI, ISA, AGP, USB) is important.

The following hardware equipment information is provided as a resource guideline to products necessary for video capture and production. There are over 1,000 equipment manufacturers, dealers, and service providers. The following only lists a small fraction.

The following cards are compatible with the Windows Media Encoder and the MPEG-4 Video High Speed Compressor Codec:

Windows 98 and Windows NT 4.0 compatible:

▸ Multimedia Access Corporation Osprey 100

▸ Hauppauge Computer Works WinCast/TV

▸ Winnov Videum

Windows 98 compatible:

▸ Philips PCA645VC USB Camera

▸ Intel Corporation Smart Video Recorder III

▸ Winnov VideumCam PCMCIA

▸ ATI Technologies Inc. All-In-Wonder

Table 3-3 provides information on general capture cards details while Table 3-4 provides specific MPEG compression capture cards.

▣ Capture Applications

Your capture card may come with an application designed to control the capture process. Many cards are shipped with Adobe Premiere, and AV Macs already have MovieRecorder installed. Follow the instructions with the software. If you do use Premiere, make sure to select the **Warn on Dropped Frames** option so you'll know if some frames are missing. For example, even though you may want to capture your video at its original 29.97fps, you may really only be getting 15fps. Dropped frames may also be sporadic, causing the video to occasionally pause for a fraction of a second at random times. There's not much you can do to fix dropped frames after the fact, so keep working to improve your system until you get zero dropped frames during your capture.

Table 3-3   Capture Cards

	Operating System	Maximum size and motion	codecs
Alaris QuickVideo Transport *www.alaris.com*	Win95/98/NT	320 × 240 30 frames per second	Cinapak, Indeo
ATI Technologies ATI-TV Wonder *www.atitech.com*	Win98	640 × 480 60 frames per second	MPEG-1, MPEG-2
Dazzle Multimedia Dazzle Digital Video Creator *www.dazzle.com*	Win95/98	320 × 240 60 frames per second	MPEG
Digital Processing Systems Spark Perception RT *www.dps.com*	Win95/98/NT	720 × 480 60 frames per second	DV, MJPEG
Matrox Matrox Marvel *www.matrox.com*	Win95/98	720 × 480 60 frames per second	MPEG, MPEG-2
Pinnacle Systems Studio DV Targa *www.pinnaclesys.com*	Win95/98/NT Mac	720 × 480 60 frames per second	MPEG, MPEG-2, DV, Indeo

Dropped frames usually result when you're trying to capture video that exceeds capture rate (Mbps) for your system, or if you have a configuration problem. Try turning down the quality of the capture to see if this fixes the problem. Test your drive to see what kind of transfer it can handle. Read the capture hardware and software manuals for more information on fine-tuning it, and refer to our tip section for some other hints on optimizing the system for capture.

Most capture cards are optimized to capture at 320 × 240 or 640 × 480. Don't capture at odd image sizes, because this often requires your computer to resize on-the-fly, which can slow down the process and cause dropped frames.

Make sure to test the capture system before capturing clips. Audio levels are often different between capturing and playback.

Table 3-4   **DVD MPEG Compression Cards**

Vendor	Name
Canopus *www.canopuscorp.com*	Amber
C-Cube Microsystems *www.c-cube.com*	CLM4740 Encoder
Digital Vision *www.digitalvision.com*	BitPack MPEG-2 Encoding Workstation
Heuris	MPEG Power Professional
Leitch *www.leitch.com*	MPEG-2 Compression System
Ligos Technology *www.ligos.com*	LSX-MPEG Encoder 2.5
Minerva Systems *www.minervasys.com*	DVD Professional
Optibase *www.optibase.com*	DVD Fab! Xpress
Optivision *www.optivision.com*	VSTOR 100 Series
NUKO information systems *www.nuko.com*	DVD Composer
Omnimedia	DVD-ROM Toolkit
Sigma Designs *www.sdesigns.com*	MPEG-2 Encoding/Decoding

■) Computer Bus Architecture

One of the important aspects of processing video is data transfer rate through the bus (ISA, EISA, MCA, PCI, USB or AGP) architecture.

■) Drive

Video editing operations are very disk-intensive applications, so it is important to have an optimal drive and controller. The IDE and their follow-on EIDE drives are common for workstations. The IDE in combination with a PCI bus can reach up to 10MBps.

SCSI will probably remain the main drive controller for servers and graphics workstations controlling both hard disks and CD-ROM units. It is important to have a fast SCSI controller and drive. The original SCSI specification was an 8-bit data path transferring about 5MBps. The SCSI-2 or fast SCSI doubled that capacity to 10MBps. Wide-SCSI/SCSI-3 68-pin cable offers data path and data transfer improvements between 20Mbps and 40MBps. Currently, all Macs and most Windows PCs have USB.

Backup Hardware

There will be many very large files that you will be required to keep for later revision and editing. Tape storage for backing up large media files is essential for development companies.

Turnkey Nonlinear Editor Systems

There are "turnkey" systems that ship with all the needed hardware and software to capture video. Preconfigured systems provide a capture card and editing software that walks you through the whole process. An example of a complete turnkey system is View-cast (www.viewcast.com) with video capture, conversion, compression, and broadcast capability. A recommended system would include a Pentium III system with high speed hard drive, Osprey-100 video capture card, and with conversion, compression, and broadcast capability.

Getting your system properly configured to capture video can often be a frustrating experience. Capturing to a fast defragmented drive will enhance performance. For high quality captures, an SCSI accelerator card and possibly a disk array are beneficial. Unnecessary devices should be removed from the system. See Table 3-5 for example systems.

Step 3: Editing and Adding Effects

Now that you have captured your video, you will need to edit it. This is the fun part of the process. Editing is where the various pieces of the movie are assembled and transitions and effects added. For complicated edits and effects, a program such as Adobe Premiere, Avid Cinema, or Strata's VideoShop are recommended. These programs use a timeline-based interface to allow arranging clips in order and use various transitions between the clips. Adobe AfterEffects is well known for special effects editing. Table 3-6 provides a list of some editing software products currently available.

Table 3-5 Turnkey Nonlinear Editing Systems

Company	System	Editing Software	Inputs/Outputs
Apple PowerMac G3 Final Cut Pro Bundle *www.apple.com*	Power Macintosh G3 400MHz 128MB Mac OS 9.0	Apple Final Cut Pro	• Firewire
Avid Avid Xpress *www.avid.com*	Power Mac 333MHz Mac OS 8.1 or Pentium II 400MHz WinNT4.0	Avid Xpress	• Composite • S-Video • Component
Compaq Presario *www.compaq.com*	Pentium III 500MHz 128MB Win98	MGI Videowave II	• Firewire • USB
DPS DPS Perception RT3Dzi-4200 *www.dps.com*	Pentium II 450MHz 128MB WinNT	DPS Video Action 6.3	• Composite • S-Video • Component
DraCo Casablanca 060 *www.draco.com*	Pentium III 500MHz 128MB WinNT	Proprietary	• Composite • S-Video • Firewire
Matrox Matrox Realtime Pro-Edit *www.matrox.com*	Pentium III 500MHz 128MB WinNT	Adobe Premiere	• Composite • S-Video • Component
Mina Mina Systems *www.mina.com*	Pentium III 450MHz 128MB WinNT	Adobe Premiere	• Composite • S-Video • Component
Pinnacle Systems Targa *www.pinnaclesys.com*	Pentium II 450MHz 128MB WinNt	Adobe Premiere	• Composite • S-Video • Component
ProMax FireMax *www.promax.com*	Power Mac G3 400MHz 192MB Mac OS 8.5	Adobe Premiere	• Composite • S-Video • Firewire
Sony VAIO digital Studio *www.sony.com*	Pentium III 550MHz 128MB Win98	Adobe Premiere	• S-Video • Firewire

Putting a video clip on your Web page is easier than you might think.

Once you have taped your video, it is necessary to conduct the editing process to get all those special effects in place for your viewer. In an editing software package such as Adobe Premiere (see Figure 3-3), choose **Capture Movie** from the menu. A new window will pop

Table 3-6   Editing Software

Adobe Systems *www.adobe.com*	Premiere 5.1
Apple Computer *www.apple.com*	Final Cut Pro
Avid Technology *www.avid.com*	Avid Xpress3.0
Crystal Graphics *www.crystalgraphics.com*	Crystal 3D Vortex
Discreet *www.discreet.com*	edit*
Image Products *www.imageproducts.com*	The Executive Producer
In-sync *www.in-sync.com*	Speed Razor RT
Strata *Strata3d.com*	VideoShop 4.0/3D
Trakker Technologies *www.trackertech.com*	Slingshot
United Media *www.unitedmediainc.com*	On-line Express 2.0
Videomedia *www.videomedia.com*	VIP-LM Logging Module

up and you can specify what dimensions you want to use to capture the clip. The current standard is 240 × 180 at 15fps. Next, press **Record** to capture your video. Save the file as an .avi or .mov. Be aware that this file is going to be really large.

Once the video clip is captured, editing begins by opening one or two player windows containing the source media—the existing content from a video library. Then creating a new video is simply a matter of selecting segments from the source movies, copying them, and pasting the clips into the new player. Drag and drop features are available for

- Selecting frames
- Replacing frames
- Multiple player windows
- Time code changes

Most of the tools you need are found under the Edit menu in most tools. But there are many shortcuts to make the job even easier. The first bit of editing you will probably undertake is postcapture editing, like clipping frames from the beginning or end of the video.

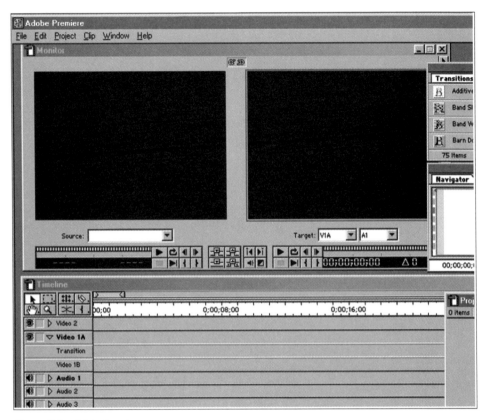

Figure 3-3   Adobe Premiere

Afterwards, you will need to do more advanced edits, like moving a video clip from one location to another or adding background sounds or voice-overs. The advanced projects will require the overlaying of graphics, titles, special effects, and transitions.

Transitions are effects for combining two adjacent scenes, moving from one to the other through a blackout, fade, blends, dissolves, or rolling effect, for example. Adobe Premiere has over 70 transitions.

MediaStudio Pro

MediaStudio Pro consists of a suite of modules including Audio Editor, CG Infinity, Video Capture, Video Editor, Video Paint, and Video Wizard. Audio Editor is a tool that can be used for editing straight audio files. The module is filled with nice touches and deals well with different sound formats. The most common audio formats are supported for importing and exporting, and the program can be easily used just for file format conversion. Basic editing functions such as cutting, pasting, and managing cue points are included. Effects also include a pitch changer, a speed changer, fade controls, and several types of echo. CG Infinity is another well-designed module for designing titles.

Video Capture is the module for digitizing your video. It includes professional features such as a waveform monitor and vectorscope combination for proper image level calibration, VTR control with SMPTE, and frame-accurate batch digitizing.

Video Editor is a very nice nonlinear editor with all the features you would expect out of a professional product. It is easy to work with and really intuitive, with two video tracks, one effects track, and up to 99 video overlay tracks. All you have to do is drag the video tracks to where you want them in the timeline, and when A and B are overlaid, the transition you select will automatically be timed to fit accordingly. Video Paint is quite a powerful paint, animation, and rotoscoping program that lets you paint over any frame in a video sequence.

How To Example

Our Web site *www.video-software.com* provides download links for *free* video players from all the major developers (RealNetworks, Microsoft, Apple, Emblaze, Bitcasting, LZX-MPEG), as well as video encoding tools, editing tools, and server software.

A CD-ROM with example code and streaming video demos is included at the back cover of this book. On the enclosed CD-ROM is an example in a directory called *How To*. It contains a sequential series of examples that takes you through the Internet video production process. The continuous production process addresses the steps described in the chapters throughout the book as follows. To produce the video, a How To talking head presentation describing all the steps was videotaped and then captured to digital in the file HowTo1.avi (also HowTo1.qt). These files are on the CD-ROM. Subsequent steps edit the .avi and .qt files into a new HowTo.avi file.

In subsequent chapters, we will show how these files are compressed into streaming format and published to Web pages on your Web site. For now we will describe the process of taping, capturing, and editing the original HowTo1.avi file.

To start looking in the How To directory, there are subdirectories called
  ▸ How To AVI, which has several avi files
  ▸ How To Graphics, which has graphics for insertion into the video during the editing process

Our equipment list includes a 200MHz Pentium pro computer with 64MB of RAM and an 8.1GB hard drive, with an Osprey-100 capture card, MS-32 sound card, VIDcap capture software included with Osprey package, audio/video connector plugs, Sony DV camcorder, and Adobe Premiere 5.1 and video compression software to be described in later chapters.

Step one is preparing the original source material. The How To video was prepared in an office with a floodlight and sunlight for background lighting and an overhead light and a key light on the subject just off-camera to reduce shadows and contrast. A DV camcorder was placed on a tripod approximately six feet from the subject at eye level. A microphone was attached and extended toward the subject just off-camera. A light and sound test was conducted and several takes were necessary to arrange the stage successfully. A ten-minute presentation was recorded using DV minitape format.

Step two is capturing the audio/video using a computer with a video capture card. The DV camcorder has a three-band plug that separates into two audio plugs and one video plug to connect into the computer sound and video capture cards, respectively. (Alternate options include an S-Video adapter and a FireWire connection.) All three of these connects were used and the video was captured by them all to compare quality.

The capture card used here was an Osprey-100 with VIDCap software (see Figure 3-4).

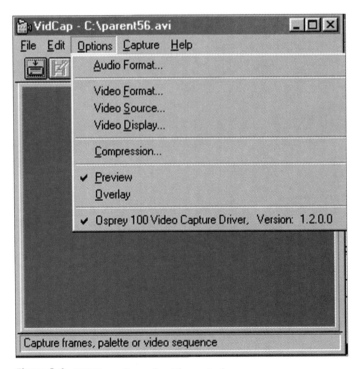

Figure 3-4   VIDCap software for video capturing

The video was captured with setting, for 15fps and 160 × 120 pixels frame size with a keyframe set at 5 and audio at 44Kbps × Hz (see Figure 3-5). The original video for 160 × 120 pixel size frames is called *HowTo.avi*.

The captured file was named *HowTo.avi* and was then edited by Adobe Premiere 5.1 (see Figure 3-3) to improve the video through the use of filters and added graphics.

Step three is editing the video and saving the large uncompressed edited file. In the graphics subdirectory, you will find several graphics that can be inserted into the video according to the Adobe Premiere project file entitled *HowToEdit.ppj*. By using Adobe premiere with the project file, you can import the video file and the graphics and then export the files to a movie called *HowTo.avi*. The conversion of the ten-minute video to the edited form by using Adobe Premiere required two hours of processing.

The encoding process of *step four* will be presented in Chapters 5 and 6. Publishing to a Web site and Internet delivery of *step five* will be presented in Chapters 8 and 9.

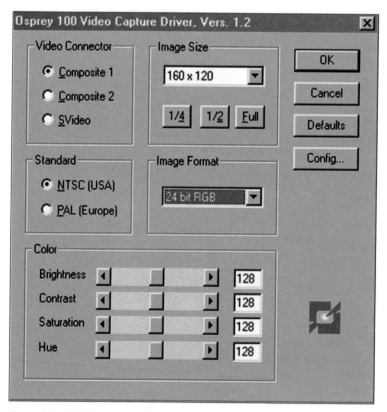

Figure 3-5   **VIDCap software for video capturing**

▶ Conclusion

The quality of analog delivery of audio and video through radio and television is based upon large clear pictures without noticeable interruption or downtime. In this chapter, the background for the development of video content and production was presented. The overall goal of creating good multimedia video is to produce a video signal with less noise, minimum camera movement, and fine detail so that the final movie will compress well and look good at a small screen size. This contributes to meeting the limitations of bandwidth resources.

On the basis of this chapter, you should conclude that the authoring, editing, and Web publishing tools for streaming video are widely available, inexpensive, and easy to use. Your participation and success in building streaming video Web sites and businesses looks great.

PART III

Video Compression

Data compression algorithms are in their infancy. By understanding the basics of how data is compressed in Chapter 4, an appreciation of how much more capability exists emerges. Then, in Chapters 5 and 6, narrowband streaming video compression technology is detailed with how to examples for the leading software compression products. Chapter 7 moves streaming compression to the next stage (MPEG compression), where it is preparing for low-end broadband (1.5Mpbs) delivery within the next few years.

Video Compression

Up until recently, capturing video involved very large file data transfer rates (1Mbps to 600Mbps), and putting them on the Internet had been prohibitive. Compression and better support of different formats is revolutionizing on-line video, both at narrowband and broadband. Developers of streaming and compression tools are targeting business application in the 28.8Kbps to 1.5Mbps range, and TV-quality video delivered in the 1.5Mbps to 6Mbps range. With each improvement in data compression, there is an equivalent effective expansion of available bandwidth. ▶

We will explain a few simple ideas of binary computer code for data types and then go on to the basic principles of data reduction through redundancy removal. Jumping from there, we advance to lossy schemes and novel approaches, starting with JPEG and continuing with wavelet, fractal, and motion compensation. This will lead to a simple perspective of compression and decompression standards and the software tools on the market today. Of course, many of today's compression software tools can be used without any knowledge of the underlying algorithms involved. But by reviewing the competing parameters driving different vendors you will appreciate the pressures on resolving standards.

◗ Data Types for Different Types of Content

The Internet had existed for decades mostly as a tool of scientific workers and the military in order to exchange text and numerical information. The modem and network connections provided reliable but slow data transfer. The priority was for accurate and reliable reproduction of the data information, and lengthy download times and excessive storage requirements were a fact of life.

Then, in 1989, the World Wide Web developed with its ability to link more than just text. It could link graphics, sound, and video to create an entire hypermedia system. Over the next couple of years, the groundwork for the Web was further developed and refined to include the Hypertext Transfer Protocol (HTTP) for linking Web documents, the Hypertext Markup Language (HTML) for formatting Web documents, and the universal resource locator (URL) system for addressing Web documents.

In order to appreciate the impact data types can make on the Web's efficient transmission of information, we need to review some basic computer science facts.

The basis of computer language and communication is binary code. The binary digital bits (0,1) were found to be eminently suitable for the electronic circuits of computers and the processing of logic information because the two values 0 and 1 can be represented reliably by the presence or absence of electrical currents, electrical charge, and magnetic fields. All data, whether sets of numbers or abstract representations, are chosen to provide efficient means of computational analysis. And a programming language representing an abstract understanding about a problem or application uses this computation power to solve our problems.

But no matter what computer language a program is written in, it has a variety of data types for storing and manipulating bits of information efficiently. These elements of storage are essential to running applications. So how is a variable used? A variable is an area in memory that stores values.

To get a picture of memory, consider a piece of graph paper. If each lined-off piece of the graph paper represents a section of memory, then a section may be a byte of memory. One kilobyte would be 1024 sections of the graph paper. When applications store and retrieve information, temporary values are placed in memory. Different types of data require different amounts of memory to hold the required information of that data type. Variables are assigned memory locations to store information, and it is necessary to store that information without wasting memory.

Information today comes in many shapes and sizes. The variety of information content is manifold. For example, content types can include personnel information, news, business sales, entertainment, and so forth, each of which may contain text, numbers, graphics, and other rich media. The storage of this information may be a simple list of a data string or a more complex collection of data in the form of records or database entries.

Let's consider text information for a start. For memory storage considerations, text should be stored in continuous adjacent locations. If the text is defined as a series of fixed-length strings, for example, then not every fixed string will be fully used since normal paragraphs contain variable-length words. Therefore, fixed-length strings could contain blank spaces and prove inefficient. If in addition to text, the information contained numerical information, the format difference between text and numbers would make their joint storage more complex. Indeed, record data types were developed to solve just this issue. Records can be complex text and numerical data types grouped and stored as units. This provides just the right elements for database-type information where the close proximity of memory-stored information and the organized pattern of that information makes retrieval and display rapid and efficient.

Our question then becomes, What are the most efficient ways of recording, storing, and transferring various data types of information?

For text and numerical information being transported over the Internet, there are additional considerations. In order to preserve the meaning of the text, the characters must be exactly reproduced. However, carriage returns, spaces, and format information may be left out without damage to the information. Compression of text then has the advantage of improving transmission rate, but has strict limitation on how greatly it can be compressed.

For audio and video data, information transfer does not have to be perfect since the human ear and eye are limited and can in many ways be fooled into accepting an imperfect reproduction. The importance of graphics, audio and video formats, and standards plays a crucial roll in reaching compression optimization. The information contained in a series of pictures is enormous when digitized for transmission. A 30-second commercial digitized without compression is almost a gigabyte of data. This is impossible for ordinary modems to download in a reasonable amount of time.

The arrival of data compression reduces the video data to more manageable levels. Now the technology has only recently reached the point where video can be digitized and compressed to levels with reasonable appearance while being distributed over digital networks. Consider compression targeted for

> *Narrowband.* Streaming video is highly compressed (up to 500:1) and allows the user to begin watching the video almost immediately when he clicks on the link. On a low bandwidth connection today, the quality will be slightly lower than downloadable, but the total experience is far more satisfying, often making the difference as to whether the video is watched at all.

Table 4-1   Application Bandwidth Requirements

Application	Approximate Compression Factor	Required Bandwidth (Mbps) (after compression)
Video conferencing	300:1	0.384
Video catalog	100:1	1.5
Corporate LAN (10Mbps Ethernet)	100:1	1.5
Digital TV (MPEG-2)		
• On demand	100:1	1.5
• Live	50:1	3
• Sports	25:1	6
Entertainment video (HDTV 1080 × 1920 × 24-bit color)	100:1	19.3 to 38.6

Broadband: Uncompressed high-definition television streams require around 1Gbps per channel for proper delivery. Several compression methods have been developed that can reduce the bandwidth requirements for video streams to levels acceptable for existing networks at the last mile delivery bottleneck of 1.5Mbps.

Table 4-1 presents the bandwidth and compression requirements for some applications of interest.

How Data Is Compressed

Data compression, itself, is a process of converting raw data into an output stream of smaller size. The process of compression requires reducing redundant information, either by a loss-less, or lossy, process. A loss-less process might be necessary for transmission of vital accounting or banking information. Lossy data compression, on the other hand, concedes a certain loss of accuracy in the exchange for greatly increased compression. Lossy compression proves effective when applied to images and digitized audio.

Due to the limitations of the human ear and eye, audio and video can accept an imperfect reproduction. Consider the following analogy. Storing and transmitting Beethoven's Ninth Symphony played by the Philadelphia Philharmonic would require a huge amount of storage and bandwidth to transmit. However, the storage and transmission of the musical score from which the music is played would be more readily handled. The question would be how well the score was played at the receiving end of the transmission when it arrived.

Nevertheless, compression of audio/video information even with the loss of some of the original information is an important improvement in Internet utilization.

Data compression consists of taking a stream of symbols and transforming them into codes. The fundamental law of compression is to assign short codes to common terms leaving the remaining longer code assignments to rarely occurring terms. If the compression is to be effective, the resulting codes will be smaller than the original symbols. The decision to output a certain code for a particular symbol is based upon a model. The model is a collection of data and rules used to process input symbols and determine which codes to output. A program uses the model to accurately define the probabilities for each symbol and the coder to produce an appropriate code based on those probabilities. The sum of modeling and coding produces data compression. Typically, however, the complete process is simply referred to as *coding*.

Braille is a well-known code consisting of groups of dots embossed on paper. It is equivalent to a 6-bit system with 64 possible groups representing letters, numbers, punctuation, and common words. Braille achieves only a very slight compression.

Another well-known code is the Morse code for telegraphs. It replaces the common letter "e" with one dot and less common letters by a series of dots and dashes. Morse code achieves a more substantial compression.

Methods of compression include the following.
- Run length encoding (RLE) is based on numerical counting of the same repeated item. If data item d occurs n consecutive times, replace it with nd.
- Statistical encoding is based upon assigning short codes to the most frequently occurring events. (Examples include Shannon-Fano, Huffman, MNP5, and Arithmetic coding.)
- Dictionary encoding selects strings of symbols and encodes each string as a token using a dictionary. The simplest example is a dictionary of the English language. (Examples include LZ77, LZ78, LZFG, and LZW.)

Most compression methods operate in streaming mode where the input is processed and continues until an end-of-file is reached. Some methods use a block mode where input is read block by block and encoded separately. Compression methods that only read the data and ignore the physical meaning of the data are called *physical*. Logical compression methods refer to special-purpose pattern substitution where the source data are replaced as recognized items.

Compression performance is measured in several ways as follows:
- Compression ratio = (size of output stream)/(size of input stream)
- Compression factor = 1/ratio

- Compression performance = $100 \times (1 - \text{compression ratio})$
- Bpp = number of bits needed to compress a pixel

There are numerous ways of implementing the compression process, some suitable for text and others for image information. A nonadaptive compression method is rigid and does not modify its operations parameters or tables in response to how effective the compression process is proceeding. In contrast, adaptive methods examine raw data and make modification accordingly.

Many methods rely on adaptive means to modify the applied method based on the particular file characteristics being compressed. The Shannon Fano coding, for example, is *n* symbols of known probability, divided into multi-subsets of equal probability.

In 1952, D. Huffman published an important optimized variable length coding technique. The length of the encoded character is inversely proportional to that character's frequency. Huffman's codes are similar to Morse code in that frequently used letters are assigned short codes. Huffman coding is also similar to Shannon-Fano, but instead of top to bottom, Huffman uses a code tree from the bottom up.

Arithmetic coding takes the complete data stream and outputs one specific code word as a floating point number between 0 and 1. In 1977, the next important step was taken with the LZW method using strings of characters.

Image Compression

Of course, many of today's compression software tools can be used without any knowledge of the underlying algorithms involved. But if you want an appreciation of the competing parameters driving different vendors and forcing various standards, you will find the following sections worthwhile.

Graphical user interfaces make it easier to run computer applications converting many types of complex information into understandable images. Each pixel occupies a small rectangular region on the screen and displays one color at a time. The pixels form a two-dimensional array. The color pixels are usually internally represented by a 24-bit number where the percentages of red, green, and blue occupy 8 bits each. Such a 24-bit number can specify 2 to the 24th power or 16.78 million colors.

Graphics file formats can be divided into two general classes: vector and bitmap. Vector graphics use a series of commands, such as **draw a circle and rectangle,** and are primarily used for monitors and printers. Their disadvantages include too many commands needed for complex images and usually a slow display rate. (An exception is vector-based Flash.)

Bitmap image formats represent images as two-dimensional arrays, where each array element represents a color at a particular location. Bitmaps produce high-quality images, but are large, as shown by their equation:

Bitmap size = (width * height * (bits per pixel) + 7) / 8

Thus an 800 $\times$ 600 image with 24 bits per pixel requires 1.44MB.

The bitmap file structure is very simple, consisting of four parts: file header, image header, color table, and pixel data.

There are many ways to represent colors numerically. One of the most common is the RGB (red-green-blue) model, where the range of colors is represented by 0 to 1 values per component in color space.

Compression techniques take advantage of patterns within the image data. Of the three compression principles, RLE, statistical methods, and dictionary-based methods, none are individually satisfactory for color compression. RLE is of some value, but statistical methods are useless where the probability of a continuous-tone color gives roughly the same probabilities. Dictionary-based methods similarly fail for continuous-tone colors, since similar tones do not produce repeatable patterns. Table 4-2 shows which compression methods are used by the most popular image file formats.

The failure of traditional compression methods has led to novel approaches, such as JPEG, quadtrees, weighted finite automata (WFA), wavelets, and iterative function systems (IFS).

Vector Quantization, (VQ), like JPEG (Joint Photographic Experts Group), breaks an image into blocks, or vectors, of $n \times n$ pixels. One advantage of JPEG is the use of many adjustable parameters.

Table 4-2   **Compression Methods Used by Various File Formats**

	BMP	*GIF*	*JPEG*
RLE	x		x
Huffman			x
LZ		x	
DCT			x

The JPEG compression encoding process includes the following.
- Color images are transformed from RGB into luminance/chrominance color space.
- Creation of low-resolution pixels.
- Pixels of each color are organized by groups of 8×8 pixel data units. The Discrete Cosine Transform (DCT) is then applied to each data unit.
- Each of the 64 frequency components in the data unit is divided by a separate quantization coefficient (QC).
- The 64 quantized frequency coefficients of each data unit are encoded using a combination RLE and Huffman coding.
- Headers are added and all JPEG parameters are saved.

The decoder reverses the entire process.

The lossy algorithm methods specializing in video compression include
- Discrete cosine transforms (DCTs)
- Discrete wavelet transforms (DWT)
- Fractals transforms
- Hybrid wavelet-fractal transforms

Compression methods can be symmetric or asymmetric. For symmetric compression methods, it takes the same amount of computational effort to perform the compression operation as it does to perform the decompression operation. Motion JPEG is an example of a symmetric compression method. Video compression methods, such as MPEG-1 and MPEG-2, are asymmetric. Since many of the video on demand applications will involve one source with many recipients, it is desirable that the compression method place most of the required computational complexity on the source side. This limits the complexity and therefore the cost of the equipment at the destination side or end user.

Discrete Cosine Transforms (DCTs)

Discrete cosine transforms (DCTs) decompose an image into coefficients assigned to basic functions. DCTs are limited to cosine functions and are computationally intensive. The beauty of the DCT-based approach is that it is compatible with current and imminent draft compression standards. H.261, H.263, MPEG-1, and MPEG-2 are all motion-compensated DCT-based schemes. However, DCT-based video delivery, with the exception of MPEG-2, possesses no inherent scalability.

Non-DCT based compression techniques, such as layered, subband, and wavelet, are intrinsically scalable.

Discrete Wavelet Transforms (DWT)

Discrete wavelet transforms (DWT) are a new form of applied mathematics. This technology has found application in many areas including acoustics, seismic analysis, crystallography, quantum mechanics, and image compression. Discrete wavelet transforms are like discrete cosine transforms since they will decompose an image into coefficients assigned to basic functions. Wavelets use a wider range of simpler functions resulting in less complex calculations. The basic compression idea of the DWT is computed and the resulting coefficients are compared with a threshold value. The compression results from packing the information into a smaller number of coefficients. The nonzero coefficients produce a loss-less encoding scheme. High compression is possible with no noticeable difference in quality.

Video compression is essentially a three-dimensional reduction scheme for a sequence of images with intraframe and interframe coding. The intraframe coding reduces correlation between pixels while the interframe coding applies the difference between successive frames in a sequence. Wavelet-based subband coding for intraframe coding produces better visual quality and higher compression ratios. The first commercial 10-bit proprietary wavelet codec was released for capture cards in March 1998.

The majority of scalable video codecs are based on subband coding techniques of which the most widely used is the *wavelet transform*.

Fractals

Fractal compression is radically different. It stores instructions or formulas for creating the image. The approaches involve extracting important subsets of the image content of each frame and only delivering the most objects. Object-based coding can achieve very high data compression rates while maintaining an acceptable visual quality in the decoded images. However, object-based coders are computationally intensive and need an image segmentation algorithm.

Temporal redundancy is unique to video compression resulting from fractal similarity on the time axis. Unfortunately, three-dimensional fractal compression algorithms are unrealistic regarding today's computer capabilities.

Hybrid Wavelet-Fractal Transforms

Wavelet image compression subband decomposition uses a local wavelet quadrature filter that transforms images to an equivalent spectrum space. The local image redundancies are then more easily extracted. A wavelet subband compression algorithm consists of the image data decorrelating transform and the data symbol entropy coding. The most efficient order for encoding entries is called *embedded zero tree*.

The most important advantage of wavelet compression over other systems is that it is a variable manipulation where the gains are reflected in two geometric aspects.

Fractal compression can be related to wavelet compression through the process of destination-reference matching of tree branches. Hybrid combinations of wavelet-fractal compression are based on these geometric properties.

▣ Image Compression Segmentation and Edge Detection

The edges of an image contain important information about the image, in particular for fractal compression. The edge tells where the objects are, their shape, size, and texture. Edge detection is the first step in segmentation. Image segmentation, a field of image analysis, is used to group pixels into regions to determine an image's composition.

The simplest and quickest edge detector determines the maximum value from a series of pixel subtractions. Gradient and second-order derivatives produce contour and localization. Edge detection in color images depends on luminance discontinuity. Full-color information can provide segmentation with coding of chrominance. This produces extremely high compression (1000:1).

In contrast to MPEG-1 and 2 (that work with rectangular effects, such as blocking), second-generation techniques concentrate on objects instead of blocks. The temporal stability of segmentation is of major importance in predictive coding and tracking. Focus and motion measurements are taken from high frequency data and edges, but intensity measurements are taken from low frequency data and object interiors. Moving foreground can be segmented from stationary foreground and moving or stationary background. Typically, the foreground contains important information. The background can be transmitted less frequently. Integration of cues improves accuracy in segmenting complex scenes and produces a sensor fusion.

▣ Motion Compensation DWT

In recent years, a fundamental goal of image sequence compression has been to reduce the bit-rate for transmission while retaining image quality. Compression is achieved through reductions in spatial and temporal dimensions.

Motion compensation discrete cosine transform (MCDCT) coding schemes have been successfully used. The basic idea of motion compensation coding is using the corresponding content of the previous decode frame as the prediction of the current frame. Using adaptive motion compensation in conjunction with DWT offers an opportunity to optimize a wavelet codec expressly for object tracking.

Compression-Decompression (codec) Standards

Wow! We've gone from a few simple ideas of binary computer code and data types to the basic principles of data reduction through redundancy removal. Jumping from there, we advanced to lossy image compression schemes and novel approaches starting with JPEG and continuing with wavelet, fractal, and motion compensation.

This book is not intended to go into each topic in detail, but only to provide a flavor. The result should be the ability to sort through subsequent discussions of advantages and disadvantages, since they will play a central role in video applications and broadband standards convergence in chapters to come.

For additional information see the following public bodies that are active in this area.

- *JTC*. Joint Technical Committee of ISO and IEC. It deals with information technology. ISO/IEC JTC1/SC29 is the subcommittee of JTC responsible for coding audio, picture, multimedia, and hypermedia information. The WG11 is the Moving Pictures Experts Group (MPEG).
- *ITU*. International Telecommunication Union.
- *IMA*. Interactive Multimedia Association.
- *DAVIC*. Digital Audiovisual Council.

A useful additional source on standards related to multimedia can be found at *http://cuiwww.unige.ch/OSG/info/MultimediaInfo/mmsurvey/standards.html*.

So let's continue by sorting out compression-decompression standards and their comparisons.

There are two main common environments for desktop video playback, QuickTime from Apple and Video for Windows (VFW) from Microsoft.

PC video:
- *AVI*. Proprietary Microsoft standard, Audio Video Interleave compression technique used to encode audiovisual information for Video for Windows for personal computers by Microsoft Corporation for Intel.
- *MOV/QT*. Proprietary Apple standard.

Table 4-3 shows the architecture for AVI.

The Video for Windows application uses software DDLs and drivers to handle low-level capture, software codec compression and decompression, and dat formats. The following is a list of compression-decompression (codec) standards.

- *H.120.* ITU codecs for videoconferencing using primary digital group transmission.
- *H.261.* ITU (International Telecom Union) video coding standard from 1990.
- *H.263.* Provisional videoconferencing ITU draft 1996.
- *H.320.* A family of standards for video adopted by ITU. Quality not as high as proprietary video compression algorithms. Most video codecs employ proprietary and standard compression algorithms. The proprietary compression is used to transmit to another *like* video unit, and the standard algorithm is used when conferencing between differing vendors.
- *H.323.* A family of standards for video adopted by ITU for sending packets of video over networks. Microsoft and Intel adapted the standard in 1996 for sending voice packets over packet networks. It is installed on Windows-based PCs and used to packetize and compress voice when callers with PCs make calls from their computers over the Internet.
- *M-JPEG.* Moving JPEG images to provide image presentation.
- *Sorenson.* Mac compression codec.
- *VRML.* Virtual Reality Modelling Language. Originally a proprietary standard developed by Silicon Graphics, but now in the public domain and formally adopted by the VRML Architecture Group (VAG). The specification has been standardized by *ISO/IEC JTC1/SC24.*
- *MPEG-1.* Targets CD-ROM at 1.5Mbps and includes Windows Media and QuickTime3.
- *MPEG-2.* For all-digital transmission of broadcast TV and DVD-based quality video at 4Mbps to 9Mbps.

Table 4-3   **Video for Windows Capture Software Architecture**

VFW capture		
AVI Capture AVICAP.DLL		
Video Channel Input		File/Stream Handler
MMSYSTEM.DLL	MSVIDEO.DLL	AVIFILE.DLL
Wave audio driver	Video capture device driver	**Codec**
Audio hardware	Video hardware	

▸ *MPEG-3.* Layer3 of MPEG-1 is a compression standard for streaming audio.

▸ *MPEG-4.* Targets very low bitrate for mobile multimedia, video phone, video mail, remote sensing, and video games.

▸ *MPEG-6.* Wireless transmission.

▸ *MPEG-7.* Content information standard for information searches.

▸ *MPEG-8.* Allows a four-dimensional description of objects.

Video Compression Methods

In 1999, the most important nonproprietary video codec standards for streaming video included H.261, H.263, MJPEG, MPEG-1, MPEG-2, and MPEG-4. Compared to video codecs for CD-ROM or TV broadcast, codecs designed for the Internet require greater scalability, lower computational complexity, and greater resiliency to network losses. The codecs must be tightly linked to servers and network delivery software to achieve the highest possible frame rates and picture quality. In fact, over the next few years, we will see a host of new flexible and scalable algorithms designed for the Internet. A more complete breakdown on standards is presented in Appendix F.

Streaming Video Codecs

Streaming is compressed information sent through an Internet connection and played in real time. An encoder compresses the stream, which is sent to the server. Instead of downloading the entire file before playing it, the file is played as it is downloaded. There are two types of streaming: live streaming sends the signal as it is happening; on-demand streaming sends a prerecorded file. The quality of stored streaming from a Web server is not as good as that from a video server. There are several products that provide streaming technology but not all support live streaming.

Video streaming is a rapidly changing technology. Universal standards have not yet been established, so each product currently available on the market is proprietary and not universally compatible (see Table 4-4).

RealNetworks and its proprietary codec has had over 80 million RealPlayers downloaded. In 1999, the company held 85 percent of the streaming media market share, which consist of about 600,000 Web pages containing streaming media. RealVideo uses a 500:1 compression ratio for data, which, when unfolded, can yield stream video at the rate of 20Kbits per second, well below the 28.8Kbps limit found on many older modems. RealNetwork's software will be presented in detail in Chapter 5.

Table 4-4   **Vendors and Codecs Standards**

Vendors	Codecs and Standards	Comments
RealNetworks *www.real.com*	RealSystems G2 • Supports a wide variety of codecs and standards and third-party plug-ins	• Wavelet-based • Fractal-based
Microsoft *www.microsoft.com*	Desktop • WAV • AVI • QuickTime • RealVideo 4.0 Codecs • Microsoft MPEG-4 • MPEG-layer3 • Vivo G.723 and H.263 • Duck TrueMotion RT • Iterated Systems' ClearVideo • VDOnet's VDOWave • Intel H.263	Windows Media
Apple *www.apple.com*	QuickTime 4.0 Sorenson	
SupeMAc	Cinepak	VQ-based
Emblaze *www.emblaze.com*	Emblaze	Java-based applet player
Digital Bitcasting *www.bitcasting.com*	MPEG-1, MPEG-2, and MP3 distribution and playback using RealNetworks RealSystem G2	MPEG multicast streaming redistribution from 300Kbps to 15Mbps
VDO	VDOLive	
VOSAIC	• H.263 • MPEG-1 • MPEG-2	
Duck corp.	TrueMotion	
Inetcam *www.inetcam.com*		
Intel	Indeo	Vector quantization
Minerva Systems *www.minerva.com*	MPEG	MPEG streaming broadcast over IP networks
Sorenson Vision *www.s-vision.com*	Sorenson QuickTime codec	
Clearband *www.clearband.com*		MPEG-2 multicast streaming redistribution from 300Kbps to 2Mbps
Wild Tangent *www.wildtangent.com*		Streaming 3D multimedia
Aware	Wavelets	Hybrid DCT and VQ

Microsoft's Windows Media Player has all the features found in most of the other multimedia players. And it supports most local and streamed multimedia file types including WAV, AVI, QuickTime, RealAudio 4.0, and RealVideo 4.0. Windows Media software will be presented in detail in Chapter 6.

QuickTime is Apple's multiplatform, industry-standard, multimedia software architecture. QuickTime is widely used by software developers and content creators to publish synchronized graphics, sound, video, text, music, VR, and 3D-media. QuickTime 4 adds strong support for real (RTSP) streaming. QuickTime software will be presented in detail in Chapter 6.

VOSAIC supports a variety of codecs, for example, H.263, MPEG-1, and MPEG-2, to suit the available bandwidth ranging from 28.8Kbps to T1. The bandwidth must be specified at encoding so that the most appropriate codec can be selected. Limited dynamic adaptation is possible through frame dropping.

VDOLive is based on a proprietary wavelet encoding that enables 10fps to 15fps, ¼ screen video replay over 28.8Kbps. It scales dynamically from 14.4Kbps modem to ISDN and cable modems.

Emblaze is a Java-based video architecture, which is unique in that it does not require any plug-ins. However, proper playback does require the latest version of Java and a high-end computer, and even then it generally falls short of other technologies.

Authoring Tools

Digital Renaissance, T.A.G., and Veon V-Active have developed new interactive Web video tools that provide clicking in the middle of a video clip to jump to another video segment, piece of text, audio clip, picture, or Web page. Interactive video has real appeal for education, advertising banners, news delivery, and electronic commerce. A QuickTime VR movie's hotspots can be used to trigger any sort of Web action. Hotspots can link to other pages, other movies, sounds, images—any kind of Web media.

Available authoring tools include the following.
- Agent 7 by 7th Level is an application that allows the user to create streamed, interactive animated characters.
- The new SMIL Tag Pack from Allaire makes it easy to author multimedia-rich Web applications and presentations using Cold Fusion, the leading Web application development system, and HomeSite, the popular code-based HTML editing tool.
- Cinax is a leading provider of desktop digital video (MPEG) software to the entertainment, multimedia, and consumer electronics industries. Cinax editing, transcoding,

and stream security technologies expose the power of digital media in the future of communications. MediaPalette Plus and MediaPalette Pro are available on the RealStore at special introductory prices.

▶ T.A.G. supports RealNetworks streaming media system.

▶ OZ.COM's Fluid3D delivers real-time streaming 3D, enabling true broadcast animation on the Internet.

▶ Sausage Software has incorporated support for RealSystem G2 and SMIL.

▣ Conclusion

Capturing video involves very large files (1Mbps 600Mbps). In this chapter, we examined how to reduce file size through data compression and make it small enough that it can be played over the Web. In addition, streaming formats and codecs were reviewed, and the latest relevant software tools were discussed.

We showed a few simple principles of data reduction through the use of redundancy removal. Jumping from there, we advanced to lossy image compression schemes and novel approaches starting with JPEG and continuing with wavelet, fractal, and motion compensation.

Data compression produces an effective expansion of bandwidth. Developers of streaming and compression tools are targeting TV-quality video delivered in the submegabit range in the right context. Media on-demand is available for TV and for PCs in the near future.

Our conclusion is that data algorithms are in the early stages of development and that there is tremendous room for orders-of-magnitude improvement. This will have a dramatic effect on effective bandwidth in the future. The variety of algorithms and their implementation will continue to produce serious competition.

On the basis of this chapter, you should conclude that new codec improvements will emerge rapidly from the numerous competing codec developers.

CHAPTER 5

RealNetworks and SMIL

The first contact most Internet users had with streaming media started with RealNetworks' (formerly Progressive Networks) release of RealAudio server and client programs. RealAudio started playing as soon as the user clicked on a selection, and it was a cross-platform program that could be played from Windows, Unix, and Mac systems. ▸

This chapter provides the basic information on how to use RealNetworks' production software and the open standard SMIL language used to encode combining text, graphics, and video. Instructional information and simple How-to examples for producing Web video with RealVideo are provided.

I n 2000, RealNetworks had over 115 million RealPlayers distributed, and the company held 85 percent of the streaming media market, which consists of about 600,000 Web pages containing streaming media. RealVideo uses a compression ratio up to 500:1, which can yield streaming video at the rate of 20Kbps.

As bandwidth increases and compression gets better, expect streaming video to scale to produce competition with TV's MPEG standards. Then the Internet will be a true mainstream entertainment medium. Until then, we must be content with the present-day tools and bandwidth limitation of 28.8Kbps to 1.5Mbps.

On the enclosed CD-ROM, an example directory called *How To* contains a sequential series of examples that takes you through the Internet video production process. The continuous production process follows the chapters throughout the book. A Web page link to most of the vendor codec developers and their player, editing, compression, and server software is included. A How To talking head presentation describes all the steps involved. The files on the CD-ROM contain each step for conversion and edited process for the .avi and .qt files and subsequent compression into RealVideo files *.rm. The HTML files for posting the streaming video in various formats are included in its directory. Finally, a SMIL directory includes .smi files for streaming RealVideo with scrolling text, graphics, and URLs. To get the most out of this chapter, it is recommended that you copy the directories from the CD-ROM to your hard drive and examine the files as they are referred to within the chapter.

▣ Background on RealNetworks' RealSystem G2

RealNetworks' RealSystem G2 is a whole new media delivery system. The codecs have been upgraded to enhance quality at all bit rates. Using the new system's SureStream technology, the bit rate is adjusted to match available bandwidth. The addition of two new data types (RealText and RealPix) helps create multimedia at narrowband delivery rates. The system supports SMIL and allows new data types to be added.

There are two basic types of file formats that can stream with RealSystem G2: Standard or open formats. Video editing programs let you export files as AVI or QuickTime, for example, but these formats are not optimized for network streaming. RealAudio and RealVideo are highly compressed formats for network streaming. You can convert a file from a standard format to a streaming format with an encoding tool. Some editing programs can also export files directly to streaming formats.

RealSystem G2 is a fully integrated encoder, server, splitter/cache, and player system with the two-way intelligence to resolve network congestion and negotiate complex Internet protocols. RealSystem G2 includes

 ▸ An automatic, variable bit-rate encoding and delivery system that can scale to megabit connection rates and will dynamically adjust the transmission rate up or down as a user's connection rate changes due to network congestion.

 ▸ Deployment in the redistribution nodes of the Internet that can serve live and on-demand streams to users from the nearest access point to reduce congestion and packet loss, increase broadcast capacity, and eliminate bandwidth constraints.

 ▸ SMIL, the W3C specification standard streaming media language that provides a time-based synchronized environment to stream audio, video, text, images, and Flash files.

 ▸ Compliance with RTSP (IETF) for control of streaming media to ensure that broadcasts can navigate across network architectures.

 ▸ Support for broadcast platforms (Alpha UNIX, FreeBSD, HP/UX, Linux, SCO Unix, SGI IRIX, Sun OS, and Win32) and emerging clients (PCs, set-top boxes, portable devices, and browsers).

RealNetworks provides several encoding tools including Real Publisher 5.0, Real Producer G2, and Real Producer Pro G2. RealProducer is best for single bandwidth encoding. RealNetworks' Surestream technology allows encoding for multiple bandwidth streams into one file, and it supports the Synchronized Multimedia Integration Language (SMIL). RealText and RealPix files stream text and graphics.

When streaming multimedia clips, the timelines must flow smoothly. The clips must be synchronized to a single presentation timeline and specific bandwidths. Audio, video, and animation have internal timelines. Each frame corresponds to a specific point in the timeline. Each second of audio is meshed with each second of the visual images throughout the clip's timeline.

The initial data that the RealServer sends to the RealPlayer before playback begins is called the *preroll.* Before it delivers a presentation, RealServer looks at the clip sizes and the timeline. The RealServer determines how much data it must receive before starting to play the presentation. The preroll helps ensure that once playback commences, it does not need to halt for more data.

The target bandwidth of a RealSystem G2 presentation is the maximum bandwidth available for a network connection, such as a 28.8Kbps modem. The presentation's total bit rate must be at or below the target bit rate.

About 25 percent of target bit rate is lost due to overhead noise, data loss, and packet overhead. Overhead can vary depending on the type of connection and general network conditions. For a 28.8Kbps connection, there is approximately 20Kbps available for video delivery.

A 28.8Kbps connection can still play a 56Kbps stream. But the modem takes about two seconds to receive the data that RealPlayer has to play every second. In other words, data has to be displayed faster than it comes in over the modem. Consequently, RealPlayer does not begin playback until it receives and stores (buffers) enough data to play the presentation without halting.

RealVideo encoders vary a clip's frame rate and image quality to produce the best possible quality for the bandwidth target. RealVideo consumes bandwidth at a flat rate for a given bandwidth target. A target of 20Kbps uses an 8Kbps RealAudio codec for the soundtrack, and the image track uses 12Kbps. By displaying RealText prior to starting the video, better use can sometimes be made of bandwidth.

RealAudio Characteristics

RealAudio is a compressed format suitable for streaming over the Internet or intranets. A RealAudio clip generally uses .rm as its file extension, but .ra is also acceptable. Start with an uncompressed sound file, such as WAV or AIFF, and then create a RealAudio clip through an encoding tool. The encoding tool should accept these input formats:

- Audio Interchange Format (.aif)
- Audio (.au)
- QuickTime (.mov)
- MPEG-1 (.mpg)
- Sound (.snd)
- WAV (.wav)

RealAudio uses a lossy compression scheme that discards parts of the audio source file to achieve a highly reduced file size. A RealAudio clip encoded from a WAV source file may be 10 to 20 times smaller than the WAV file. Carefully choosing codecs minimizes the loss of audio quality of compression.

A RealAudio encoding tool uses a codec to compress the original sound file and create a RealAudio clip. RealPlayer uses the same codec to decompress the streamed RealAudio clip for playback. RealAudio uses different codecs for music and spoken voice. Voice codecs focus on the standard frequency range of the human voice. Music codecs have broader frequency response to capture more of the high and low frequencies.

The audio stays synchronized by using a codec's optimum sampling. It prevents pitch shifting in audio resampling. Audio quality requires the optimum sampling rate or a multiple of that rate.

When encoding RealAudio clips with a RealSystem G2 encoding tool, you simply set parameters such as audio type (voice or music). Specify multiple bandwidth targets for the clip, such as both 28.8Kbps modems and ISDN connections. The tool then chooses the best codec to use.

A single RealAudio clip can be encoded for up to six bandwidths with SureStream technology. The encoding tool encodes the clip for your selected bandwidths.

RealVideo Characteristics

A RealVideo clip uses the file extension .rm and includes an embedded soundtrack as RealAudio. The encoding tool uses direct input from a capture device or from an existing file, such as one of the following input formats (preferably uncompressed):

- AVI (.avi)
- QuickTime (.mov)
- MPEG-1 (.mpg)

Like RealAudio, RealVideo uses a lossy compression scheme that discards parts of the source file during encoding. When encoding with the new RealVideo standard codec, the encoding tool crops the video window to multiples of 4 pixels, so a 176×132 video stays its original size. Encoding tools also permit manually cropping the image.

RealSystem can stream several video formats in addition to RealVideo, including Vivo. RealPlayer G2 also supports operating systems Windows, Macintosh, and UNIX.

How to Encode Using RealProducer

It's simple to create audio and video clips, presentations, and live broadcasts for Web pages using RealProducer. RealSystems G2 producer provides wizards and is straightforward and user friendly. It allows you to

- Create RealMedia files
- Automatically insert the RealMedia files into HTML Web pages
- Publish the RealMedia Web pages to a Web server or RealServer or
- Send RealMedia e-mail

The basic process to add streaming media to a Web site starts with

1. Selecting video content from
   - .avi or .mov file formats
   - media devices, video camera, videotape, or live feed

2. Encoding the source content into streaming format by using
   - Wizards
   - Templates

3. Creating a Web page with
   - RealPlayer
   - Embedded RealPlayer

4. Delivering RealMedia Web pages
   - To a Web Server
   - To a RealServer
   - Via e-mail

The process is user friendly and follows a logical sequence of input windows.

Our Web site *www.video-software.com* provides downloadable links for *free* video players from all the major developers (RealNetworks, Microsoft, Apple, Emblaze, Bitcasting, LZX-MPEG), as well as video encoding tools, editing tools, and server software.

A CD-ROM with example code and streaming video demos is included at the back cover of this book. On the enclosed CD-ROM is an example on a directory called How To. It contains a sequential series of examples that takes you through the Internet video production process.

◖▷ How to Create the RealMedia Clip

In Chapter 3, we presented the steps necessary to develop content appropriate for video capture and encoding into streaming video. Those steps are summarized as follows.

1. Capture the source by shooting a scene with a video camera of the best available quality.

2. Use a fast hard drive and controller along with a fast bus especially made for audio and video work.

3. Use a capture card with appropriate high throughput.

4. It is best to capture video at the planned delivery size.

5. It is better to work with uncompressed source formats.

6. Keep your actors as static as possible.

7. Keep the camera rock-steady.

8. Keep the background simple.

9. Keep the area well lit and don't allow a lot of contrast.

10. Shoot tests of the material.

Once the content is prepared and the video taping completed, capture it to your computer's hard drive as an .avi or .mov file. For our example on the enclosed CD-ROM, this was the HowTo.avi file in the How To directory. Using editing software, we modified the file to include an appropriate timeline, graphics, and special effects (Chapter 3). Now we are ready to convert that file into a compressed streaming RealVideo format.

We will provide our example for RealProducer Plus G2, although the other Real encoding tools follow a similar routine.

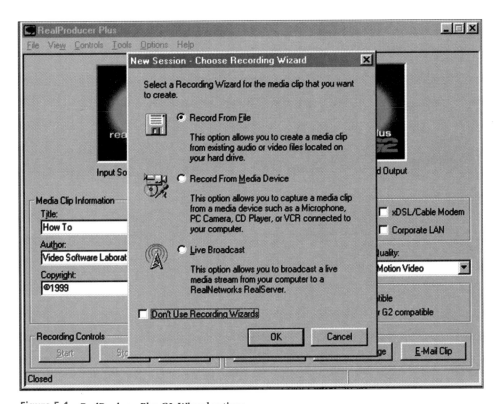

Figure 5-1   **RealProducer Plus G2: Wizard options**

If you haven't already done so, start RealProducer Plus G2, from the **Start** menu on your desktop window. When RealProducer Plus G2 starts, a wizard opens for the new session. It presents a choice of input sources (**Record from File, Record from a Media Device, Live Broadcast**) (see Figure 5-1). For our How To example, choose **Record from File** and select **OK**.

Use the **Browse** button to find the file named How To.avi in the How To AVI directory (see Figure 5-2).

Then select **Next** and enter your title, author, and copyright information (see Figure 5-3). Then select **Next** again.

Before you even begin to compress and optimize your clip, you must think about your audience. Is your clip going to be seen by the masses? Is it for corporate environments with T1 lines? Is it for a music site where the audio demands are much higher?

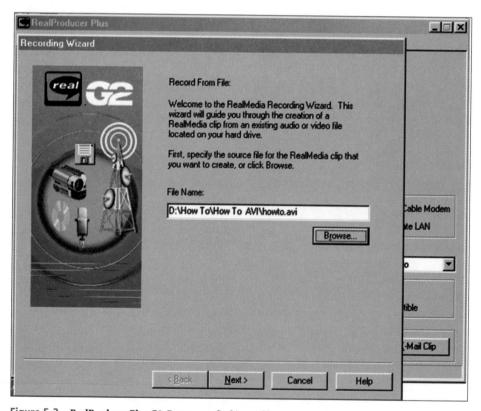

Figure 5-2   **RealProducer Plus G2: Browser to find input file**

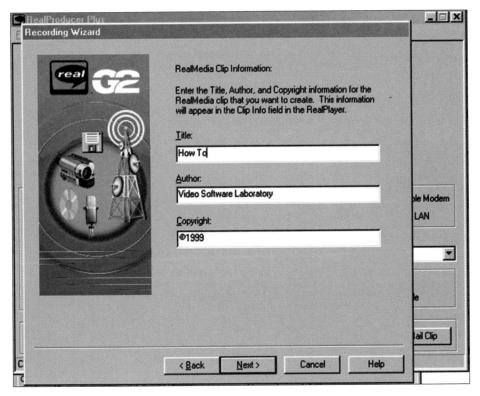

Figure 5-3   RealProducer Plus G2: Input your title, author, and copyright

At this point you can choose to encode to a single stream or to create a SureStream file with multiple bandwidths from the options presented. Choose **Single rate** for this example, then select **Next.** Now you'll be asked what bandwidth you'd like. Remember that 28.8Kbps is the lowest quality; 56Kbps encoding is better, but will probably mean a lot of time spent buffering. Choose based on your target audience. For our example, choose **56K Modem,** then select **Next.**

Next, options for audio include **Voice Only, Voice with Background Music, Music, and Stereo Music.** For our example, select **Voice Only,** then select **Next.**

For video **Normal Video** should be selected for mixed talking heads and motion. **Smooth** should be chosen for talking head shots, while **Sharpest** should be chosen for motion shots. **Slide Show** can be chosen for video that has lots of still nonmoving images. For our example, choose **Normal, Motion Video,** then select **Next** (see Figure 5-4).

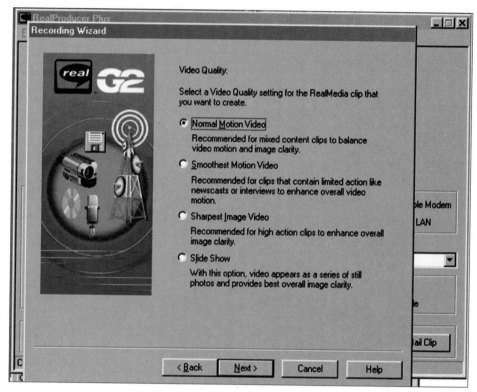

Figure 5-4   RealProducer Plus G2: Select smooth playback

Then, choose an output file name. For our example, select **Howto.rm** and select **Next** (see Figure 5-5). The Prepare to Record screen shows the input and output file names and the compression characteristics you have selected. Press **Finish** to continue.

This returns you to the main screen. Now we are ready for compression into streaming format (see Figure 5-6).

Simply press <u>**Start**</u> and you will see the audio levels fluctuate and the video playing slowly in both windows (see Figure 5-7). When the producer is done, the Play button will activate for a preview of the compressed file.

Now you are ready to select from the following simple options:

 ▶ Create Web page
 ▶ Publish Web page
 ▶ E-mail clip

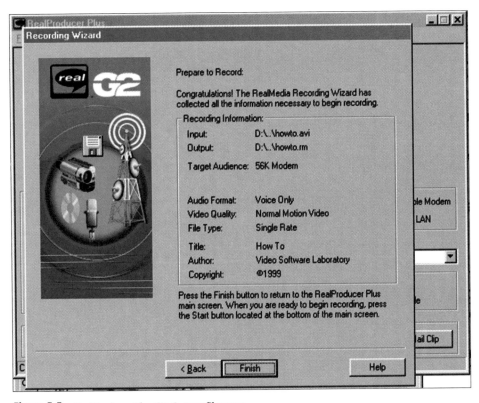

Figure 5-5 **RealProducer Plus G2: Output file name**

▪◗ How to Create a Web Page Example

Return to the main screen (see Figure 5-6) and select the **Create Web Page** button on the bottom of the screen. On the introductory screen, select **Next** and then **Browser** to enter the file name Howto.rm. Then select **Next.** The choice is then to embed the player in the Web page or display as a pop-up player. For our example, select **Pop-up Player** (see Figure 5-8), then select **Next.** This provides options for the display of the player controls. For our example, select **Standard Player** and check the **Auto Start** check box. This starts the video immediately when the page is loaded. Now select **Next.** This screen allows you to type in the title for your Web page and select whether to dispay it above or below the video. For our example, type *How To Stream Video* as the title and select **Above,** then select **Next.**

The next screen lets you name the output Web page. For our example, type *Howto.html,* then select **Next.** This leads to the Web Page Wizards Results, which summarizes the selections you made and allows you to preview the page. Select **Preview,** then select **Finish.**

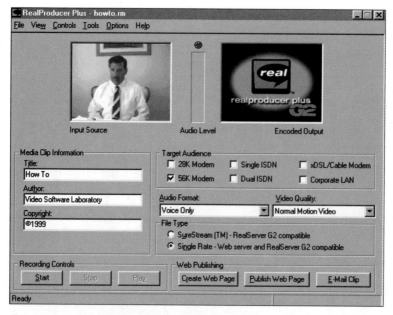

Figure 5-6   RealProducer Plus G2: Ready for compression

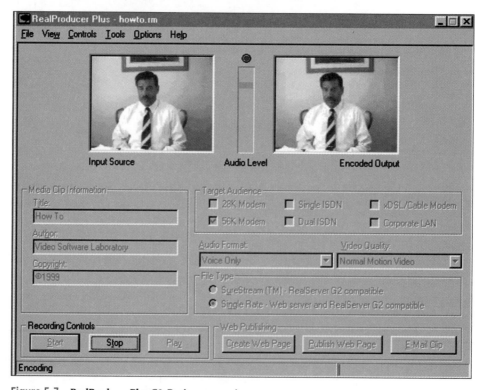

Figure 5-7   RealProducer Plus G2: Begin compression

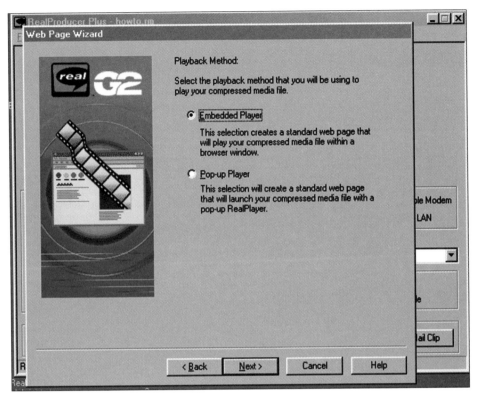

Figure 5-8   **RealProducer Plus G2: Embed or pop-up player**

▶ How to Publish a Web Page Example

Return to the main screen (see Figure 5-6) and select the **Publish Web Page** button on the bottom of the screen. An introductory screen appears. Select **Next.**

Your first choice is to identify the source HTML page or browse to select it. For our example, select **Browse** and find the HTML file you just completed above. Then select **Next.** Now select **Generic** for profile, then select **Next** (see Figure 5-9). You can now choose to "Stream media clip from a RealServer," then select **Next.**

This will be followed by the ftp screen information (see Figure 5-10). You must add the ftp address and directory and your user ID and password, then select **Next.**

Now the Web page server name and directory are inputted. The following screen is for the RealServer and includes the server name, directory, user ID, and password. (This information is available from your server administrator if you do not know it.) Then select **Next.**

The next screen is for media clip server and directory information. Select **Next.**

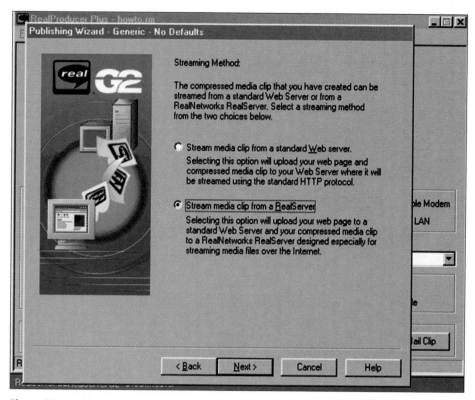

Figure 5-9   **RealProducer Plus G2: Streaming**

In the following screen select **Next** to start to ftp upload process, then select **Next** again. This uploads the video files and the HTML file to the appropriate Web and RealServer.

When this is done, you can **Preview** the page (see Figure 5-11), and then select **Finish.**

▓ What Is SMIL (Synchronized Multimedia Integration Language)?

You can use Synchronized Multimedia Integration Language (SMIL) to coordinate multimedia presentation containing multiple clips—such as a slide show and a video played together. The key to SMIL is that it relies on one of the Web's basic building blocks, XML (eXtensible Markup Language). Pronounced "smile," SMIL is an XML compliant markup language that coordinates when and how multimedia files play. SMIL allows integrating a set of independent multimedia objects into a synchronized multimedia presentation. Using SMIL, you can

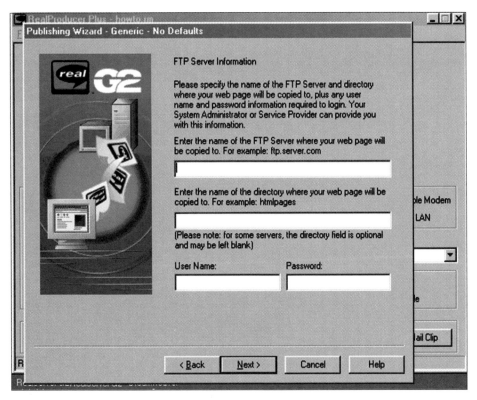

Figure 5-10   RealProducer Plus G2: FTP settings

▶ Describe the temporal behavior of the presentation
▶ Describe the layout of the presentation on a screen
▶ Associate hyperlinks with media objects

Early work on SMIL began in December 1995, and it became an officially recommended standard of the World Wide Web Consortium on June 15, 1998 (www.w3.org/tr/rec-smil).

SMIL players are client applications that receive and display integrated multimedia presentations. SMIL servers are responsible for providing content channels and serving presentations to clients.

Although SMIL itself is an open technology, some of the players and servers use proprietary techniques to handle multimedia streaming and encoding. There are essentially two types of players available: those that support SMIL and the standard multimedia formats used by SMIL presentations, and those that also support vendor-specific extensions. The most commonly used SMIL players include GRiNS (GRaphical iNterface to SMIL)

Figure 5-11   **RealProducer Plus G2: Finished Web page**

(www.cwi.nl/grins), HPAS (Hypermedia Presentation and Authoring System) (www.research.digital.com/src/HPAS), and RealPlayer G2.

GRiNS and HPAS are versatile, but RealNetwork's RealPlayer G2 is a full-featured player that supports SMIL as well as RealNetwork's streaming multimedia formats, RealText and RealPix. It is available for Windows 95, 98, and NT or Macintosh from *www.real.com*.

Delivering SMIL presentations is the job of specially configured multimedia servers, such as RealServer from RealNetworks. These servers are configured to handle multiple forms of media including text, audio, video, and animation, and they understand hypertext links.

A SMIL file (extension .smil) can be created with a text editor and be saved as a plain text output file. In its simplest form, a SMIL file lists multiple media clips played in sequence:

```
<smil>
 <body>
  <videosrc="rtsp://yourRealserver.yourcompany.com/video1.rm"/>
  <video src="rtsp:// yourRealserver.yourcompany.com/video2.rm"/>
    <video src="rtsp:// yourRealserver.yourcompany.com/video3.rm"/>
 </body>
</smil>
```

The master SMIL file is a container for the other media types. It provides the positions for the RealPix graphics files to appear, and it starts and stops the RealVideo. It is divided into three sections.

- ▸ *Head.* The head element contains information that is not related to the temporal behavior of the presentation. The *head* element may contain any number of *meta* elements and either a *layout* element or a *switch* element. The head contains the meta information, including copyright information, author of the page, and the title.
- ▸ *Regions.* The different regions, which are defined inside the `<REGION>` tags, control the layout in the RealPlayer window.
- ▸ *Body.* The body of the SMIL file describes the order in which the presentations will appear. The `<PAR>` tags mean that the VideoChannel, PixChannel, and TextChannel will be displayed in parallel.

The regions are arranged in a layout similar to the cells in a table. The *left* and *top* attributes control the position of the different regions along with *height* and *width* attributes that specify their size.

▶ **SMIL General Rules**

SMIL has many similarities to HTML, but also has some important differences. The SMIL markup must start with a `<smil>` tag and end with the `</smil>` closing tag. All other markup appears between these two tags.

Rules

A SMIL file can include an optional header section defined by `<head>` and `</head>` tags. It requires a body section defined by `<body>` and `</body>` tags. A tag that does not have a corresponding end tag (for example, the `<smil>` tag has the end tag `</smil>`) will close with a forward slash. For example:

```
<video src="video1.rm"/>
```

Attribute values must be enclosed in double quotation marks. File names in SMIL must reflect the file name exactly. A file name can consist of upper-, lower-, or mixed case but must be identical with how it appears on the server. SMIL files are saved with the extension .smi or .smil. As in HTML, the SMIL comment tag starts with `<!--` and ends with `-->`.

When a RealSystem G2 video streams over a network, the media clips reside on the RealServer. Each source clip's src attribute gives the clip's URL. For example:

```
<video src="rtsp://yourrealserver.yourcompany.com/videos/video1.rm"/>
```

For using many clips that are on the same server, it is possible to make each URL relative to a base target that is defined in the header:

```
<head>
<meta name="base" content="rtsp:// yourRealserver.yourcompany.com/"/>
</head>
<body>
 <video src=" videos/video1.rm"/>
 <video src=" videos/video2.rm"/>
 <video src=" videos/video3.rm"/>
</body>
```

To use a clip hosted on a Web server, use a standard HTTP URL as follows in a clip source tag:

```
<video src="http://www.yourcompany.com/videos/video1.rm"/>
```

Sequential and Parallel Tags

The SMIL `<seq>` and `<par>` tags allow you to structure your media. Use the `<seq>` tag to play various clips in sequence. In the following example, the second video clip begins when the first video clip finishes:

```
<seq>
 <video src="videos/video1.rm"/>
 <video src="videos/video2.rm"/>
</seq>
```

To play two or more clips at the same time, use the `<par>` tag. Here the video clip is playing while the text of the lyrics are scrolling in synchronization:

```
<par>
 <video src="videos/video1.rm"/>
```

```
    <textstream src="lyrics/words.rt"/>
  </par>
```

When RealServer G2 streams parallel groups, it ensures that the clips stay synchronized. If some video frames don't arrive, RealServer either drops those frames or halts playback until the frames do arrive.

SMIL timing elements let you specify when a clip starts playing and how long it plays. If you do not set timing events, the clips start and stop according to their normal timelines and their positions within <par> and <seq> groups. The easiest way to designate a time is with shorthand markers of h, min, s, and ms.

You can use the *begin* attribute for any clip or group to start a clip at a specific point within the timeline:

```
    <video src="videos/video1.rm" begin="30s"/>
```

Were this clip in a <par> group, the *begin* attribute would start the clip playing back 30 seconds after the group starts. If the clip were in a <seq> group, the attribute would delay the clip's normal playback by inserting 30 seconds of blank time. Therefore timing is relative to the start of the <seq> or <par> group, not the start of the overall presentation.

Switch Element

The switch element allows specification of a set of alternative elements. An element is acceptable if the element and all of the test attributes evaluate to *true*.

An element in a switch may be selected if it is the first acceptable element as the player evaluates the elements in the order in which they occur. Thus, authors should order the alternatives from the most desirable to the least desirable. Furthermore, authors should place a relatively fail-safe alternative as the last item in the <switch> so that at least one item within the switch is chosen.

The <switch> tag allows specification of multiple choices. For example, the following permits selection between different language settings:

```
  <switch>
   <video src="french/ video1.rm " system-language="fr"/>
   < video src="german/ video1.rm " system-language="de"/>
   < video src="spanish/ video1.rm " system-language="es"/>
   < video src="english/ video1.rm "/>
  </switch>
```

To serve different clips to viewers with different connection speeds, the <switch> tag can define options allowing the player to choose between available bandwidth. As shown below, you can group clips with <par> tags, using the system-bitrate attribute to list the approximate bandwidth (in Kbps) each group consumes:

```
<switch>
 <par system-bitrate="75000">
  <!--for dual isdn and faster-->
  <video src="videos/video1.rm"/>
  <textstream src="lyrics/words1.rt"/>
 </par>
 <par system-bitrate="47000">
  <!--for single isdn-->
  <video src="video//video2.rm"/>
  <textstream src="lyrics/ words2.rt"/>
 </par>
 <par system-bitrate="20000">
  <!--for 28.8 modems--/>
  <video src="video/video3.rm"/>
  <textstream src="lyrics/words3.rt"/>
 </par>
</switch>
```

The SMIL file header can use <meta> tags to provide title, author, and copyright information:

```
<head>
 <meta name="title" content=" Your Video"/>
 <meta name="author" content=" Your Name"/>
 <meta name="copyright" content" Your Company"/>
 <meta name="abstract" content="Your Description "/>
</head>
```

This example defines a title, author, copyright, and abstract. The title displays at the top of the RealPlayer window and in the run list under the RealPlayer File menu.

Root-Layout Element

The *root-layout* element determines the value of the layout properties of the root element, which in turn determines the size of the window in which the SMIL presentation is rendered.

With the `<root-layout.../>` tag, you specify the size of the entire playback area in pixels (percentages are not accepted for the root-layout region). You cannot display images or play clips in the root-layout region, as it is meant to set the overall playback area. The example shown below creates a root-layout region 250 pixels wide by 230 pixels high. When the presentation begins, the RealPlayer window expands to this size. Other regions measure their top and left offsets from the upper left-hand corner of this root-layout region:

```
<head>
 <layout>
  <root-layout width="250" height="230"/>
 </layout>
</head>
```

Layout Element

The *layout* element determines how the elements in the document's body are positioned on an abstract rendering surface. A SMIL document can contain multiple alternative layouts by enclosing several layout elements within a *switch* element. This can be used, for example, to describe the document's layout using different layout languages. The following example shows how CSS2 can be used as an alternative to the SMIL basic layout language:

```
<smil>
 <head>
  <switch>
   <layout type="text/css">
    [region="r"] { top: 20px; left: 20px }
   </layout>
   <layout>
    <region id="r" top="20" left="20" />
   </layout>
  </switch>
 </head>
 <body>
  <seq>
   <img region="r" src="http://www.video-software.com/image/logo.gif "
dur="10s" />
  </seq>
 </body>
</smil>
```

SMIL basic layout is consistent with the visual rendering model defined in CSS2. SMIL basic layout only controls the layout of media object elements. The type identifier for SMIL basic layout is text/smil-basic-layout.

Layout Fixed Property Values

The following style sheet defines the values of the CSS2 properties *display* and *position* that are valid in SMIL basic layout. These property values are fixed:

```
a          {display: block}
anchor      {display: block}
animation   {display: block;
            position: absolute}
body       {display: block}
head       {display: none}
img       {display: block;
            position: absolute}
layout    {display: none}
meta       {display: none}
par       {display: block}
region    {display: none}
ref         {display: block;
            position: absolute}
root-layout {display: none}
seq        {display: block}
smil     {display: block}
switch    {display: block}
text      {display: block;
            position: absolute}
textstream {display: block;
            position: absolute}
video     {display: block;
            position: absolute}
```

Note that as a result of these definitions, all absolutely positioned elements (animation, img, ref, text, textstream, and video) are contained within a single containing block defined by the content edge of the root element (smil). SMIL basic layout defines default values for all layout-related attributes. These are consistent with the initial values of the corresponding properties in CSS2.

Region Element

The region element controls the position, size, and scaling of media object elements.

In the following example fragment, the position of a text element is set to a 5 pixel distance from the top border of the rendering window:

```
<smil>
 <head>
  <layout>
   <region id="a" top="5" />
  </layout>
 </head>
 <body>
  <text region="a" src="text.html" dur="10s" />
 </body>
</smil>
```

Region Element Attributes

The *region* element can have the following attributes:

▶ *Background-color.* The use and definition of this attribute are identical to the background-color property in the CSS2 specification, except that SMIL basic layout does not require support for *system colors*. If the background-color attribute is absent, the background is transparent.

▶ *Fit.* This attribute specifies the behavior if the intrinsic height and width of a visual media object differ from the values specified by the height and width attributes in the *region* element. This attribute does not have a 1-1 mapping onto a CSS2 property, but can be simulated in CSS2. Fit has the following attributes.

  ▶ *Fill.* Scale the object's height and width independently so that the content just touches all edges of the box.

  ▶ *Hidden.* If the intrinsic height (width) of the media object element is smaller than the height (width) defined in the *region* element, render the object starting from the top (left) edge and fill up the remaining height (width) with the background color. If the intrinsic height (width) of the media object element is greater than the height (width) defined in the *region* element, render the object starting from the top (left) edge until the height (width) defined in the *region* element is reached, and clip the parts of the object below (right of) the height (width).

  ▶ *Meet.* Scale the visual media object while preserving its aspect ratio until its height or width is equal to the value specified by the height or width attributes, while none of the content is clipped. The object's left top corner is positioned at the top-left coordinates of the box, and empty space at the left or bottom is filled up with the background color.

▸ *Scroll.* A scrolling mechanism should be invoked when the element's rendered contents exceed its bounds.

▸ *Slice.* Scale the visual media object while preserving its aspect ratio so that its height or width are equal to the value specified by the height and width attributes while some of the content may get clipped. Depending on the exact situation, either a horizontal or a vertical slice of the visual media object is displayed. Overflow width is clipped from the right of the media object. Overflow height is clipped from the bottom of the media object.

The default value of *fill* is *hidden*.

▸ *Height.* The use and definition of this attribute are identical to the *height* property in the CSS2 specification. Attribute values can be *percentage* values and a variation of the *length* values defined in CSS2. For *length* values, SMIL basic layout only supports pixel units as defined in CSS2.

▸ *Id.* A region element is applied to a positionable element by setting the region attribute of the positionable element to the id value of the region.

▸ *Left.* The use and definition of this attribute are identical to the *left* property in the CSS2 specification. Attribute values have the same restrictions as the attribute values of the *height* attribute. The default value is zero.

▸ *Title.* Values of the title attribute may be rendered. It is recommended that all *region* elements have a *title* attribute with a meaningful description.

▸ *Top.* The use and definition of this attribute are identical to the *top* property in the CSS2 specification. Attribute values have the same restrictions as the attribute values of the *height* attribute. The default value is zero.

▸ *Width.* The use and definition of this attribute are identical to the *width* property in the CSS2 specification. Attribute values have the same restrictions as the attribute values of the *height* attribute.

▸ *Z-index.* The use and definition of this attribute are identical to the *z-index* property in the CSS2 specification, with the following exception.

If two boxes generated by elements A and B have the same stack level, then if the display of an element A starts later than the display of an element B, the box of A is stacked on top of the box of B (temporal order). If the display of the elements starts at the same time, and an element A occurs later in the SMIL document text than an element B, the box of A is stacked on top of the box of B (document tree order as defined in CSS2).

Playback regions for media clips are created with `<region>` tags. These regions must lay within the root-layout region. Any part of a region that lays outside the root-layout region is cut off. Each `<region.../>` tag must define top, left, width, and height attributes. The example below defines two regions named *videoregion* and *textregion*:

```
<head>
 <layout>
  <root-layout background-color="red" width="250" height="230"/>
  <region id="videoregion" top="5" left="5" width="240" height="180"/>
  <region id="textregion" top="200" left="5" width="240" height="20"/>
 </layout>
</head>
```

In this example, both regions are offset 5 pixels to the right of the root-layout region's left edge. The video region displays 5 pixels down from the top of the root-layout region, and the text region displays 200 pixels down. All regions used in the presentation must be defined in the header.

Body Element

The *body* element contains information that is related to the temporal and linking behavior of the document. It implicitly defines a *seq* element for a definition of the temporal semantics of the *body* element.

Hyperlinking Elements

The link elements allow the description of navigational links between objects. SMIL provides only for in-line link elements. Links are limited to unidirectional single-headed links (that is, all links have exactly one source and one destination resource). All links in SMIL are actuated by the user.

Handling of Links in Embedded Documents

The presentation of a SMIL document may involve other applications or plug-ins. For example, a SMIL browser may use an HTML plug-in to display an embedded HTML page. Vice versa, an HTML browser may use a SMIL plug-in to display a SMIL document embedded in an HTML page. In such presentations, links may be defined by documents at different levels and conflicts may arise. In this case, the link defined by the containing document should take precedence over the link defined by the embedded object. If a link is defined in an embedded SMIL document, traversal of the link affects only the embedded SMIL document.

If a link is defined in a non-SMIL document that is embedded in a SMIL document, link traversal can only affect the presentation of the embedded document and not the presentation of the containing SMIL document. This restriction may be released in future versions of SMIL.

Addressing

SMIL supports name fragment identifiers and the # connector. This means that SMIL supports locators as currently used in HTML (that is, it uses locators of the form http://foo.com/some/path#anchor1).

Linking to SMIL Fragments

A locator that points to a SMIL document may contain a fragment part (that is, http://www.w3.org/test.smi#par1). The fragment part is an id value that identifies one of the elements within the referenced SMIL document. If a link containing a fragment part is followed, the presentation should start as if the user had fast-forwarded the presentation represented by the destination document to the effective beginning of the element designated by the fragment.

Within a SMIL file you can define hot spots using an <anchor> tag. The <a> tag turns the entire media source clip into a link; the <anchor> tag turns only a defined area into a link. With <anchor> tags you can create links similar to those in HTML image maps. But SMIL links can be temporal as well as spatial. A link might be valid for just ten seconds during a source clip's timeline, for instance.

The <anchor> tag differs from the <a> tag in that you place it within the media source tag rather than before it:

```
<video src="video.rm" region="videoregion">
<anchor href="rtsp://yourrealserver.yourcompany.com/video2.rm" .../>
</video>
```

An <anchor> tag ends with a closing slash. But the media source tag does not end with a closing slash. Instead, the source tag and its subsequent <anchor> tags are followed by a closing source tag, such as </video>. The <anchor> tag includes an href attribute that uses rtsp:// if the linked clip streams from RealServer, or http. The <anchor> tag's *coords* attribute defines spatial coordinates for the hot-spot rectangle. Coordinate values in pixels or percentages define the rectangle's offset from the upper left-hand corner of the media source clip as shown in this example:

```
          <video src="video1.rm" region="videoregion">
    <anchor href="..." coords="10,20,40,60"/>
    </video>
```

The coordinate values for the hot-spot rectangle follow this order:

- Left-side pixel or percentage value
- Top pixel or percentage value
- Right-side pixel or percentage value
- Bottom pixel or percentage value

The sample above uses pixel values to define a hot spot 30 pixels wide (40 pixels minus 10 pixels) and 40 pixels high (60 pixels minus 20 pixels).

In addition to defining spatial coordinates, the `<anchor>` tag can set temporal attributes that specify when the link is active. If you do not include temporal attributes, the link stays active as long as the source clip appears on screen. To add timing attributes, use the SMIL begin and end values. (You cannot use dur, clip-begin, or clip-end.)

Synchronization Elements

The sychronizing elements are seq, par, and clock value. The children of a *seq* element form a temporal sequence. The seq element can have the following attributes:

- *Author.* The region attribute on *seq* elements cannot be used by the basic layout language for SMIL defined in this specification.
- *Title.* It is recommended that all *seq* elements have a *title* attribute with a meaningful description. The children of a par element can overlap in time. The textual order of appearance of children in a par has no significance for the timing of their presentation.

The *par* element can have the following attributes:

- *Abstract.* A brief description of the content is contained in the element.
- *Author.* The name of the author of the content is contained in the element.
- *Begin.* This attribute specifies the time for the explicit begin of an element. The attribute can contain the following two types of values:

1. *Delay-Value.* A delay value is a clock-value measuring presentation time. Presentation time advances at the speed of the presentation. It behaves like the time code shown on a counter of a tape deck. It can be stopped, decreased, or increased either by user actions or by the player itself. The semantics of a delay value depend on the element's

first ancestor that is a synchronization element (that is, ancestors that are *a* or *switch* elements are ignored):

If this ancestor is a *par* element, the value defines a delay from the effective begin of that element.

If this ancestor is a *seq* element, the value defines a delay from the effective end of the first lexical predecessor that is a synchronization element event-value.

The element begins when a certain event occurs. The element generating the event must be *in scope*. The set of in scope elements S is determined as follows:

Take all children from the element's first ancestor that is a synchronization element and add them to S.

Remove all *a* and *switch* elements from S. Add the children of all *a* elements to S, unless they are *switch* elements.

Clock values have the following syntax:

```
Clock-val           ::= Full-clock-val | Partial-clock-val | Timecount-val
Full-clock-val      ::= Hours ":" Minutes ":" Seconds ("." Fraction)?
Partial-clock-val   ::= Minutes ":" Seconds ("." Fraction)?
Timecount-val       ::= Timecount ("." Fraction)?
                        ("h" | "min" | "s" | "ms")? ; default is "s"
Hours               ::= 2DIGIT; any positive number
Minutes             ::= 2DIGIT; range from 00 to 59
Seconds             ::= 2DIGIT; range from 00 to 59
Fraction            ::= DIGIT+
Timecount           ::= DIGIT+
2DIGIT              ::= DIGIT DIGIT
DIGIT               ::= [0-9]
```

The following are examples of legal clock values:
- Full clock value: 02:30:03 = 2 hours, 30 minutes, 3 seconds
- Partial clock value: 02:33 = 2 minutes, 33 seconds
- Time count values:
  3h = 3 hours
  45min = 45 minutes
  30s = 30 seconds
  5ms = 5 milliseconds

A fraction x with n digits represents the following value:

$x * 1/10^{**}n$

Examples:

> 00.5s = 5 * 1/10 seconds = 500 milliseconds
>
> 00:00.005 = 5 * 1/1000 seconds = 5 milliseconds

Element-event value:

An *element event* value specifies a particular event in a synchronization element. An element event has the following syntax:

> Element-event   ::= "id(" Event-source ")(" Event ")"
>
> Event-source   ::= Id-value
>
> Event   ::= "begin" | Clock-val | "end"

The following events are defined:

▶ *Begin.* This event is generated at an element's effective begin.

Example use: begin="id(x)(begin)"

▶ *Clock-val.* This event is generated when a clock associated with an element reaches a particular value. This clock starts at 0 at the element's effective begin. For *par* and *seq* elements, the clock gives the presentation time elapsed since the effective begin of the element. For media object elements, the semantics are implementation dependent. The clock may either give presentation time elapsed since the effective begin or the media time of the object. The latter may differ from the presentation time that elapsed since the object's display was started, that is, due to rendering or network delays, and is the recommended approach. It is an error to use a clock value that exceeds the value of the effective duration of the element generating the event.

The following example creates two temporal links for the clip video1.rm. The first link is active for the first five seconds of playback. The second link is active for the next five seconds. Because no spatial coordinates are given, the entire video is a link:

```
<video src="video1.rm" region="videoregion">
 <anchor href="rtsp://.../video2.rm" begin="0s" end="10s"/>
 <anchor href="rtsp://.../video3.rm" begin="10s" end="20s"/>
</video>.
```

A SMIL file can define a link to another SMIL file or another part of itself. For example, a video played through a SMIL file may link to another SMIL file so that when a viewer clicks the video, a new presentation starts up in RealPlayer. To do this, you simply set the href attribute for the <a> or <anchor> tag to the new SMIL file's URL.

You can also link to portions of a SMIL file. The following example from a target SMIL file uses id attributes (such as those used in regions to create region names) to define a target name for a <par> tag that groups a video and a text clip. This id attribute functions like a name attribute in an HTML <a> tag:

```
<par id="text_and_video">
 <video src="video2.rm" region="newsregion"/>
 <textstream src="text.rt" region="textregion"/>
</par>
```

Media Object Elements

Media object elements include ref, animation, audio, img, video, text, and textstream elements. They allow the inclusion of media objects into a SMIL presentation. Media objects are included by reference. Anchors and links can be attached to visual media.

When playing back a media object, the player must not derive the exact type of the media object from the name of the media object element. Instead, it must rely solely on other sources about the type, such as type information contained in the type attribute, or the type information communicated by a server or the operating system.

Authors, however, should make sure that the group into which the media object falls (animation, audio, img, video, text, or textstream) is reflected in the element name. This is in order to increase the readability of the SMIL document. When in doubt about the group of a media object, authors should use the generic *ref* element.

You can use the <anchor> tag's time coordinates to create a timeline offset in a linked clip. To link a video to another video at 30 seconds into the second video's timeline, you define an <a> or <anchor> link from the first video to a SMIL file that contains the second video. In the second SMIL file, the video's <anchor> tag defines the timeline offset using SMIL timing parameters.

Here is a sample of the link in the first SMIL file:

```
<a href="rtsp://yourRealserver.yourcompany.com/media1.smil#vid2">
 <video src="video.rm" region="videoregion"/>
</a>
```

Producing Animation

RealFlash makes it easy to put animation on the World Wide Web. Combining the power of Macromedia Flash with the clarity of RealNetworks' RealAudio, RealFlash produces visually arresting animations with superb sound. This chapter explains how to create RealFlash content for different bandwidths. It also provides tips for optimizing RealFlash clips.

RealFlash is well-suited for linear presentations that have continuous audio and images synchronized along a timeline, including the following:

- Full-length, television-like cartoons for entertainment and education
- Internet or intranet demonstrations, training courses, and product overviews
- Product advertisements
- Movie trailers
- Karaoke

A RealFlash clip consists of two separate files streamed in parallel: a Shockwave Flash animation file and a RealAudio soundtrack. To create these components, you develop animation in Macromedia Flash 2.0 or 3.0 and synchronize it with an imported sound file, such as a WAV or AIFF file. You then export a Shockwave Flash file that contains the animation and generate a RealAudio file from the soundtrack. RealServer streams the clip to RealPlayer, ensuring that animation and sound stay synchronized.

Our How To Example

Let's look at our CD-ROM "HowTo" example for smil:

```
<smil>
<head>
<meta name="title" content="How To" />
<meta name="author" content="Video Software Laboratory" />
<meta name="copyright" content="(c) 1999 " />
<layout>
<root-layout width="408" height="368" background-color="black" />
        <!-- Logo Region -->
<region id="logo" left="16" top="2" width="130" height="60" fit="fill"
z-index="2" />
        <!-- Links Region -->
        <region id="headlines" left="16" top="62" width="130" height="30"
        fit="fill" background-color="black" z-index="2" />
<region id="links" left="16" top="82" width="130" height="124" fit="fill"
background color="#160f60" z-index="3" />
        <!-- Video region -->
<region id="video_background" left="159" top="3" width="214" height="262"
background-color="black" z-index="1"/>
<region id="video_border" left="160" top="26" width="184" height="153"
fit="fill" background-color="black" z-index="2" />
```

```
<region id="video" left="162" top="30" width="240" height="180"
background-color="black" z-index="3" />

        <!-- Ticker Region -->

<region id="last_updated" left="16" top="217" width="343" height="20"
fit="fill" background-color="#160f60" z-index="2" />

<region id="ticker_background" left="16" top="237" width="343"
height="25" background-color="black" z-index="2"/>

<region id="ticker" left="16" top="237" width="343" height="125"
z-index="2" />

</layout>

</head>

<body>

<par>

        <!-- Play these streams concurrently (in parallel). -->

<a href="http://www.video-software.com/" coords="0,0,15,15" show="new" >

<img src="pix/vsla.gif" region="logo" fill="freeze" /></a>

<text src="text/title_last_updated.rt" region="last_updated" fill="freeze" />

<text src="text/title_headlines.rt" region="headlines" fill="freeze" />

<video src="video/howto.rm" region="video" fill="freeze" />

<text src="text/ticker.rt" region="ticker" />

</par>

</body>

</smil>
```

Let's take a look at this code to get a better idea of how it works.

The master SMIL file (with the .smi file extension) acts as a container to hold the other media types mentioned above. The SMIL file gives the positioning where the RealPix graphics files will appear, it places the RealVideo, and it also tells the RealAudio when to start and stop. The master file is really divided into three sections: the head, regions (which define the layout), and the body.

As you can see, the entire file is surrounded by the <SMIL> </SMIL> tags, much like the start and end <HTML> tags found in a standard HTML document.

The Head

The first area is the head. It contains the meta information. The title, author, and copyright are identified in the meta tags of the head section in the <meta ... ./> format.

The Regions

The second part of the head defines the different regions, which are defined inside the <REGION> tags. Regions control the layout in the RealPlayer window. The layout information about regions is included in the head area between the <layout> and <layout/> tags.

The root-layout defines the total region within which all the text graphics and video regions reside. Each subsequent region (logo, links, video, and ticker) is then specified.

The regions are defined by the following tag:

```
<region id="" left="" top="" width="" height="" fit="" z-index="" />
```

Care must be exercised in locating the regions to avoid overlap and to stay within the root-layout defined space.

The Body

The body of the SMIL file describes the order in which the presentations will appear. The body section defines the sequence of display as either sequential <seq> or parallel <par>. The <par> tags mean that the video and ticker will be displayed in parallel.

The presentations can mix and match any of the available media types. It is necessary to transfer all standard animation, video, and audio file formats to streaming formats, such as RealFlash, RealVideo, and RealAudio.

With RealPix or RealText, timing tags set the appearance of each image or text block. Images and text can remain stationary for indefinite periods until new images and text replace them.

Timing a presentation with SMIL can be a matter of simply starting one clip as soon as another one stops. When your presentation plays clips simultaneously, use SMIL to define the layout. SMIL files can insert ads into your presentation, either in a separate ad banner or between clips playing in sequence.

The presentation layout determines how you divide the screen space. Like Web browsers, SMIL players have a viewing area or window. When a SMIL presentation plays only one type of media at a time, the media can be displayed fully in the viewing window and automatically resized as necessary. To play multiple media types simultaneously, miniwindows within the main viewing area, called *regions,* are created.

After the layout, create a timeline to coordinate the playing of media elements. SMIL provides two ways to play media elements in parallel, where multiple files can play simultaneously. When you present files in parallel, you can synchronize elements to create smooth transitions. Descriptive text files can be used to highlight key moments in a video clip.

SMIL provides many features for controlling the timing of media playback.

RealPix

RealPix are a general classification for any graphics supported by the G2 Player, including GIF, JPEG (slightly modified), and BMP files. Animated GIFs are not supported. JPEG files need to be slightly modified in order to be optimized for streaming. This is done using a program called JPEGTRAN. JPEGTRAN is a DOS command-line program that only converts one file at a time using the syntax that follows.

Graphics for RealSystem G2

RealPix is the graphics portion of the RealSystem G2. It lets you stream images across the Web in combination with audio and text. Image software such as Adobe Photoshop lets you create images in formats RealPix can stream. RealPix can stream images in the following formats.

Both interlaced and noninterlaced GIFs will work, but RealPix does not take advantage of any features of interlaced GIFs. Noninterlaced GIFs are therefore recommended. RealPix can use RGB baseline and grayscale JPEGs. Progressive JPEGs are not supported.

JPEGTRAN is a freeware program provided by RealNetworks that optimizes JPEG (.jpg) images for streaming with RealPix. It modifies them so that if a packet of image data is lost, RealPlayer can still decode and display remaining packets. If you do not use JPEGTRAN on your images, RealPlayer cannot decode packets following a lost packet, and a substantial part of the image may not display.

To use JPEGTRAN, first create JPEG-format. Then run JPEGTRAN from the command line on Windows. From the directory that holds the JPEGTRAN program, use the following command to process an image:

```
jpegtran -restart 1B -outfile output.jpg input.jpg
```

Here is an example in which the input is image1.jpg and the output is newimage1.jpg:

```
jpegtran -restart 1B -outfile newimage1.jpg image1.jpg
```

Image Tag

All information in the file occurs between an opening <imfl> tag and a closing </imfl> tag. This is the only tag that uses an end tag. You can set the display window size with the RealPix <head> tags and the width and height attributes. Attribute values must be enclosed in double quotation marks. For example:

```
<head width="256" height="256".../>
```

Duration

The required duration attribute sets the length of the entire RealPix presentation. For example, the following value sets a duration of 50 seconds:

```
<head duration= 50".../>
```

All RealPix effects stop immediately when the duration elapses. When the duration time exceeds the time required to complete the effects, the last effect stays frozen in the display window.

RealPix tags and attribute values can create the RealPix timeline and visual effects. A typical RealPix tag looks like this:

```
<fadein start="3" duration="1" target="1"/>
```

The tags and attribute names must be lowercase. A tag that does not have a corresponding end tag closes with a forward slash (/): `<fadein.../>`

Background

The optional background-color attribute sets an initial background color. The default color is black. You can subsequently change the background color with the `<fill/>` tag. The following example sets the initial background color to a shade of red:

```
<head background-color="#E00000".../>
```

Image

For each image you use in the RealPix presentation, you must add an `<image/>` tag after the `<head/>` tag. The `<image/>` tag provides the image file location and assigns a unique handle number to the image. An `<image/>` tag looks like this:

```
<image handle="2" name="image1.jpg"/>
```

Handle

The required handle attribute assigns a positive integer to the image. Each handle number within the file must be unique. The RealPix effects then refer to the handle number rather than the file name. Here is an example:

```
<image handle="2".../>
```

Name

The name attribute is required. It specifies the image file name and a path relative to the location of the RealPix file on RealServer or the local machine. The following example designates an image file that resides in the same directory as the RealPix file:

```
<image name="image1.jpg".../>
```

This next example indicates that the image file resides one level below the RealPix file in the "images" directory:

```
<image name="images/image1.jpg".../>
```

Fill

The `<fill/>` tag displays a colored rectangle in the display window. This is useful at the beginning of a presentation or anytime you want to paint over all or part of the display window. A `<fill/>` tag is:

```
<fill start="0" color="red"/>
```

Start

The start attribute is required. It specifies the time from the beginning of the RealPix timeline that the fill occurs. The following example starts the fill 30 seconds into the presentation timeline:

```
<fill start="30".../>
```

Destination Rectangle

There are four attributes that define what portion of the source GIF appears in the destination rectangle. The entire source image will display in the destination rectangle, if they are left out. To use only a portion of the source image, set the source rectangle's x and y coordinates, as well as its height and width in pixels.

- *Srcx.* X coordinate of the source rectangle
- *Srcy.* Y coordinate of the source rectangle
- *Srcw.* Width of the source rectangle
- *Srch.* Height of the source rectangle

The following example selects from the source GIF a source rectangle 234 pixels wide by 58 pixels high. The source rectangle starts 117 pixels to the right of the source image's left edge and 1 pixel down from its top edge:

```
<animate srcx="117" srcy="1" srcw="234" srch="58".../>
```

URL Link

This attribute sets a hyperlink URL for the GIF. When the user clicks the image, the user's default Web browser opens the URL. This URL value overrides the presentation default set in the <head/> tag only for the duration of the effect. Use a fully qualified URL like the following:

```
<animate url="http://www.video-software.com".../>
```

Image Controls

The next area defines the images we will be working with in the How To example. It defines the source images and the reference URL links.

```
<a href="http://www.video-software.com/" coords="0,0,15,15" show="new" >
<img src="pix/vsla.gif" region="logo" fill="freeze" /></a>
```

Layout and Control

The code for layout control from our example is highlighted below:

```
<root-layout width="408" height="368" background-color="black" />
        <!-- Logo Region -->
<region id="logo" left="16" top="2" width="130" height="60" fit="fill"
z-index="2" />
        <!-- Links Region -->
<region id="headlines" left="16" top="62" width="130" height="30"
fit="fill" background-color="black" z-index="2" />

<region id="links" left="16" top="82" width="130" height="124" fit="fill"
background-color="#160f60" z-index="3" />
        <!-- Video region -->
<region id="video_background" left="159" top="3" width="214" height="262"
background-color="black" z-index="1"/>

<region id="video_border" left="160" top="26" width="184" height="153"
fit="fill" background-color="black" z-index="2" />

<region id="video" left="162" top="30" width="240" height="180"
background-color="black" z-index="3" />
        <!-- Ticker Region -->
<region id="last_updated" left="16" top="217" width="343" height="20"
fit="fill" background-color="#160f60" z-index="2" />

<region id="ticker_background" left="16" top="237" width="343"
height="25" background-color="black" z-index="2"/>

<region id="ticker" left="16" top="237" width="343" height="125"
z-index="2" />

</layout>
```

The features of interest are region ids, fit, and z-index. The region ids allow the region to be referred later in the smil file. The fit allows stretching of the image to fill the assigned area. The z-index allows overlaying of items. The layout for our example has a general region for the whole display called the root-layout and individual regions for logo display, link listing and URL hot links, a video region for showing the movie, and a ticker region for scrolling text associated with the video.

The root-layout reserves area for the complete display. Then the logo region reserves the upper-left corner for the logo image, the links layout reserves the lower left area for the list of links, the video region reserves the main portion of the area for the video, and the ticker layout reserves the bottom area for the scrolling text ticker. The backgrounds are individually identified.

RealText

RealText makes a great addition to any SMIL presentation because it takes up so little bandwidth. In our example on page 123, the duration of the text presentation is 10 seconds. The underlining of links can be turned off or on. The total duration of the text presentation is 10 seconds; after that, it freezes into place. The font tags and sizes should be familiar from HTML. The new elements are the time begin and pos tags.

The time tag begin controls when the text appears, relative to the start of the presentation. Headline 1 will appear at the beginning, Headline 2 appears three seconds into the presentation, and Headline 3 at six seconds. The pos tag controls the positioning of the text, based on x, y coordinates. Headline 1 will be positioned at 10 pixels from the left side of the window and 5 pixels down from the top.

RealText provides a number of window styles depending on how you want to display text.

- A generic window has no preset parameters. You can use it to create any RealText display allowed by the RealText mark-up.
- A ScrollingNews window is preset to have text scroll from the bottom of the window to the top at a set rate for the entire presentation.
- Text in a TickerTape window crawls from the right side of the window to the left. It can also loop back around to the right. It does not scroll up or down, however. Text displays next to the window's top or bottom edge.
- The Marquee window is like the TickerTape in that text crawls from right to left and can loop.
- A TelePrompter window behaves like a generic window except that text arriving at the bottom edge of the window causes the text above it to move up just enough to display the new line.

To Create a RealText File

Open a new file in a text editor, and at the top of the file add the <window> tag with necessary options. Add the </window> tag at the bottom:

```
<window>
    <br/><time begin="3"/> your text line one
    <br/><time begin="6"/> line two
    <br/><time begin="9"/> line three
</window>
```

Save the text file as yourtext.rt in the text subdirectory.

Here's the code for our example:

For links:

```
<window
        type="generic"
        duration="0:59"
        bgcolor="#444444"
        underline_hyperlinks="true"
        link="white"
        width="130"
        height="124">
<font size="-1" face="arial" color="white">
<br/>
<!-- when the user clicks this link, the player will seek to the 5 second point in the
timeline. -->
-
<a href="command:seek(0:05.0)" target="_player"> Beginning Link</a>
</font>
</window>
```

For ticker:

```
<window
type="scrollingnews"
duration="59"
bgcolor="black">
```

```
<font face="arial" size="3" color="yellow">

<br/><br/>

PRESENTATION

May 27, 1999:

<br/><b><u>HELLO AND WELCOME</u></b>

<p></p>

to Video Software laboratory's streaming
video presentation series. Today on the
World Wide Web video can be used in the
most exciting ways;

<p></p>

<a href="http://www.video-software.com/future.htm">

From on-line education and entertainment,
to product demos and corporate training. </a>

<p></p>

In this series of lectures, Video Software
Laboratory will present the information
necessary to bring your web pages alive
by adding streaming video and audio.</font>

</window>
```

For headlines:

```
<window

     type="generic"

     duration="0:03"

     bgcolor="#0000FF"

     underline_hyperlinks="true"

     link="black"

     width="130"

     height="30">

<!-- Position the text at x=3 pixels and y=0 pixels. -->

<pos x="3" y="0"/>

<font color="yellow" face="arial" size="2"><b>Streaming

Video</b></font>

</window>
```

For last update:

```
<window

     type="generic"
```

```
            duration="0:03"
            bgcolor="#0000FF"
            underline_hyperlinks="true"
            link="black"
            width="343"
            height="20">
<font color="yellow" face="arial" size="2">
<b>
<time begin="0"/>
<clear/>
<!-- Position the text at x=3 pixels and y=3 pixels. -->
<pos x="3" y="3" >updated: 07:12 est
<!-- Position the text at x=263 pixels and y=3 pixels. -->
<pos x="253" y="3" >June 3, 1999</b>
</font>
</window>
```

Set the window type to tickertape. The duration controls how long it takes the text to fully move across the screen. If you'd like the text to loop through many times, then set loop to true. The crawl rate parameter sets the scroll speed. If you omit this parameter, it crawls at 20 pixels per second.

Scrolling News

You can see that most of the programming is built in and that by setting window type to scrollingnews, the text follows a preprogrammed course. You can also set the duration for the text to travel from the bottom to the top of the screen and set the bgcolor of the background.

Video for Our Example

Here's the code for playing a source video, howto.rm, in the video region. The fill="freeze" means that the last image is displayed after the video is completed:

```
<video src="video/howto.rm" region="video" fill="freeze" />
```

Inserting Ads with SMIL

With SMIL, you can create ads in any format. You can treat the ads the same way you treat your media clips. Lay out your presentation and time when each media clip and ad appears. Because a SMIL file lists separate URLs to each clip, your ads can be on any server.

And because a SMIL file is a plain text file, you can dynamically generate it by any means to present different ads for each page visitor.

The following example creates a video region with an ad banner above it. When a user plays the presentation, the video plays uninterrupted while ads appear in the ad banner twice a minute. The video and ads play simultaneously as specified in a <par> group. Within the <par> group, ads are nested within a <seq>. Each ad links to a different HTML page that displays in the browser when the user clicks the ad graphic:

```
EXAMPLE:
<smil>
  <head>
    <!--presentation with video clip and ad banner-->
    <layout>
      <root-layout width="330" height="330" background-color="black"/>
      <region id="adregion" top="5" left="5" width="320" height="72"/>
      <region id="videoregion" top="85" left="5"width="320"
height="240"/>
    </layout>
  </head>
  <body>
    <par>
      <video src="howto.rm" region="videoregion"/>
      <par>
        <seq>
          <!--Display new linked ad banner every 30 seconds-->
          <a href="http://www.video-software.com/ads/ad1.htm"
show="new">
            <img src="ad1.gif" region="adregion" dur="30s"/></a>
          <a href="http://www.video-software/ads/ad2.htm" show="new">
            <img src="ad2.gif?bitrate=1000" region="adbanner"
dur="30s"/></a>
          <a href="http://www.video-software/ads/ad3.htm" show="new">
            <img src="ad3.gif?bitrate=1000" region="adregion"
dur="30s"/></a>
          <a href="http://www.video-software/ads/ad4.htm" show="new">
            <img src="ad4.gif?bitrate=1000" region="adregion"
dur="30s"/></a>
        </seq>
```

```
          </par>
        </par>
      </body>
    </smil>
```

Inserting Ads in a Clip

The following example inserts three ad videos into our example video, howto.rm. The effect is like a television program with commercial breaks. Each ad video links to an HTML page that displays in the browser when the user clicks the ad:

```
<smil>
 <head>
  <!--video clip with commercial breaks-->
  <meta name="author" content="H. P. Alesso"/>
  <meta name="title" content="How to Stream Video"/>
  <meta name="copyright" content="(c)1999 H. P. Alesso"/>
 </head>
 <body>
  <seq>
    <video src="howto.rm" clip-end="3.0min"/>
     <a href="http://www.video-software /ads/ad1.htm" show="new">
    <video src="commercial1.rm"/></a>
    <video src="Howto.rm" clip-begin="3.0 min" clip-end="6.0 min"/>
     <a href="http://www.video-software /ads/ad2.htm" show="new">
    <video src="commercial2.rm"/></a>
    <video src=" Howto.rm" clip-begin="6.0 min" clip-end="9.0 min"/>
     <a href="http://www.video-software /ads/ad3.htm" show="new">
    <video src="commercial3.rm"/></a>
    <video src=" Howto.rm" clip-begin="24.5min"/>
  </seq>
 </body>
</smil>
```

As shown above, the three ad clips and the main video clip, howto.rm, are in a <seq> group. The howto.rm video begins at its normal beginning and plays for 3.0 minutes. It then stops while the commercial1.rm ad plays. The howto.rm clip then resumes where it left off, breaking at later intervals for commercial2.rm and commercial3.rm. Because no timing elements are specified for the ads, they play from their normal beginnings to normal ends and may be any length.

Using RealPix for Ads

Instead of streaming ads to RealPlayer directly through SMIL, you can use RealPix to assemble JPEG and GIF images into ad presentations. RealPix lets you create exciting transitions, such as fades, wipes, zooms, and pans. You can create these effects through the RealPix mark-up with regular JPEG or GIF images. You do not need to use animated GIFs.

RealPlayer G2 does not maintain a disk cache, but does cache images in memory for the duration of the RealPix presentation. A RealPix presentation that reuses an ad graphic does not use bandwidth after RealPlayer has received the graphic. Images streamed directly through SMIL are not cached, though, and RealServer must stream each image each time it appears in the presentation.

Conclusion

In this chapter, we presented the background of the development of RealVideo and its impact on digital technology. It is the driving force demanding compatibility and interactivity with greater and greater efficiencies.

On the basis of this chapter, you should conclude that:
- RealNetworks will dominate narrowband streaming codec for several more years with its easy-to-use publishing tools and its compatibility with the open standard SMIL.
- SMIL provides a very effective rich media experience.

CHAPTER 6

Windows Media, QuickTime, and Other Formats

Streaming media started with the Internet's first streaming audio player, RealAudio, in April 1995, which allowed listeners to hear audio as it was being downloaded. The first Internet streaming video player was Xing Technologies' StreamWorks, released in August 1995 and followed shortly by VDOLive from VDOnet Corp. In early 1997 Progressive Networks, renamed RealNetworks released RealVideo along with an all-in-one audio/video player called *RealPlayer.* ▶

In this chapter, Windows Media, QuickTime, Emblaze, VDOlive, and StreamWorks formats are presented and examples provided. A table comparing different format features is included.

A s the use of streaming media has increased, competition for customers in the streaming media market has intensified. While RealNetworks has emerged as the clear leader in 1999, rapid changes in codecs produced many new challengers. Increasingly, however, the question is asked, How do Windows Media and other formats stack up against RealNetworks?

🔊 Windows Media

Microsoft entered into the streaming video market in 1997 with its buyout of WebTV Networks and Vxtreme. Microsoft introduced its own format called *Active Streaming Format (ASF)*. This format provides a standard method of synchronizing audio, video, and multimedia within an ASF file. Competition between ASF and RealNetworks emerged as the World Wide Web Consortium (W3C) endorsed the open standard Synchronized Multimedia Integration Language (SMIL).

Windows Media (once called *NetShow*) is the latest version of Microsoft's streaming media. This new version provides both live and on-demand content. It offers two levels of streaming quality: a standard unicast and a multicast streaming (streaming real-time content to an unlimited number of users). More than 17 million consumers have the Windows Media Player, which is distributed free with the Windows operating system.

Streaming media files can be synchronized into interactive multimedia presentations via ASF. Through the use of multibitrate streams, intelligent transmission, and video playback enhancement, Windows Media can detect network connection speeds, adjust to changing network conditions, and automatically improve video stream quality on the fly.

Windows Media provides all the encoding tools for free, including Windows Media Player, Content Creation Tools, and Windows Media Server.

The Windows Media Player supports a variety of formats: ASF, Real Video/Real Audio version 4.0 (pre-1997), MPEG-1, MPEG-2, WAV, AVI, MIDI, MOV, VOD, AU, MP3, and QuickTime files.

The Windows Media Encoder turns content (such as live audio or video, or stored media files) into an ASF stream or file. The Windows Media Author combines and synchronizes audio and image files into a streaming ASF presentation. The Windows Media ASF Indexer graphically edits ASF files by adding indexing, properties, markers, and scripts. The Windows Media Encoder can encode video content live at over 5 megabits per second (Mbps), achieving a 30-frame-per-second (fps) frame rate, or it can scale down to 22Kbps.

The Adobe Premiere and PowerPoint plug-ins let you create ASF files from within those applications. The On-Demand Producer provides Save as Windows Media and Publish

Windows Media wizards for easy encoding and Web page creation/publishing of AVI and WAV files.

The ASF Conversion Tools are a set of DOS command-line utilities that let you convert AVI or MOV files as well as WAV and MP3 files into ASF. And there are utilities for editing, verifying, and checking ASF files.

ASF files send the first part of an audio or video clip down the *pipe* first. While that is playing, the rest of the data flows down, arriving in time to be played. To make sure playback isn't interrupted if the network slows, the player collects a buffer before it starts playing.

The On-Demand Producer converts content from other formats to ASF and provides basic audio and video editing capabilities. It has features for adding synchronized script commands for building high-impact multimedia presentations. It also includes a wizard-based publishing tool to build an HTML template and upload everything to the server.

Converting Existing Digital Video to ASF

The associated Web site *www.video-software.com* provides download links for *free* video players from the major developers (RealNetworks, Microsoft, Apple, Emblaze, Bitcasting, LZX-MPEG), as well as, their video encoding tools, editing tools, and server software.

A CD-ROM with example code and streaming video demos is included at the back cover of this book. On the enclosed CD-ROM is an example on a directory called How To. It contains a sequential series of examples that takes you through the Internet video production process.

Let's look at our CD-ROM How To example for Windows. Our example was videotaped and digitally captured to an AVI file on the CD-ROM. So now that you have the AVI file, let's put it through the encoder.

The first thing we need to decide is just how much bandwidth to send out. Since most users connect with a 56Kbps modem, we'll assume that we're creating content for these users, even though higher bandwidth means higher quality files.

Start the Windows Media Encoder by going to the **Start** button, point to **Programs,** point to **Windows Media Services,** and click **Windows Media Encoder** (see Figure 6-1) followed by OK.

When you create scalable video, you are creating files that are meant to be streamed from a Windows Media Services Server. They are really files that contain multiple video tracks for a given bandwidth. If network congestion causes your users to fail to receive all of the information for your clip, Windows Media Services is smart enough to start sending down

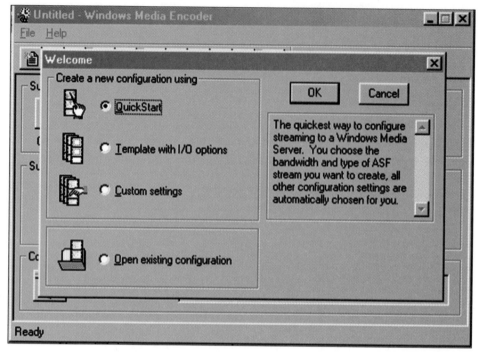

Figure 6-1   Microsoft Encoder: Opening the Encoder

less information. This wouldn't be possible from a Web server. Media streaming enables a user to watch a clip with reasonable quality—even when the Internet is busy—without having to wait and have the clip constantly buffer. It is highly recommended that you use scalable video whenever possible, so make sure to use a scalable template.

Since we are creating 56Kbps content, we now have three options, a high-motion template, a music video template, or a presentation template. How important is the audio to your clip? Since you have a fixed amount of bandwidth, you must evaluate the trade-off between allocating resources between the audio and the video.

In the Welcome window select **56K Dial-up Modem Video** (see Figure 6-2). The details and description of the codec and files is listed below the selection. Now select **Next.** The next screen asks you to select a live or file source. For our example select **AVI/WAV/MP3 File,** then select **Next.** An input screen now asks you to view your Browser and select your input file name. For our example go to the How To AVI directory and select the **Howto.avi file** then select **Next.** The next screen asks for the output file name. For our example, input "Howto.asf" then select **Next.** You can now start the encoding process by pressing the arrow > from the icon menu. Statistics are displayed as the process proceeds.

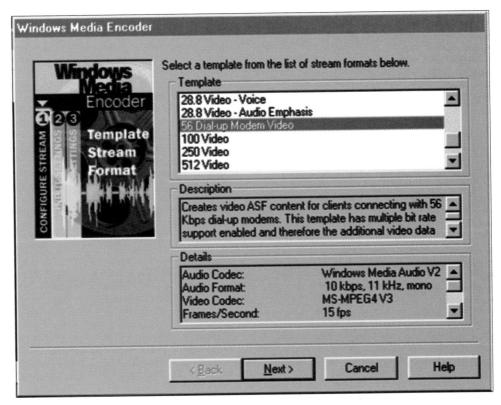

Figure 6-2   Microsoft Encoder: Selecting Codec

The setup is now complete (see Figure 6-3). Once you click on the **Start** button, it will become shaded, and the **Stop** button will be available. You will know that your file is finished when the **Stop** button becomes shaded and the **Play** button returns. Now it is time to play the file. Simply open up the directory where you stored your ASF, and double-click it. The media player will then open.

How to Publish a Web Page Example

Now you are ready to create a Web page and publish to your Web site.

Click on the file in your source folder with the new ASF extension. Your file will begin playing. To place a link to your ASF file from your Web page, you will need to create an ASX file. An *ASX file* is a text-based metafile that provides a link between your page and the ASF file. Open your text editor. Copy and paste this code:

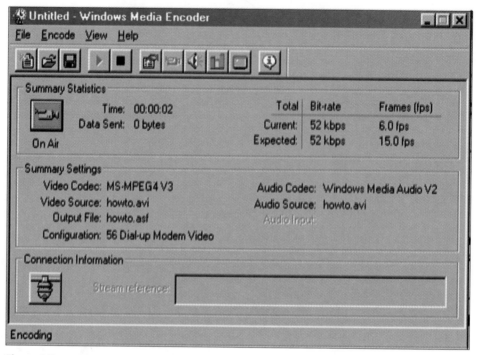

Figure 6-3   Microsoft Encoder: Start encoding

```
<ASX version="3">
 <Entry>
 <ref HREF="http://www.video-software.com/howto/howto.asf"/> </Entry>
 </ASX>
```

Save the file into the same folder as the ASF file. Change the path in the <REF HREF> tag so that it points to your file. The extension must be changed from .txt to .asx. Test this ASX file by clicking it. Add an < A HREF> tag to your Web page that points to the ASX file, for example:

```
<ref HREF="http://www.video-software.com/howto/howto.asx"/>
 Start Windows Media Presentation
 </a>
```

Test your Web page by viewing it in your Browser, and clicking your link to the ASX file.

To post to an HTTP server, place both the ASX and ASF files in the same folder as your Web page. To post to a Windows Media Services Server, install Windows Media Services and place the ASF file in an ASF root directory. Place the ASX file in the same folder as the Web page.

For clients to view your media, they need to have certain settings called MIME types correctly configured. Installation of the Windows Media Player on most browser configurations usually takes care of these settings.

Embedded Windows Media Files in Both Internet Explorer and Netscape

Use the code below to create Web pages that can play embedded streaming media files in the Windows Media Player in both Internet Explorer and Netscape Navigator. This code will embed the Windows Media Player within your Web page, using an ActiveX control for Internet Explorer and a plug-in for Netscape Navigator.

Add the code below to your Web page between the <BODY> and </BODY> tags. Replace "howto.asx" with the path of a file on your local hard drive or a file on a Windows NT Server running Windows Media Services.

```
<OBJECT ID="MediaPlayer"
 classid="CLSID:22d6f312-b0f6-11d0-94ab-0080c74c7e95"
CODEBASE="http://activex.microsoft.com/activex/controls/mplayer/en/
nsmp2inf.cab#Version=5,1,52,701"
 standby="Loading Microsoft Windows Media Player components..."
 TYPE="application/x-oleobject">
  <PARAM NAME="FileName" VALUE="<ref HREF="http://www.video-
software.com/howto/howto.asx"/>">
 <PARAM NAME="AnimationatStart" VALUE="true">
 <PARAM NAME="TransparentatStart" VALUE="true">
 <PARAM NAME="AutoStart" VALUE="true">
 <PARAM NAME="ShowControls" VALUE="1">
 <Embed TYPE="application/x-mplayer2"
pluginspage="http://www.microsoft.com/windows95/downloads/contents/
wurecommended
        /s_wufeatured/mediaplayer/default.asp"
      SRC="<ref HREF="http://www.video-software.com/howto/howto.asf"/>"
      Name=MediaPlayer
      ShowControls=1
      Width=160
      Height=120 >
   </embed>
 </OBJECT>
```

```
<BR><BR>
<ref HREF="http://www.video-software.com/howto/howto.asx"/>
```

🔟 Start the Streaming Media Presentation in the Stand-alone Player

Add the following JavaScript code after the </TITLE> tag. This will refresh the Netscape Navigator plug-in and load the MAYSCRIPT applet, which monitors the plug-in for scripting events.

```
<script language="JavaScript">
<!--
  if ( navigator.appName == "Netscape" )
  {
    navigator.plugins.refresh();
    document.write("\x3C" + "applet MAYSCRIPT
Code=NPDS.npDSEvtObsProxy.class" )
    document.writeln(" WIDTH=5 HEIGHT=5 NAME=appObs\x3E \x3C/applet\x3E")
  }
//-->
</script>
```

Netscape Enable

Now you should have a Web page that can play embedded files in the Windows Media Player in both Internet Explorer and Netscape Navigator. Your ActiveX control can receive script events and play them back in Internet Explorer 3.*x* or later. You will need to add more code to get these events to work in Netscape Navigator.

Add the following JavaScript function between the </HEAD> and <BODY> tags. This code first checks to see whether the current browser is Netscape Navigator. If yes, a small Java applet (downloaded in above) will monitor the Netscape Navigator plug-in for script events.

```
function RegisterEventObservers() {
  if(navigator.appName == "Netscape") {
    var plugin = document.MediaPlayer;
    document.appObs.setByProxyDSScriptCommandObserver(plugin, true);
  }
}
```

To run this code when the Web page loads add an OnLoad event for the RegisterEventObservers function inside the <BODY> tag, as follows:

```
<BODY onLoad="RegisterEventObservers()" BGCOLOR="#000000" LINK="#000066">
```

Put Your Streaming Media Files into Media Services Server

Put your streaming media files into the ASFROOT directory of the Windows Media Services Server. Now that your media clips are on your Windows Media Services Server, you need to add elements into your HTML and on your Web server so that you can access these files. You can either have your users use the Windows Media Player as a stand-alone application, or put the player directly into the Web page.

A simple, yet effective method of playing Windows Media is to simply reference an ASF Stream Redirector (ASX) file. An ASX file is an Extensible Markup Language (XML)–based text file. It references a Uniform Resource Locator (URL) for a piece of media content. An ASX file is a shortcut to media content that resides on your Web server.

An ASX file should always be used to reference media content for the stand-alone player because browsers other than Microsoft Internet Explorer do not intrinsically understand the Microsoft Media Server (MMS) streaming protocol. As such, they cannot locate or obtain information about the Media File. Without an ASX file, content cannot stream to the stand-alone media player. When you click on a link in a browser, that file is downloaded to the browser's cache. However, when you click on a link to an ASX, the ASX (which is a very small download) gets downloaded into the cache and then launches the helper application associated with the ASX MIME type for the Windows Media Player.

ASX files are very similar to HTML. They use tags in a way that is very similar to HTML, and some of the tags are even the same. Here's the basic syntax:

```
<ASX version="3.0">
<TITLE>Simple ASX</TITLE>
  <ENTRY>
     <TITLE>An Entry in a Simple ASX</TITLE>
     <AUTHOR>Your Name Here</AUTHOR>
    <REF HREF="mms://windowserver/howto/howto.asf"/>
  </ENTRY>
</ASX>
```

To reference an ASX file, add the following code to your Web page:

```
<A HREF="http://webserver/howto/howto.asx">
    Link to Streaming Content
</A>
```

The browser will open this file and then launch the Windows Media Player.

Windows Media T.A.G. Author

Gather your media. Insert all of your media (images and audio tracks) into a folder labeled *source*. If you don't have an existing audio track, use Sound Recorder for your audio (start > programs > accessories > entertainment > Sound Recorder), or another sound editor. For your images, JPG images will produce the best results.

Start the Windows Media T.A.G. Author. A welcome window will appear. Choose the third radio button on the list labeled **Create a New Project.**

Go to your Source folder. Drag all of your audio into the white holding bin area. Move your mouse over the files, and notice the thumbnail image of the file and attributes in the upper left window. In the center of the first row of buttons in the title bar, you are given bandwidth choices (28.8Kbps or 56Kbps). Choose the modem speed equivalent to your connection.

Drag an audio track into the timeline window at the bottom of the T.A.G. Author. The Audio Conversion dialog box appears with a list of compression choices. Choose the option applicable to the connection you selected above. Click **OK.**

The green bar in the timeline window represents your audio file. The numbers across the top represent the time code of your presentation in seconds. For example, if the green bar starts at 12 and ends at 34, then your audio track will begin 12 seconds into the presentation and end 34 seconds into the presentation.

If you choose to, you can add more than one audio file, but they cannot overlap in the time code.

Test your presentation by clicking **File** > **Preview** > **Media.**

Collect your images from your source folder and drag the first image into the timeline window.

The load time of your image file is represented by the blue line. The image will not appear in the presentation until the image is done loading. If you choose to compress the image more, it will appear smaller in the timeline window.

To compress the image, right click on the blue line and select **Convert.** Change the text area labeled **Quality** to 50. The image is now compressed by 50 percent. Notice the change in appearance of the blue area; it is now cross-haired and smaller in length.

Since you cannot have two images loading at the same time, ensure that the blue areas in the timeline window do not overlap. If the blue line turns red or white, compress the image more or remove one of the images.

Test your presentation by clicking File > Preview > Media. Go to File > Save, and save your presentation in your Source folder.

Your file will be assigned an .aep extension, not ASF. The AEP file is the project file, while the ASF file is the finished product. Many other files will be created with the AEP file. Keep these files in the same folder and the same directory structure. Don't delete or move them.

Comparison of Formats

The following table (Table 6-1) compares the feature of Windows Media and RealSystems G2.

Table 6-1   Comparison of Windows Media and RealSystems

Feature	Windows Media Technologies 4.0	RealSystem G2
W3C SMIL Standards-compliant	No	Yes
Encoder platform	Windows	Windows, SUN, Mac, Linux, UNIX
Input format	AVI, WAV, MOV, MP3	AVI, WAV, MOV, MPEG
Server communication protocol	TCP/HTTP	TCP
Player scriptable from JavaScript, VBscript	Yes	Yes
URL hot spots	Yes	Yes
Adobe Premiere plug-in	Yes	Yes
Third-party tool support	Sound Forge, Digital Renascence, Ulead, Veon, Terran	Digital Renascence, Oz Interactive, Veon, Live Picture
Transmission protocols	UDP, TCP, HTTP	UDP, TCP, HTTP, RTSP
Multicast support	Yes	Yes

◗ Microsoft TV Platform Adaptation Kit (TVPAK)

Microsoft's Windows Media Technologies will be an integral part of the Microsoft TV Platform Adaptation Kit (TVPAK). Microsoft's client/server television software—will enable listening and viewing for consumers using televisions or set-top boxes based on future TVPAK technology. TVPAK technology is based on the Windows CE operating system, Internet Explorer browser technology, and WebTV technology.

When IP Multicasting becomes broadly available on the Internet, customers with Windows Media Technologies will be able to take advantage of the scalability and bandwidth derived from single-stream, multiuser connections.

Microsoft TVPAK consists of Microsoft client/server software for the television industry. The client software, Microsoft TV, operates a range of TV-centric appliances from Internet terminals and advanced set-top boxes to integrated televisions. The server software, Microsoft TV Server, will be used by network operators to deploy and manage a rich, scalable, enhanced TV service.

◗ QuickTime

Apple's QuickTime VR technology is one of the most attractive technologies to happen to digital imaging in five years. With it, you can produce and view 360-degree panoramas of real or computer-generated scenes, without the need for expensive panoramic cameras or any other fancy equipment usually associated with VR.

You create a panorama by photographing a scene with a standard 35mm camera atop a tripod, taking 12 to 18 photographs to capture a full 360-degree view. Then, using Apple's software, you "stitch" these images into a single PICT file, which is then processed further to create the final, user-navigable movie, playable on both Macintosh and WINTEL personal computers.

QuickTime is the centerpiece of the Mac and is what makes the Macs so popular with artists and developers. Its sophisticated, time-based engine makes it easy to create and edit projects. QuickTime VR (QTVR) is Apple's panoramic extensions to QuickTime and lets ordinary QuickTime files become one large static panoramic scene. QTVR works by stitching together a series of photographs into a panoramic 360-degree view. Once that is done the file must be completely downloaded before playing.

An excellent application of Apple's QuickTime VR technology is real estate walk-thru by iPIX. See *www.ipix.com/merger/index.html*.

QuickTime 4.1 features ad insertion, improved firewall navigation, AppleScript, and support of Synchronized Multimedia Integrated Language (SMIL).

QuickTime Streaming Server 2 features password protection and a plug-in architecture. It will also support third-party analysis tools that provide consolidated server reporting. The QuickTime Streaming Server is an open-source standards-based Internet streaming solution.

QuickTime Compression

To compress video with QuickTime Encoder (see Figure 6-4):

Figure 6-4   **QuickTime Encoder**

▸ Choose **Export** from the File menu. In the dialog box that appears, choose our example video, Howto.avi. If you don't see compression choices, click **Settings.**

▸ Select a type of compression. Each compression method has strengths and weaknesses. Some methods are more appropriate for storing certain types of media. Some compression methods introduce more distortion in the final product than others. Some compress slowly and decompress quickly, while others compress and decompress at the same rate. Some methods can compress a file to one one-hundredth of its original size, while others decrease the file size very little. Compressors included with QuickTime include: Apple Video, Cinepak, Component Video, H.261, H.263, Intel Indeo Video 4.4, Microsoft Video, Microsoft RLE, MPEG-1.

▸ Click **Options** to set video and sound options that affect how the file is exported.

When you save a movie file to be used on the Web with the current version of QuickTime and QuickTime Movie Player, add the extension .mov to the end of its name. This allows a Web browser to recognize the movie file type and play the movie properly. Save the movie in a QuickTime format.

To compress .avi to .mov files with the QuickTime Player and Encoder:

1. Using the file menu, select **open movie** and open the provided example, How to edit.avi.

2. Click **Export** from the File menu.

3. Type in the save name and location for the How To.mov file.

4. Use the Options button to set up the compression codec.

Table 6-2 compares the pros and cons associated with converting files to QuickTime.

Table 6-2   QuickTime

Converting Media Files to QuickTime	
PROs	CONs
• QuickTime editing applications exist on all platforms and are among the most used products in the industry.	• Bandwidth needs are more difficult to estimate than in other technologies.
• QuickTime Pro can open AVI files and export to QuickTime without the need of a major video editing package.	• Only QuickTime Pro will give a kb/sec dialog for the Sorensen Codec. The audio component bandwidth needs to be tested, because QuickTime Pro doesn't show a composite bandwidth total for video and audio combined.
• Works reliably on PC and Mac.	

The only really serious problem of QuickTime in comparison to Real and Microsoft, is the lack of a variable frame rate codec. When the action in a low-bandwidth clip picks up, QuickTime stoically sticks to the preset frame rate. This causes loss of image detail into blobs. Smarter codecs like Real and Microsoft's MPEG-4 allow for a variation in frame rates to accommodate some image detail at the expense of smoothness as needed.

StreamWorks

StreamWorks is the oldest streaming video player and is well known for its MPEG video. StreamWorks has two components: the client and the server. There is a third element for real-time transmission of live content.

The cross-platform software player is free and available for Windows, Macintosh, and UNIX platforms. The StreamWorks server software works alongside Web server software and uses UDP protocol. It sends real-time transmissions of MPEG video as unicast or multicast. The optional hardware MPEG encoder encodes incoming audio or video and is called Xing's MPEG encoder.

VDOlive

One of the first streaming video players after StreamWorks was VDOLive by VDOnet Corp. VDOLive is a client/server solution that can handle HTTP streaming. It consists of VDOLive Player, VDOLive Tools, VDOLive On-Demand, and VDOLive Broadcast.

VDOLive Player has a television-like appearance with just start/stop controls on the bottom. The player is a plug-in and an Active-X control for Internet Explorer.

VDOLive Tools includes VDO Capture and VDO Clip that capture and compress files. The first step is to capture the video as an AVI file with VDO Capture. It is a very basic capture program using sources from a VCR, camcorder, TV, or digital camera. The new AVI file is then ready to compress with VDO Clip converter, which produces a VDO format with an AVI file extension. This allows editing in Adobe Premiere.

With VDOLive one file can scale to play at different speeds though VDO does not support IP multicast. All streams are sent unicast.

Emblaze

Emblaze is both a serverless and clientless streaming video system. Emblaze creates streaming Web multimedia, including audio, video, text, and graphics. Emblaze video player is a 50KB Java applet downloaded with the HTML of the Web page.

Emblaze is designed to deliver streaming media using existing standards and protocols rather then proprietary ones. This is achieved using Rapid Media algorithms and mechanics that stream the media packets as standard TCP/IP datagrams and through regular HTTP Web servers. With a simple drag and drop operation, video or audio content is uploaded to the site and becomes an integral part of the HTML Web page.

Emblaze requires no special Web server software or hardware and no installations or any reconfigurations on the ISP or server side. Emblaze has dynamically scalable bandwidth from 28.8Kbps to full broadcast quality, full screen, full motion, CD quality stereo over LAN and wideband networks. Emblaze is also MPEG-4 compliant.

The Emblaze encoding product is Emblaze Creator.

Emblaze Encoding

To compress .avi and .mov files with the Emblaze Producer (see Figure 6-5):

1. Using the file command press the large Open Marble and open the selected .avi or .mov file.

2. Click **Open** for the selected file.

3. Click on the appropriate frame size and FPS (frames per minute) fields.

4. To add video controls check the Control Panel box under the create HTML box.

5. To create HTML with the associated file for compression, check the create HTML box.

6. Finally press the Compress Marble.

7. You must copy the Java Class files to the Emblaze Video Player Folder (including CyclicDecoredStream.class, EmblazeAudio.class, EmblazeVideo.class, Exec.class, Jsdec.class, Ev.bin, Xbuttons.gif).

Note: Do not place the class files in the same folder as other Emblaze product class files.

Inetcam

Java applet applications are becoming popular because they can provide simple and easily accessible live video delivery packages. A new example is Inetcam.

Unlike conventional video conferencing systems, the new Inetcam system requires no proprietary software or downloads to view video. The Inetcam video is Web accessible through Windows, UNIX, and Mac platform, as well as, LCD phones. The Inetcam soft-

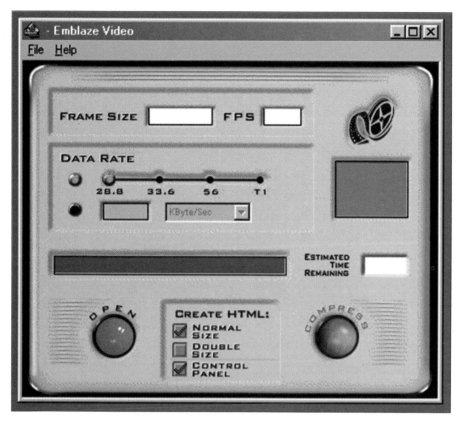

Figure 6- 5   Emblaze Producer

ware package allows you to capture and serve live video in real time using a Java applet. Inetcam works with any hardware camera or video source that is compatible with Video for Windows. It allows multiple camera and is compatible with either static- or dynamic-allocated IP addresses (www.inetcam.com).

Conclusion

In this chapter, we presented the background of the development of software and its impact on digital technology. It is the driving force demanding compatibility and interactivity with greater and greater efficiencies.

On the basis of this chapter, you should conclude that

▶ RealNetworks will dominate narrowband streaming codec for several more years, but Microsoft Windows Media will grow rapidly and aggressively target the 1.5Mbps and above delivery. In addition, new codec improvements will emerge rapidly from the numerous competing codec developers (see Chapter 7 for streaming MPEG plug-ins for RealNetworks and Windows Media).

▶ There are a few issues that handicap Java-based streaming video. First, there needs to be a Java standard for all operating systems. Microsoft has already optimized Java for Windows virtual machine. This has produced divergent Java camps.

CHAPTER 7

MPEG
Streaming

Outside of the Internet, MPEG is the world video standard. MPEG-1 video is already the standard for transmitting video over satellites or cable television. MPEG-2 is being used for DVD feature films. So why isn't it being used over the Internet? ▶

In this chapter, we outline the MPEG standards and where they are being used and developed. We describe the commercial products scaling MPEG from narrowband streaming to high definition TV.

The main problem is that the two most popular computer systems, Apple and Wintel, already have their own video format standards, QuickTime (MOV) and Video for Windows (AVI /ASF), respectively. The tide is shifting, however, with software MPEG encoders becoming available. While the MPEG codec can be played within the Windows and QuickTime formats, a more MPEG-centric format may emerge.

▶ Standards

Moving Picture Experts Group (MPEG) standards are used for audio and video. The ITU (International Telecommunications Union) formed the Moving Picture Exerts Group in 1991 to develop compression standards for playback of video clips and digital TV.

The Moving Picture Experts Group is a working group under International Standards Organization (ISO/IEC, see Appendix A) in charge of the development of international standards for compression, decompression, processing, and coded representation of moving pictures and audio. MPEG plenary and their subgroups meet on Requirements, Systems, Video, Audio, SNHC, Test, and Implementation on a routine basis. The meeting includes 300 experts from 20 countries.

So far MPEG standards have produced the following.

> *MPEG-1.* A standard for storage and retrieval of moving pictures and associated audio on storage media
> *MPEG-2.* A standard for digital television
> *MPEG-4.* A standard for multimedia applications
> *MPEG-7.* A content representation standard for information search

Readers can go to the MPEG Web site to obtain the latest information on MPEG standards at *http://drogo.cselt.it/mpeg*.

MPEG-1 Standard

The MPEG-1 (ISO/IEC 11172) video encoding standard was designed to support video encoding at bit rates of approximately 1.5Mbps (this is the standard connection speed of DSL and cable modems). MPEG-1 video compression makes use of the Discrete Cosine Transform (DCT) algorithm to transform 8 × 8 blocks of pixels into variable length codes (VLC). The quality of the video achieved with this standard is roughly similar to that of a VHS VCR. This level of quality is generally not acceptable for broadcast quality video. It is expected that most video over ATM network applications will use MPEG-2 rather than MPEG-1.

MPEG-1 is intended to be generic (although the initial target applications envisaged and applications parameters defined were constrained to digital storage media). Generic means that the standard is independent of a particular application and therefore comprises mainly a toolbox. It is up to the user to decide which tools to select to suit the particular application. This implies that only the coding syntax is defined and therefore the decoding scheme is standardized. MPEG-1 defines a hybrid DCT coding scheme with motion compensation similar to the H.261 standard. Further refinements in prediction and subsequent processing were introduced to provide the functionality required for random access in digital storage media.

MPEG-2 Standard

The MPEG-2 (ISO/IEC 13818) standard is an extension of the MPEG-1 standard. MPEG-2 was designed to provide high-quality video encoding suitable for transmission over computer networks.

MPEG-2 video compression makes use of the Discrete Cosine Transform (DCT) algorithm to transform 8×8 blocks of pixels into variable length codes (VLC). These VLC's are the representation of the quantized coefficients from the DCT.

Transmitting motion changes requires fewer bits but can only succeed as long as luminance and color do not change too much. Real-time encoders have the most trouble recording rapid motion, such as sporting events. Some techniques work better than MPEG-2 for compression, but they have to find a way into the standards and chips for commercial use.

MPEG-2 uses compression video on a frame by frame basis, but treats some frames differently. It begins by encoding a single Intra, (I frame) as JPEG and then for subsequent frames encodes just the difference in frames due to motion between it (Bidirectional, B frames) and the previous frames (Predictive, P frames).

I frames use only intraframe compression and they are much larger than P or B frames. P frames use motion-compensated prediction from the previous I or P frame. B frames use motion-compensated prediction by either forward predicting from future I or P frames, backward predicting from previous I or P frames, or interpolating between both forward and backward I or P frames. B frames achieve the highest degree of compression.

MPEG-2 is expected to be the primary compression protocol used in transmitting video over ATM networks. There are two main options for mapping MPEG-2 bit streams into ATM cells.

  ▸ Constant bit rate (CBR) transmission adaptation layer 1 (AAL 1) and transmission over AAL 5. This video would probably be carried as IP packets over ATM and would be encoded in proprietary formats, such as QuickTime or AVI. The AAL 5 would provide no quality of service guarantees from the network for this class of video.

- ▶ Variable bit rate (VBR) traffic that is native to the ATM network. This video would be able to benefit from AAL 5 quality of service guarantees.

Compression squeezes the video signals into small enough units so that the studio-quality television can be sent on standard digital television channels. The HDTV displays 1080 horizontal lines and 1029 vertical scanned lines. Computerized compression reduces the 1.5Gbps to 19.3Mbps. However, the person seeing the TV image perceives the image to be almost as clear as the original. Because of this powerful codec, very little quality is lost to the viewer.

Where will we see MPEG in everyday life? Just about wherever you see video today.

DBS (Direct Broadcast Satellite) and the Hughes/USSB DBS service use MPEG-2 video and audio. Despite conflicting options, the CATV (cable television) uses MPEG-2 video.

MPEG-4 Standard

The MPEG-4 standard is directly related to scalable video codec. The MPEG-4 standard is based on next-generation techniques, such as subband coding, model-based coding, and knowledge-based coding. While wavelet transforms for data compression for streaming video have been tried by several organizations, their performance has not yet demonstrated the full extent of expected major technological improvement.

The MPEG-4 standard includes algorithms and tools for coding and flexible representation of audiovisual data to meet the challenges of future Multimedia applications. In particular, MPEG-4 addresses the need for the following.

- ▶ Multimedia audiovisual data need to be transmitted and accessed in heterogeneous network environments, possibly under severe error conditions (e.g., mobile channels). Although the MPEG-4 standards will be network (physical-layer) independent in nature, the algorithms and tools for coding audiovisual data need to be designed with awareness of network peculiarities.
- ▶ Future multimedia applications will include flexible, highly interactive access to and manipulation of audiovisual data.
- ▶ Next-generation graphics processors will enable multimedia terminals to present both pixel-based audio and video data together with synthetic audio/speech and video in a highly flexible way. MPEG-4 will assist the efficient and flexible coding and representation of both natural (pixel-based) as well as synthetic data.
- ▶ For the storage and transmission of audiovisual data a high coding efficiency, meaning a good quality of the reconstructed data, is required. Improved coding efficiency,

in particular at very low bit rates below 64Kbps, continues to be an important functionality to be supported by the MPEG-4 video standard.

Bit rates targeted for the MPEG-4 video standard are between 5Kbps and 64Kbps for mobile or PSTN video applications and up to 2Mbps for TV/film applications. Seven new (with respect to existing or emerging standards) key video coding functionalities have been defined that support the MPEG-4 focus and provide the main requirements for the work in the MPEG video group.

MPEG-4 is designed for use in broadcast, interactive, and conversational environments. Its strong points are inherited from the MPEG-1 and -2 standards (broadcast-grade synchronization and the choice of on-line/off-line usage) and VRML.

TV/Web integration is therefore a domain where the MPEG-4 technology can be successfully applied.

MPEG-7 Standard

MPEG-7, formally named *Multimedia Content Description Interface,* aims to create a standard for describing the multimedia content data. It will support some interpretation of the information's meaning accessed by a device or a computer code. MPEG-7 is not aimed at any one application in particular. It supports as broad a range of applications as possible.

Readers can go to the MPEG Web site to obtain the latest information on MPEG standards at *http://drogo.cselt.it/mpeg/standards/mpeg-7/mpeg-7.htm.*

◖◗ Broadband Applications

The Internet Engineering Task Force (IETF) has defined specific types for the Real-Time Transport Protocol (RTP) that can be used to deliver MPEG-2 encoded, TV quality video over IP networks.

The video outputs of such systems can be displayed directly on regular TV sets. As the Internet backbone and the residential access bandwidths increase, similar systems can be used to transmit high-quality video over the Internet to residential users. Since this approach requires layer-three functionality at the receivers, it may not be optimal for the transmission of regular TV broadcast channels, a task that requires multi-gigabit-per-second data processing. On the other hand, it opens significant new avenues for video on demand as a part of information-on-demand and narrowcasting applications to justify its existence along with other means to carry broadcast TV channels.

One problem with the broadcast video is the sequential access. For example, we have to listen to an entire news program although we may be interested in only specific news items. A much better way of viewing news programs can be made possible through a descriptive index to the news with links for video on demand of the various segments. AT&T's Pictorial Transcripts application generates a digital multimedia library of TV programs automatically using scene change detection and closed captioning information. Pictorial Transcripts used together with MPEG-2 over IP provides on-demand, non-sequential playback on a regular TV set with video quality.

Another set of applications that benefits from MPEG-2 over IP is based on narrowcasting specialized programs using IP multicast. This way, practically everyone can run a private TV studio, and programs that may be of high interest to a small group of people can be made available to them. For such applications the Internet can provide sophisticated directory and search services.

Both IP-based high-quality video on demand and narrowcasting applications can be developed based on the existing set of Internet protocols. In particular, RTP/RTCP (see Chapter 8) can be used for the transport, Session Description Protocol (SDP) can be used for transmitting the session information to the receivers, and RealTime Streaming Protocol (RTSP) can be used for session control including VCR type control functionality. A guideline document describing the use of these protocols to implement a complete system may be needed to help the implementers.

A second application targets automatic extraction and use of the URL information embedded in broadcast TV pictures. Currently, URL references are used in many TV programs providing additional information on the subject matter of the program. Accessing the Web pages pointed by these requires manual transfer of the displayed URLs from the TV to the Web accessing device. The URL embedded in the picture is extracted through image analysis and character recognition and transmitted to the Web accessing device, which downloads the indicated page automatically.

TV over Copper

Telecommunications service providers are operating in an exciting industry and are beginning to experiment with offering (currently only in Canada) TV over copper wire. Their core capabilities, along with the large amounts of bandwidth that service providers have at their disposal, make it possible for them to offer bundled multiple services to their subscribers using MPEG video content from broadcasters and IP resources already in place.

The system takes in uncompressed and compressed video feeds from any video source, adapts them as needed, and then transmits the MPEG-2 video signals natively or within an IP multicast format over an ATM infrastructure.

TV content is direct from a direct broadcast satellite (DBS) service provider. Channels from the DBS service provider's lineup, that have already been MPEG-2 compressed, are demodulated, descrambled, and sent out over the network to set-top boxes at customers' homes.

Narrowband MPEG Streaming

Streaming MPEG across a scale from several hundred kilobits per second to multi-megabits per second is now taking place. The following information will provide some examples.

A How-To Example for Streaming MPEG

Our Web site, *www.video-software.com*, provides download links for *free* video players from all the major developers (RealNetworks, Microsoft, Apple, Emblaze, Bitcasting, LZX-MPEG), as well as video encoding tools, editing tools, and server software.

A CD-ROM with example code and streaming video demos is included at the back cover of this book. On the enclosed CD-ROM is an example on a directory called How To. It contains a sequential series of examples that takes you through the Internet video production process.

Let's look at our CD-ROM How To example for Streaming MPEG compatible with RealVideo: Bitcasting.

How to Compress to MPEG

Compress .avi to .mov files with the Bitcasting Player and Encoder (see Figure 7-1) as follows.

1. Using the File menu, select **Open Movie,** and open the provided example, How to edit.avi.

2. Click **Export** from the File menu.

3. Type in the save name and location for the How To.mpg file.

4. Use the **Options** button to set up the compression codec.

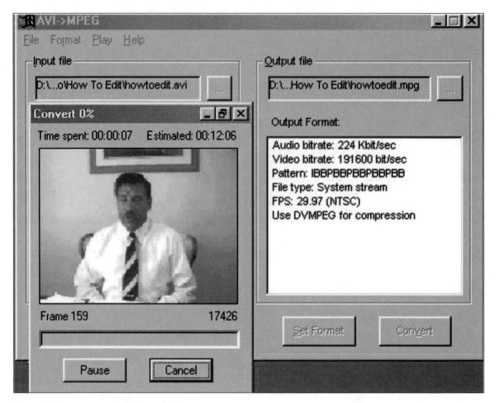

Figure 7-1   Bitcasting MPEG Encoder

The compression codec options include parameters, such as frame rate, video stream data rate, and frame size. This is the information (referred to as Profile) that will control the encoding process.

Suppose we have an AVI file that is a little over 400Kb, and we want to encode it to MPEG and ultimately distribute it over the Internet. The easiest way to do this when first starting out with the LSX-MPEG Encoder (see Figure 7-2) is with the Profile Manager. The Profile Manager includes some predefined Profiles, and also allows you to create and store Profiles for later use. Open it from either the pulldown File menu item or the **Open Profile Manager** button on the toolbar.

When the Profile Manager is opened, you will see a two-part interface. The left side is a list box that displays predefined and custom MPEG-1 and MPEG-2 Profiles with descriptive names. To deliver this piece of video over the Internet to many people, we will want a low bandwidth Profile, but hopefully one that has nearly the same quality of the original AVI file. Click on the Profile MPEG-1 Internet 28.8K higher bandwidth on the left side. The right side displays information on this Profile, and it looks like a good match for our intended application (distribution over the Internet). Click on the **Load Profile** button, to return to the main window.

Now we need to select our Input File to convert and encode to MPEG. Near the Input File box, click on the **Browse** button. A standard Windows file dialog is displayed, prompting you to choose an AVI file for encoding. Select the file HowTo.avi from the How To subdirectory, and click the **Open** button. This file can show off the excellent compression capability of MPEG.

An Information pop-up appears with an analysis of the HowTo.avi file. Click **OK** to continue. In addition to the Input File box being filled in, the Output File is now automatically named HowTo.mpg, saved in the same folder.

To preview the file, click on the **Preview** button to the left of the Input File box. A window appears and plays back the clip. Close the movie window.

Figure 7-2   **LSX-MPEG Encoder**

As you can see, the parameters in the main window have been adjusted to match the Input File and the Profile we chose.

Click on the **Start MPEG Encoding** button on the toolbar. A Warning pop-up appears regarding the low bitrate of the output settings. Click **Yes** to continue. The application will begin encoding the video portion of the stream. A new section of the interface, MPEG Video Encoding in Progress, will appear. Meters will display a frame-by-frame accounting as each is encoded and show information on image quality, current frame quality, and elapsed encoding time. The application will then show a meter for the encoding progress of audio, followed by a meter for the multiplexing of audio and video. When finished, the Multiplexing Encoding Completed box is displayed, presenting a summary of information regarding the process. Close the dialog.

To play the file, click on the **Play** button to the left of the Output File box. A window appears to play back the clip. Click **Play.** As you can see, it is nearly the same quality as the AVI file we input. A quick check on the file size (using Windows Explorer) shows the resulting size. Close the movie window.

◐ Conclusion

In this chapter, we outlined the MPEG standards and where they are being used and developed. We described the commercial products scaling MPEG from narrowband streaming to high definition TV. We included an illustration of using MPEG-2 TV transmission over copper VDSL lines and the protocols required.

On the basis of this chapter, you should conclude that

- ▸ Both RealNetworks and Microsoft may scale their codecs to streaming MPEG standards, perhaps in cooperation with Digital Video and LSX-Mpeg, respectively.
- ▸ MPEG will become widely available, scaling from narrow to broadband.

PART IV

Video Delivery

The networks and servers supporting Internet video are critical in delivering high performance and quality for the viewing experience and are an integral part of the Webcasting production process.

CHAPTER **8**

High-Speed Networks Prepare for Video

When it comes to networks, how fast is fast enough? It seems to be always just a little more than anyone ever gets. In particular, video has very demanding and unique network and software protocol requirements that we are only now beginning to adequately address. ▶

In this chapter, we differentiate three issues currently underway in network development: bandwidth expansion, intelligent networks, and caching servers providing local access for video content.

The natural evolution of building bandwidth is discussed through a brief background on network architecture in order to establish the point of departure between data/voice requirements and the newer video delivery issues. This step describes the relationship of the network's transmission media, switches, routers, and protocol requirements. In so doing, it ties together the delivery of streaming video to the network bandwidth—from the fiber backbone to the last mile connections.

▶️ Building Bandwidth

The earliest computers were stand-alone unconnected machines. To transfer information from one system to another, it was necessary to store the data in some form and physically carry it to the second compatible system and read it into the computer. During the past decade, mergers, takeovers, and downsizing have led to a need to consolidate company data in a fast, seamless, integrated database for all corporate information. Moreover, as companies discovered that their data could be moved from expensive mainframes to small machines on more economical local area networks and wide area networks, their executives started pressuring the Information Technology (IT) organizations to port applications and databases. With these driving forces, intranets and local networks began to increase in size and sought ways to interface with each other.

Today, speed is still the principal constraint between accessing Internet networks and residences. The growing complex network architectures and protocols operate to reach out to access homes and businesses. With the speed of today's computer networks, it is normal for a piece of e-mail or corporate data to travel around the world to many computer recipients almost instantly.

The vast intertwine of networks is composed of several different types of transmission media including:
- Fiber optic
- Twisted pairs (copper)
- Coaxial cable
- Microwave
- Infrared

The two dominant media for data transmissions are fiber optic cabling and unshielded twisted pair (copper). The fiber is faster but more expensive. Fiber optics provides higher speed and larger capacity due to its nonelectric medium. In contrast, not only is copper slower, but it acts as an antenna picking up noise and interference. In addition, new electronics in fiber-optics networks, called *dense wavelength division multiplexing* (DWDM), are improving capacity.

The advantages of fiber include

- ❱ Security—resistance to electromagnetic taps
- ❱ Small size
- ❱ Light weight
- ❱ Low attenuation
- ❱ High bandwidth

The disadvantages of fiber include

- ❱ Component costs higher than copper
- ❱ Local power required
- ❱ Fiber not as flexible for bending around corners

But how is the vast interlacing structure of fiber and wire organized? Let's start by differentiating the network types into a hierarchy based on bandwidth and physical extent as follows.

- ❱ LAN (local area network) typically interconnects computers within a small area of 5 km to 10 km, such as a building or campus at speeds from 10Mbps to 100Mbps.
- ❱ MAN (metropolitan area network) connects many LANs in a larger geographical area of 10 km to 100 km at speeds of 1.5Mbps to 150Mbps.
- ❱ WAN (wide area network) interconnects computer systems over 100 km to 1000 km at speeds from 1.5Mbps to 24Gbps.
- ❱ GAN (global area network) connects networks between countries, across continents, and around the globe at speeds ranging from 1.5Mbps to 100Gbps.

It is typical to find a modern computer facility with LAN links to other systems. LANs are commonly used for small areas but can run over copper wire, fiber optic cable, infrared, or radio waves. A diversity of operating systems, such as UNIX, Linux, or Windows NT platforms administer the LAN server systems.

Intranets are networks connecting computing resources at a school, company, or other organization, but unlike the Internet, they restrict users. On a broadcast network, such as Ethernet, any systems on the cable can send a message. Ethernets can support 10Mbps, but traffic usually reduces this capability. When messages collide and become garbled, it is a problem. The extra load on the system due to collisions affects transmission rate. The high speed Ethernets include the following.

- ❱ Fast Ethernet is a shared protocol that reaches speeds of 100Mbps, ten times the standard Ethernet used by most LAN.
- ❱ Switched Ethernet is a nonshared service. Devices are given their own dedicated paths within a LAN.
- ❱ Gigabit Ethernet works with existing LAN protocols at 1000Mbps and requires fiber optic cabling. On LANs, it is mainly used by high-speed servers.

LANs typically connect to WANs through a gateway. A gateway is a computer or device with multiple network connections. It converts data traffic to appropriate format to and from networks.

Routers play an important role by communicating with one another dynamically and passing information about which computer routes are up or down and providing directions for messages to reach destinations. Routers connect and translate protocols between LAN and WAN and determine the best path for data traffic to take to reach a destination.

Most connections on a WAN are through a point-to-point link, using cable, radio, satellite, or wire links. The advantage of point-to-point links is that the links are limited and well understood. The disadvantage is that each system typically can be equipped for a small number of links. They often use serial lines and modems or parallel ports.

The Internet has recently been upgraded to accommodate demand. Transfer rates of gigabits per second on experimental networks already exist and will soon be put into use.

Figure 8-1 shows a hierarchical illustration of the Internet.

On a token ring network, such as Fiber Distributed Data Interface (FDDI), only one system can send a message at a time. A token is constantly being passed from one host to another around the ring to establish whose turn it is to send. This prevents collisions. If the ring is large, however, it can impact performance. The peak data rate of FDDI networks is 100Mbps.

Fiber Distributed Data Interface, FDDI, was the first 100Mbps transport protocol for LANs and is a significant departure from IEEE 802 specifications. FDDI uses a frame type differ-

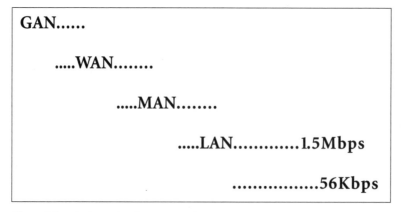

Figure 8-1   The hierarchy of connections from the backbone of the Internet to your home

ent from IEEE 802.3 (Ethernet) or IEE 802.5 (Token Ring) standards. FDDI is an expensive protocol to implement; however, it is highly scalable.

ATM (Asynchronous Transfer Mode)

ATM (asynchronous transfer mode) is a dedicated-connection switching technology that organizes digital data into 53 cells or packets and transmits them over a medium using digital signal technology. Individually, a cell is processed asynchronously relative to other related cells and is queued before being multiplexed over the line.

Because ATM is designed to be easily implemented by hardware (rather than software), faster processing speeds are possible. The specified bit rates are either 155.520Mbps or 622.080Mbps.

Ethernet, or FDDI workstations, use TCP/IP protocol to communicate over ATM switches. ATM switches are used to control information flow from video/multimedia digital servers through telecommunications and digital video/data gateways to cable TV clients. The signal flows along fiber optic cable to fiber hubs, through fiber nodes, then on Ethernet over traditional coaxial cables to individual subscribers.

Is it a big deal to take a standard H.320 stream, package it, and transport it over a frame relay service? No. And the economics for video over frame (or any packet/cell technology) are compelling in the same way that they are for voice communications.

The potential technical problems with video over frame are jitter, the variation in delay between frames, and discarded packets. Video requires a constant bit stream to maintain an image, so extreme variations in delay can be problematic. Jitter can occur when a video frame arrives in a network switch buffer and waits while other packets are processed. Frame relay packets are variable in length, so the delay is not predictable. In addition to jitter, too many dropped frames can cloud the images and cause disruptions in the accompanying voice communication.

In practice, these potential issues don't pose much of a threat to video traffic. The higher the speed of the network, the less the delay is likely to be and most carriers run very high-speed backbones. Many of these backbones are cell-based, which reduces the likelihood of too much jitter because of the predictability of fixed-length ATM cells.

The Audiovisual Multimedia Services Technical Committee of the ATM Forum released the Video on Demand Specification 1.1, in March 1997. This document represents the first phase of a study of multimedia issues relating to ATM. Specification 1.1 only addresses issues relating to the transport of constant packet rate MPEG-2 Single Program Transport Streams

(ISO/IEC 13818-1) over ATM networks. While the scope of the document is very limited, many believe it will serve as a guide for carriage of a wide range of video over ATM networks.

Like ATM, Switched Multimegabit Data Service (SMDS) is another cell-based service provided by the Regional Bell Operating Companies (RBOCs).

Quality of Service

Quality of Service (QoS) includes consideration of availability, accuracy, priority, and delay. QoS evaluates the availability of bandwidth. If a customer wants fewer delays on video and voice they need the option for selecting a quality of service which has greater bit rate and fewer delays. ATM cell's 5byte header allows for level of service information.

Standards are being developed for service specifications such as constant bit rate, real-time variable bit rate, nonreal-time variable bit rate, available bit rate, and unspecified bit rate.

Switching

Switches and routers are the essential joints of the Internet's muscle that relay information. Switches forward information from one host to another without knowing anything about the paths between the hosts. Routers understand the Internet layer protocol used between hosts. WAN services are provided through three primary switching technologies.

- Circuit-switched networks are dedicated to link users during a particular time using TDM methods. The telephone industry is an example. While circuit switching for the telephony industry has been losing out to IP switching over Ethernet, there has been a rebirth of circuit switching technology through optical circuit switching which is able to function complementarily with IP packets.
- Packet-switched networks allow end stations to share bandwidth. Ethernet and token rings are examples. Packet switching services do away with fixed virtual circuits. Data is transmitted one packet at a time through a network, with each packet able to take various paths through the network. Switching is generally thought to be a layer 2 function maintaining a virtual link between two network end points. Because there is no predetermined virtual circuit, packet-switching can increase effective bandwidth. The emergence of IP switching is occurring where network nodes fake the establishment and maintenance of IP connections between end points. They do so by tracking packet flows through a node, taking note of common destination addresses and building tables to route subsequent packets.
- Cell-switched networks move fixed-sized data called cells using Statistical Time Division Multiplexing (STDM) and Time Division Multiplexing (TDM)–based access. ATM and SMDS are examples of cell-switched technology.

Data can be transmitted across cellular networks using either circuit-switched or packet-switched connections. Each type of connection has unique characteristics and appropriate uses.

A telephone voice connection uses a circuit-switched connection. Circuit-switched connections provide a temporary dedicated line, or circuit, between two end points. A circuit is dedicated from the moment the caller dials a phone number and makes a connection until he or she hangs up. However, circuit-switched connections are appropriate for voice calls that tend to be long, two-way, and highly interactive. This makes circuit-switched connections appropriate for data transactions. Data is received in the order sent and is not likely to be lost, separated, or incomplete. For example, a file transfer that requires the use of a network connection for a long period of time would be best served by a circuit-switched connection. Circuit-switched can take time to establish since a direct connection must be made. For example, a modem connection might take up to 40 seconds to establish, depending on modem protocols.

In contrast to circuit-switched connections, Internet Protocol (IP) packet-switched connections do not use a dedicated circuit between two end points. Rather, packet-switched connections allow multiple simultaneous users access to multiple locations across a network. Packages of data (packets) are sent from source to destination using the quickest route available. While circuit-switched connections operate the same as a phone call, packet-switched connections are much like sending a series of letters through the mail. Because each packet contains a source and destination address, packets that make up a single transaction can be sent out of order and along different routes. Although packets can be of any size, typical packet sizes range from 100 bytes to 1500 bytes.

Transmitting information in packets can result in vastly increased efficiency and reduced costs to users. All packet-switched services require a connection from the customer site to the access point of the packet-switched network or a connection via the Internet.

Whether to choose circuit switching or packet switching depends upon the type of traffic on the networks and the costs involved. Traffic such as video is sensitive to delays and needs guaranteed bandwidth of circuited-switched service. Unfortunately this is expensive.

The battle between IP and ATM has been basically the battle between the data communication industry and the telephony industry. IP comes from the bottom; it is a protocol that solves a relatively local problem, multiplatform minicomputer networking, and has gotten extended for larger applications.

ATM comes from the top; it is a protocol of slow evolution, far-sighted but ponderous, slow, and inflexible. ATM developed so slowly that it gave IP/Ethernet an opportunity to come up with Ethernet switching and fast 100Mbps Ethernet transmission.

By 1999, IP and Ethernet were too firmly entrenched for the corporate marketplace to bypass them in favor of ATM. Some of the problems presented by IP/Ethernet disappear as they move to local switching paradigms. ATM multiplexing and switching will ultimately force frame relay aside for WAN networking. ATM and IP/Ethernet will continue to coexist and struggle in their continuing protocol war for some time to come.

SONET Networks

The Synchronous Optical Network, SONET, is the U.S. standard for synchronous data transmission on optical media. It consists of a WAN interface to the public network carriers with an internationally supported physical layer transport scheme. The international equivalent of SONET is synchronous digital hierarchy (SDH). Together, they ensure standards so that digital networks can interconnect internationally.

SONET currently provides standards up to the maximum line rate of 9.953Gbps. Actual line rates approaching 20Gbps are possible. ATM runs as a layer on top of SONET as well as on top of other technologies.

Traditional SONET solutions require numerous network element types to handle traditional voice-centric traffic. They do not easily support data traffic, do not easily scale, and typically support only a single topology. These equipment limitations force transport networks to pay a premium for high-capacity systems, often purchasing bandwidth well in advance of anticipated demand in order to avoid costly, cumbersome equipment upgrades.

Clearly, the access demand continues to outstrip the ability of service providers using traditional SONET technology to keep up with this explosive growth. Transparent optical networking offers service providers a way to migrate to a new transport foundation and will enable the carriage of high-speed access services to the large bandwidth pipes of the core networks.

Ethernet Networks

The 1000Base-T is the fiber-based version of Gigabit Ethernet that will have the most dramatic impact on the market. It has long been acknowledged that Ethernet dominates the desktop. The availability of inexpensive Gigabit Ethernet connections running over Category 5 copper will cement Ethernet's dominance of the LAN. However, Gigabit Ethernet over long-haul fiber will take Ethernet into WANs and metropolitan area networks (MANs).

Ethernet will give ATM, SONET, and other traditional MAN technologies a run for their money over the next several years, particularly for data-oriented applications.

Gigabit Ethernet's low cost and ease of operation relative to other MAN technologies make it appealing to enterprises that want to extend their LANs across a metropolitan or wide area.

The Gigabit Ethernet MANs deployed to date have been private networks. Certainly private Gigabit Ethernet MANs offer their users benefits, but the market for Ethernet-based MANs will really take off when public services are readily available.

Ethernet's ability to continue to scale in terms of bandwidth is crucial to its long-term viability in multiple markets, particularly compared with ATM. Currently, carriers and service providers are the main targets for this technology. WAN equipment makers would like the speed to match OC-192 SONET (9.58Gbps), thus allowing them to use existing technology and presumably reduce the complexity of connecting Ethernet LANs to MANs and WANs.

Although some industry players would like Ethernet to evolve to be more SONET-like, others want Ethernet to remain the relatively simple technology it has always been. Indeed, Ethernet's simplicity has been its key strength.

Multiplexors

Network nodes play a fundamental role in networking maximizing the use of expensive lines connecting them together. A node has a high-speed line and multiple slow lines. The node multiplexes information from the slower speed line on to high speed lines. Analog signal, such as television, voice, or data signals can be frequency division multiplexed (FDM) by assigning each incoming channel to a specific frequency. Digital signals can be time division multiplexed (TDM) by positioning each incoming channel to a fixed time slot of the high-speed outgoing channel. Neither FDM nor TDM makes any effort to gain bandwidth efficiency.

Multiplexors are used at network access points aggregating traffic and moving data over lines. Each line terminates in a port. Any port tends to support one networking protocol only.

In general, networking nodes move packets from input port to output port by routing or switching. Switching requires establishing a prior path between nodes and sending a variable-length packet, a fixed-length cell, or a time slot in a multiplexed data stream. Routing does not establish a prior path but treats packets as individuals providing destination addresses rather than node addresses.

Routers have several advantages. They do not need complicated time-consuming connection set-up and tear-down protocols. They are not committed to a single path. Routers can be rerouted around a congested area.

■● Signals

Digital signals are categorized as DS digital signals (DS0,1,2,3,4) while optical signals are categorized as OC optical channels (OC1,3,9,12,18,24,36,48,96,192,768), where the number represents a multiple of 672 channels at 64kbps each. Table 8-1 provides a specific breakdown.

The optical networks provide all the basic network requirements in the optical layer, such as capacity, scalability, reliability, survivability, and manageability. Today, the wavelength is the fundamental object of the optical network. Basic network requirements can be met through a combination of the optical transport layer that provides scalability and capacity beyond 10Gbps, and the SONET/SDH transport layer. The long-term vision of an "all-optical network" is of a transparent optical network where signals are never converted to the electrical domain between network ingress and egress. The more practical implementation for the near term will be of an opaque optical network that works to minimize optical/electrical/optical conversions.

The natural evolution of optical transport is from a DWDM-based point-to-point transport technology to a more dynamic networking technology. Optical networking will use any one of a number of optical multiplexing schemes to multiplex multiple channels of information onto a fiber and to the optical transport layer provided by SONET/SDH.

In all, 200,000 km a year of new optical fiber is going underground or undersea. Dense wavelength division multiplexing (DWDM) equipment is being installed at a rate of $8 billion per year. The next trans-Atlantic cable is rated at 4.8Tbps.

Fiber networking companies, such as Global Crossing, use multiple OC-48 lines (2.5Gbps) with OC-192 lines (10Gbps) in high traffic areas and through DWDM can achieve speeds of 1.28Tbps on a single fiber. This is accomplished by using state-of-the-art hyper-DWDM,

Table 8-1   SONET/SDH Bit Rates

Bit rate	SONET	SDH
51.84Mbps	OC-1	--
155.52Mbps	OC-3	STM-1
622.080Mbps	OC-12	STM-4
2.488Gbps	OC-48	STM-16
9.9532Gbps	OC-192	STM-64

which can split a single fiber into 128 separate wavelengths of light, to give one fiber a total capacity of 1.28Tbps.

Satellites

The hundreds of satellites in operation support television broadcasts and radio and Internet communications from three types:

- Geo-stationary satellites 22,000 miles up directly over the equator
- Low earth orbit (LEO) in small circular orbits over the geographical poles
- Elliptical orbit satellites moving in orbits around the earth

These can provide bidirectional or unidirectional data transmission.

Expanding the Internet

Across the United States efforts are underway to upgrade the network infrastructure. Universities are connecting to the next generation of the Internet, called Internet-2. About 20 corporate partners are currently involved with 154 universities in establishing Gigabits per second points of presence nationwide. The payoff will come when this wide bandwidth can produce powerful Web applications.

In late February 1999, Internet-2 went live, with speeds up to 2.4Gbps. Colleges and universities must now upgrade campus networks to fiber-optic cabling to take advantage of the Gigabit speeds promised by the high-speed network.

Packet-switching equipment doubles in performance every 10 months or so, but circuit switches takes four times as long. With Internet traffic doubling every six months, only packet switches can keep up. As a result, ever-expanding data networks are exerting a gravitational pull on voice communications. And the long-awaited convergence of telecommunications and computing is becoming a reality. With IP data packets increasingly dominating telephone networks, a circuit-switched infrastructure optimized for voice just doesn't make sense. The only real difference of opinion revolves around how fast the IP wave is coming and how it will clear some significant obstacles. We could start seeing significant data and voice convergence by 2005. Can video be far behind?

How is it that IP, which was designed for something entirely different, is succeeding at convergence? IP may not be the best technology, but it's everywhere. It has become the corporate intercommunication standard. There are countless companies working on new features for IP equipment and related software. IP has reached critical mass.

◑ New Bandwidth Economics

There is a new economics dominating the decisions for bandwidth. A new generation of routing switches is handling massive amounts of IP packets at dramatically better performance and cost. In 1999, prices for data network equipment dropped by a factor of 10, while performance rose by about the same amount.

Circuit-switched networks divide bandwidth into rigid 64Kbps pipes and assume only a certain percentage of subscribers will be accessing the network at once. Packet voice allows many conversations to take place over the same pipe simultaneously. And what takes 64Kbps on a traditional voice network can be compressed into 8Kbps to 12Kbps without any loss of quality.

When we packet audio, we are using computing power. Following Moore's Law, we get twice as much for the same price every 18 months. Packet nets are also more flexible than circuit-switched networks. A smart PBX on an IP network can watch traffic levels and implement compression mechanisms in real time when the network gets overloaded. The line quality drops a bit, but everyone still gets a connection. Compressing voice in real time wasn't feasible even five years ago, but it is now.

In general, carriers can offer multiple services more efficiently by moving them onto a single, improved infrastructure. As bandwidth becomes a low-margin commodity, service bundles and value-added features will become imperative for corporate survival.

That's a significant change in thinking from just a few years ago when IP telephony was first introduced. The voice quality of the initial products was poor. Many traditional carriers held the belief that IP telephony could not deliver business-quality voice. There have been big improvements since then, and on international calls some of the products can give about the same Quality of Service, QoS, as circuit-switched networks.

IP/Ethernet packet switching uses routers and achieves a 10-fold increase in data flow on average over ATM cell-switching using switches to establish a single continuous circuit. Packets on average move faster based on statistical routing to avoid congestion and errors. However, as such they are subject to line overloads and congestion problems from time to time.

Fiber optics are not subject to electromagnetic interference and can perform with only 1 error in 10 trillion bits of data transmitted in comparison to copper wire with a 1 in 10 million bit error rate. In addition, fiber optics make transmission speed so fast that lines are no longer limiting in transmission. The limits are the nodes between lines such as switches and routers.

Cable TV companies can carry IP on their plants without much modification. Unlike other telephony-over-cable solutions, IP is widespread, cheap, and works well. It's actually a very efficient transport protocol. The bandwidth for running IP telephony on their own two-way fiber-optic networks allows cable TV companies to keep up with demands. The second beauty of the IP standard is that it is addressable. Each device on the network has a unique IP address.

Today most of the equipment required for IP telephony is already in place. The backbone routers are commercially available. The cable modems are going to be based on a proprietary standard for adding the additional functionality of converting voice to IP packets. So the only innovation is integration of modems and chips.

Will IP telephony-over-cable succeed? Technically, it certainly can. However, there are still a few problems, such as the cable TV companies' lack of experience in running residential telephone networks and consumer unwillingness to give up old-style telephone service.

The IP-based telephony systems works as follows

- Caller dials a toll-free number and an ID number that connects a gateway computer, a bridge between regular phone network and the Internet. The call then travels the phone network to the gateway.
- The gateway digitizes the caller's voice, turning it into the ones and zeros of computer language.
- The gateway breaks the digitized voice into packets of 10 ms to 30 ms of conversation and codes each packet with the second party's phone number.
- The gateway then compresses the packets and thrusts the compressed packets onto the Internet.
- The packets travel the Internet passing through routers, computers that read the addresses on each packet, and assign a transmission line to them.
- The packets finally arrive at the destination gateway that decompresses them and converts the digital signal back to analog.

The gateway transfers the call to the local phone network, which delivers it to the second party.

Although there are still some standards issues being wrestled with, the only real question that remains to be answered about IP telephony-over-cable is not if it will arrive, but when.

Real-time traffic, such as voice and video, should be given priority over more routine transmissions such as file transfers and e-mail. Several methods are possible, including setting priority by IP address, setting priority by protocol, or using a reservation mechanism such as the Resource Reservation Protocol. However, not all routers are configurable to support such schemes.

In the corporate environment, convergence is at least as much about new applications as it is about cheaper voice calls. Convergence enables developers to build integrated voice/data applications that were impossible to implement economically over discrete voice and data networks.

Once workstations are enabled with H.323, an emerging standard for multimedia communication across packet-based networks, people can just click on a button to talk and enable a data or video session.

Competing access options include traditional modems, ISDN, digital subscriber line (DSL), cable modems, and wireless technology. The front-runner for future buildout is xDSL.

Last-mile services to customers must be integrated, providing voice, video, and data, because the backbone is integrated. However, even if DSL meets the most optimistic expectations, it will hook up a mere one million or so subscribers over the next couple of years. There will still be a vast number of people coming in over analog modems, and those calls will have to be circuit-switched. The service provider that best uses the legacy edge network, which has an aggregate $20 to 30 billion in assets, including 130 million copper pairs, will gain a huge advantage.

A convergence impediment is the per-port cost of IP switches. Transmission is cheaper, but the end point equipment is still a lot more expensive. IP telephony equipment costs about $1,000 per line, compared with $150 for analog lines.

An important issue is scalability. Circuit switches typically have about 10,000 ports, but the highest density found in IP switches is 96 ports. While IP ports handle multiple calls, the industry will need to develop bigger IP switches to replace traditional equipment.

▶ Integrating Separate Networks within the Optical Domain

Today more than $20 billion a year is expended on a worldwide basis in constructing and upgrading transmission network infrastructure. Current expenditures are spread across fiber deployment, fiber multiplication products, and SONET/SDH transmission equipment.

Looking at some U.S. statistics, interexchange carriers have more than 125,000 fiber route miles laid while local telephone companies have over 225,000 fiber route miles in the ground. Less than a third of this fiber is actually lit.

In the last few years, dense wavelength division multiplexing (DWDM) has exponentially increased fiber capacity by delivering the technology to transform each fiber strand into many parallel optical lightpaths.

The real issue lies in transforming that capacity into usable bandwidth that can be exploited for service delivery. It is this transformation where technical limitations in conventional network architectures are constraining network growth.

Today, the transmission network is comprised of three elements:

- Fiber that provides the raw capacity
- DWDM multiplexers that increase raw capacity on a specific fiber route by dividing a fiber strand into multiple lightpaths
- SONET transmission equipment that provides the network intelligence and converts the capacity into usable/salable bandwidth

Dense Wavelength Division Multiplexing

Telecom carriers are responding to the ever increasing demand for network capacity by upgrading their long-distance, single-channel fiber links with optical, multi-channel dense wavelength division multiplexing (DWDM) technology. With wavelength division multiplexing, a light stream is split into multiple frequencies, called *colors*, just like a prism.

The use of DWDM requires optical filters for adding and dropping single wavelength channels at certain network nodes. In 1999, DWDM achieved 96-channels at 240Gbps. A single 96-channel strand can carry over 3 million phone calls.

The advantages of DWDM include

- Higher capacity with fewer strands of fiber
- Lower network upgrade costs
- Lower maintenance costs

DWDM systems are vitally important for the Internet, virtual private networks, and public data networks. It provides the capacity to carry traffic associated with e-commerce including voice, data, and video.

This technology is currently too expensive for the short-distance and private market, but it is likely that the continuing rapid increase in traffic will soon necessitate DWDM in the metropolitan area networks (MANs) of alternative city carriers and within large private campus backbones. Suitable architectural concepts and low-cost technologies are necessary for the deployment of DWDM in such networks.

An optical (analog) multiplexing technique is used to increase the carrying capacity of a fiber network beyond what can currently be accomplished by time division multiplexing (TDM) techniques. Different wavelengths of light are used to transmit multiple streams of information along a single fiber with minimal interference. Typical DWDM systems available today for long-distance transmission offer 16 to 40 wavelengths at 2.5Gbps (OC-48 SONET or STM-16 SDH) or 10Gbps (OC-192 SONET or STM-64 SDH) per wavelength. DWDM has been mainly deployed as a point-to-point, static overlay to the optical TDM network to create *virtual fiber.* As such, DWDM is the precursor to optical networking. DWDM has drastically reduced the cost of transport by reducing the number of electrical regenerators required and sharing a single optical amplifier over multiple signals through the use of Erbium-Doped Fiber Amplifiers.

A key enabling technology of DWDM, Erbium-Doped Fiber Amplifiers (EDFA), allows the simultaneous amplification of multiple signals in the 1500 nanometer region. EDFAs drastically increase the spacings required between regenerators, which are costly network elements because they (1) require optical/electrical/optical conversion of a signal and (2) operate on a single digital signal, that is, a single SONET or SDH optical signal. DWDM systems using EDFAs can increase regenerator spacing of transmissions to 500 km to 800 km at 2.5Gbps.

◗ Lightpath Switching

Analogous to virtual circuits in the ATM world, a lightpath is a virtual circuit in the optical domain that could consist of multiple spans each using a different physical wavelength for transmission of information across an optical network.

The vision of the *all optical network* is a network in which a signal is transported from source to destination entirely in the optical domain. Signals are amplified, shaped, demultiplexed, remultiplexed, and switched in the optical domain with no regard to the digital content of the signal, that is, bit rate, modulation scheme, or protocol. Transparent optical networks are limited in two ways: (1) by analog signal limitations (that is, gain tilt, ASE noise, chromatic dispersion, and crosstalk) that accumulate over distance; and (2) by the difficulty of monitoring performance and isolating faults as a signal traverses a network.

Currently, traffic from voice and data networks is multiplexed by a SONET/SDH ADM (add/drop multiplexer) or SONET/SDH Terminal and converted from an electrical signal to an optical signal for transport over fiber. Since the fiber itself is just a physical medium and has no intelligence, the process to move the traffic is laborious.

At each network transit point the traffic is fed back into a SONET Network Element converted to an electrical signal and examined to see which traffic should be terminated at this juncture. Terminated traffic is extracted, and new traffic is added. The entire stream is converted back to an optical signal for transport to the next network element.

The burden of converting all traffic from electrical to optical at each network juncture adds enormously to the cost and complexity of the network. Scaling a SONET network is also a challenge since SONET equipment is speed sensitive.

In the optical network, the lightpath becomes the transport medium versus the physical fiber strand. Services are mapped directly onto lightpaths without any intervening transmission equipment. With the removal of a layer of transmission equipment, the network is greatly simplified and service providers can quickly add new services or increase bandwidth without impacting existing traffic.

Video Networks

Today's video networks are one-way broadcast video sent via coaxial cable or wireless media. About 60 percent of U.S. homes receive video service through cable. The CATV (cable television or community antenna television) has become popular in providing entertainment services. The *last mile* accounts for 50 percent of the total investment for network upgrades.

Table 8-2 provides a breakdown of the evolution of networks going from the top of the table with analog networks and transitions over time down the table to the bottom, where we reach fiber-based broadband (data/voice/video) networks competing with IP/ETHERNET over ATM/SONET.

Internet Transfer Protocols

Is that it? Is the Internet really just fiber, wires, routers, and a lot of holes dug in the ground? Is it just hardware? Of course not. The only thing changing as fast as the infrastructure of the Internet is the intelligence of the underlying controlling software. Now it is time for us to present the basic elements of the protocols and standards that rule the flow of data around the world.

One of the most important technical issues necessary for the Internet is TCP/IP, Transmission Control Protocol/Internet Protocol. TCP/IP actually refers to a collection of protocols that are used for data transfer and are in most UNIX networks. TCP/IP was developed in 1973 but was published as a standard in 1983 as the standard protocol for the ARPAnet wide area network, which was the forerunner of the Internet. It was used for academic networks.

Table 8-2 **Evolutionary Path of Networks**

Analog Technology		
Data Services	*Voice Services*	*Video Services*
N/A	Analog technology POTs—3kHz (plain old telephones) Modems enable analog lines to carry data from digital computers	Analog coax-based-video network Cable TV—700MHz Broadcast local and satellite TV and Internet data

Digital Technology		
Data Services	*Voice Services*	*Video Services*
Frame-relay-based network: T-3, up to 45Mbps, frame relay, fiber optics or digital microwave	x-DSL up to 6Mbps Digital subscriber line Residential and small business access	Fiber and coax-based switched network (HFC) Cable modem 1.5Mbps Residential and small business access
Fast Ethernet (100Mbps)	ATM/SONET network ATM—Up to 13.22Gbps Asynchronous Transfer Mode—Voice, data, and video	
Gigabit Ethernet (1Gbps)	SONET—Up to 13.22Gbps—Synchronous Optical Network SONET with dense wave division multiplexing (DWDM)—Up to 240Gbps	
IP/ETHERNET over ATM/SONET	ATM/SONET network	Fiber and coax-based switched video network
Fiber-based Broadband (data/voice/video) network versus IP/ETHERNET over ATM/SONET		

The Department of Defense first developed the four-layer TCP/IP suite protocol model in 1970 for the ARPA project. Almost every computer today provides support for at least part of this suite. The International Standards Organization (ISO) developed a layered reference model called *Open Systems Interconnection* (OSI) in the 1980s. The four-layered TCP/IP and the seven-layered OSI are the two most referenced network protocol models.

To exchange information over a network, computers must use a protocol or common language. Transmission Control Protocol/Internet Protocol (TCP/IP) is the dominant one. IP is the native language of the Internet. TCP is the special dialog along with User Datagram Protocol (UDP).

Other network protocols include Serial Line Internet Protocol (SLIP), Point-to-Point (PPP), and Parallel Line Internet Protocol (PLIP). These protocols were designed to work efficiently over serial/parallel lines, in part by compression/decompression data to make the most of limited bandwidth.

TCP/IP is an open standard (see Table 8-3) that will run a wide range of hardware, including Ethernet, Token Ring, and X.25 on varying computer platforms such as UNIX, Windows, Macintosh, and mainframe. It contains a standard method of addressing unique units on a vast network and can route data via a particular route to reduce traffic. The TCP/IP protocol has four layers as shown in the following table in comparison to the ISO model.

The application layer (SMTP, FTP, Telnet, and SNMP), the transport layer (TCP, UDP), the internet layer (ICMP, IP, ARP), and the network interface (media access and transmission) are in rough correspondence to the aligned ISO layers in the table. In both models each layer provides a function or group of functions. While the functions in the models are similar, they are incompatible. The TCP/IP protocol suite has proven to be the best approach for inter-networking mixed technologies.

The Internet layer, IP, shields the higher levels from network architecture and establishes, maintains, and terminates connections between systems.

Table 8-3 TCP/IP Comparison to ISO Model

TCP/IP Model			ISO/OSI Model
Remote file service	Server message	Network file system	7. Application
SMTP	FTP	TELNET, SNMP	6. Presentation
			5. Session
Transmission Control Protocol (TCP)		User Datagram Protocol (UDP)	4. Transport
Internet Control Messaging Protocol	Internet Protocol	Address Resolution Protocol	3. Network
Media Access			2. Data link
(Unicast, Multicast, Broadcast)			1. Physical layer
Transmission Media			
(Ethernet, FDDI...)			

Ipv4 provides a single 32-bit address space. It is divided into classes, class "D" of which is for multicasting. The next generation of IP protocol is a 128-bit address space which fully supports IP multicasting called Ipv6. Ipv6 reserves a range of addresses for multicast that is larger than Class D service.

As a data packet passes through the application layers, each layer adds header and footer information. Once the complete packet is transmitted to the next node, it is passed up the layers with the information headers stripped off one at a time. Finally the packet arrives at the application layer of the destination.

The packets that are passed over the network are called *datagrams.* Each datagram contains a header of relevant information necessary to deliver the datagram correctly. It includes the source and the destination port numbers between computers. There is also a sequence number that allows the destination computer to reconstruct the datagrams in the correct sequence.

Transmission Control Protocol HTTP (Hypertext Transfer Protocol) uses TCP as the protocol for reliable document transfer. If packets are delayed or damaged, TCP will effectively stop traffic until either the original packets or backup packets arrive. Hence it's unsuitable for video and audio.

TCP imposes its own flow control and windowing schemes on the data stream, effectively destroying temporal relations between video frames and audio packets. Reliable message delivery is unnecessary for video and audio—losses are tolerable and TCP retransmission causes further jitter and skew.

UDP (User Datagram Protocol) is the alternative to TCP. RealPlayer, StreamWorks, and VDOLive use this approach. (RealPlayer gives you a choice of UDP or TCP, but the former is preferred.) UDP forsakes TCP's error correction and allows packets to drop out if they are late or damaged. When this happens, you will hear or see a dropout, but the stream will continue. Despite the prospect of dropouts, this approach is arguably better for continuous media delivery. If broadcasting live events, everyone will get the same information simultaneously. One disadvantage to the UDP approach is that many network firewalls block UDP information. While Progressive Networks Xing and VDOnet offer work-arounds for client sites (revert to TCP), some users simply may not be able to access UDP files.

Within a network with TCP/IP protocols, when data is transferred, it uses one port to transfer data to another port. The port number is a 16-bit number in the range of 1 to 32767; some port numbers are used for particular applications. For example, HTTP Web server application is almost always port 80; Telnet server application is port 23.

A socket identifies a particular networking session by IP address and port address. For any network session there are always two sockets defined, as source and destination.

◐ Unicast and Multicast

When data is broadcast, a single copy of the data is sent to all clients on the network. When the same data needs to be sent to only a portion of the clients on the network, both of these methods waste network bandwidth. Unicast wastes bandwidth by sending multiple copies of the data. Broadcast wastes bandwidth by sending the data to the whole network whether or not the data is wanted. Broadcasting can also needlessly slow the performance of client machines. Each client must process the broadcast data whether or not the broadcast is of interest.

Multicasting takes the strengths of both of these approaches and avoids their weaknesses. Multicasting sends a single copy of the data to those clients who request it. Multiple copies of data are not sent across the network, nor is data sent to clients who do not want it. Multicasting allows the deployment of multimedia applications on the network while minimizing their demand for bandwidth. The following graph compares the network load per client when unicasting an 8Kbps PCM audio stream and multicasting the stream, and shows how a multicast saves bandwidth.

Multicasting can dramatically reduce the network bandwidth that multimedia applications require. Servers do not require hardware upgrades in order to take advantage of multicasting.

Today, the most widely known and used multicast enabled network is the Internet Multicast Backbone, the MBone. The MBone is a virtual network consisting of those portions of the Internet, sometimes called *multicast islands,* on which multicasting has been enabled. Multicasts that must travel across areas of the Internet that are not yet multicast-enabled are sent as unicasts until they reach the next multicast-enabled island. This process is referred to as *tunneling.*

The MBone has been in place since 1992 and has grown to more than 2,000 subnets. It has been used to multicast live audio and video showing Internet Engineering Task Force conferences, NASA astronauts working in space, and the Rolling Stones in concert. The MBone has successfully demonstrated the practicality and utility of using multicasting to send multimedia across the network.

The hardware for multicasting, chiefly multicast-enabled routers and their software, has reached a point where corporations can take advantage of multicasting on their own LANs and WANs. The technology is of benefit in any scenario where several (or hundreds or thousands of) individuals need the same information. Because such information can be multicast live, multicasting is the ideal method to communicate up-to-date information to a wide audience. Events such as a product introduction or an important press conference could be multicast. Multicasts can also support bidirectional communication, allowing, for example, individuals in widely dispersed locations to set up a live conference that includes audio, video, and a whiteboard.

Multicast groups provide several advantages. Groups are dynamic: clients can join or leave at any time. No elaborate scheme is required to create or disband a group. When a group has no members, it ceases to exist on the network. Groups also scale upward easily because as more clients join a multicast, it becomes more likely that the multicast is already being routed close to them.

When a client joins a group, it initiates two processes: First, an IGMP message is sent to the client's local router to inform the router that the client wants to receive data sent to the group. Second, the client sets its IP process and network card to receive the multicast on the group's address and port. Multicast addresses are Class D IP addresses ranging from 224.0.0.0 to 239.255.255.255. Class D IP addresses map automatically to IEEE-802 Ethernet multicast addresses, which simplifies the implementation of IP multicasting on Ethernet. When a client leaves a group and is the only one receiving the multicast on that particular subnetwork, the router stops sending data to the client's subnetwork, thereby freeing bandwidth on that portion of the network.

To enable multicasting, the network's routers and the protocols they run do most of the work. Multicasting can be enabled on such routers by simply updating their software and adding memory.

There are several multicast routing protocols in use today: Distance Vector Multicast Routing Protocol (DVMRP), Multicast Open Shortest Path First Protocol (MOSPF), and Protocol-Independent Multicast (PIM). The task of these protocols is to create efficient multicast delivery paths through the network. Multicast routing protocols use varying algorithms to achieve efficiency.

An efficient delivery path implies that multicast data travels only to those clients who want to receive it and takes the shortest path to those clients. If data travels elsewhere through the network, bandwidth goes to waste needlessly. You can visualize the network as a tree structure. The source of the multicast sends data through the branches of the tree. The routers are responsible for sending data down the correct branches to other routers and to the subnetworks where members of a group are waiting for data. Routers prune off branches where no one wants data and graft branches back to the tree when a client in a new subnetwork joins the group. Routers can also stop data from traveling to their own subnetworks when it is not wanted.

A new generation of multimedia applications that provide enhanced communication through the use of audio and video are ready to move onto the network. Multicasting provides an efficient way to enable these applications on the network. Because routers of recent vintage already support multicasting, enabling multicasting on a network is practical and cost-effective.

◖◗ Multicast

The TCP/IP protocols were designed for reliable transmission of data with minimal or no delay constraints. However, multimedia and multicast traffic possesses different characteristics and requires different protocols to provide the necessary services. For example, if a receiver has to wait for a TCP retransmission, there can be a noticeable and unacceptable gap in play of the real-time data, whether audio or video. In addition, the "slow start" TCP congestion-control mechanism can interfere with the audio and video "natural" play rate. Since there is no fixed path for datagrams to flow across the Internet, there is no mechanism for ensuring that the bandwidth needed for multimedia is available between the sender and receivers, so quality of service cannot be guaranteed. In addition, TCP doesn't provide timing information, a critical requirement for multimedia support.

The unicast-based protocols require one source and one destination. To send to multidestinations, different communication paths are needed between the source and each destination. Therefore, each copy of audio and video stream would need to be made separately. Clearly this is an inefficient process.

The broadcast-based protocols send only one copy out at a specified time to all computers on a LAN. While it is effective for a LAN it suffers serious problems over the Internet. In addition, while it saves a lot of bandwidth, it is at the expense of flexibility.

The multicast solution:
  ◗ Allows data to be sent to multiple Internet receivers avoiding per-receiver copies
  ◗ Is not constrained by network limits
  ◗ Differentiates transmission to only interested receivers

The host sends data only once and only the hosts interested in this data receive it. Multicast addresses are Class D addresses.

Multimedia applications can generally forego the complexity of TCP and use instead a simpler transport framework. Most playback algorithms can tolerate missing data much better than the lengthy delays of retransmissions, and they do not require guaranteed in-sequence delivery. A number of protocols have been developed to enhance the Internet architecture and improve support of applications like audio, video, and interactive multimedia conferencing.

The real-time oriented protocols, RTP, RTCP, RSVP, and RTSP, are designed to be used over both multicast or unicast network services. Many real-time applications can conserve network and server resources by using IP Multicast. The special requirements of IP Multicast are scalability, multicast routing, and accommodation of large numbers of receivers and heterogeneous receivers.

The main higher level protocols used in IP multicasting for reliable data transmission and multimedia include

- Real-Time Transport Protocol (RTP)
- Real-Time Control Protocol (RTCP)
- Real-Time Reservation Protocol (RTVP)
- Resource Streaming Protocol (RTSP)
- Reliable Multicast Protocol (RMP)
- Reliable Multicast Framework Protocol (RMF)
- Reliable Adaptive Multicast Framework Protocol (RAMP)
- Reliable Multicast Transport Protocol (RMTP)

Real Time Protocol is the Internet-standard protocol (RFC 1889, 1890) for the transport of real-time data, including audio and video. RTP consists of a data and a control part called RTCP. The data part of RTP is a thin protocol providing support for applications with real-time properties such as continuous media (that is, audio and video), including timing reconstruction, loss detection, and security and content identification. RTCP provides support for real-time conferencing of groups of any size within an intranet. This support includes source identification and support for gateways like audio and video bridges as well as multicast-to-unicast translators. It offers Quality-of-Service feedback from receivers to the multicast group as well as support for the synchronization of different media streams. Initially designed for video at T1 or higher bandwidths, it promises more efficient multimedia streaming than UDP.

RSVP is an Internet Engineering Task Force (IETF) proposed standard for requesting defined Quality-of-Service levels over IP networks such as the Internet. The protocol was designed to allow the assignment of priorities to streaming applications, such as audio and video, which generate continuous traffic that requires predictable delivery. RSVP works by permitting an application transmitting data over a routed network to request and receive a given level of bandwidth. Two classes of reservation are defined: a controlled load reservation provides service approximating "best effort" service under unloaded conditions; a guaranteed service reservation provides service that guarantees both bandwidth and delay.

SMRP, or Simple Multicast Routing Protocol, supports conferencing by multiplying the data to a select group of recipients like IP mulitcasting.

RTCP, or Real-Time Control Protocol, is a Quality-of-Service (QoS) protocol for providing end-to-end guarantee of quality.

Models of IP over ATM

To run IP on top of ATM networks, it is necessary to overlay TCP/IP protocol layers on top of ATM protocol layers. In the overlay model, the ATM networks have their own addressing scheme and routing protocols. The ATM address space is not logically coupled with the IP addressing space, and there will be no arithmetic mapping between the two. Each end system typically has an ATM address and an unrelated IP address as well. Since there is no nature mapping between the two addresses, the only way to figure out one from the other is through some addressing resolution protocol.

ATM is connection-oriented. Once the connection is set up, all data is sent along the connection path. IP is connectionless so that no connection is needed and each IP packet is forwarded by routers independently on a hop-by-hop basis. When we need to transport IP traffic over an ATM network, either a new connection is established between two parties or the data is forwarded through preconfigured connections. With the first approach, when the amount of data to be transferred is small, the expensive cost of setting up and tearing down a connection is not justified. On the other hand, with the second approach the preconfigured path(s) may not be an optimal path and may become overwhelmed by the amount of data being transferred.

Quality of Service is an important concept in ATM networks. It includes the parameters like the bandwidth and delay requirements of a connection. Such requirements are included in the signaling messages used to establish a connection. Current IP (IPv4) has no such concepts and each packet is forwarded on a best-effort basis by the routers. To take advantage of the QoS guarantees of the ATM networks, the IP protocol needs to be modified to include that information.

IPv6 and IP Integrated Services over ATM

The application-level Real Time Streaming Protocol, RTSP, aims to provide a robust protocol for streaming multimedia in one-to-many applications over unicast and multicast, and to support interoperability between clients and servers from different vendors. RTSP is intended to control multiple data delivery sessions, providing a means for choosing delivery channels such as UDP, TCP, IP Multicast, and delivery mechanisms based on RTP. RTSP is being designed to work on top of RTP to both control and deliver real-time content. Thus RTSP implementations will be able to take advantage of RTP improvements, such as the new standard for RTP header compression. RTSP can be used with RSVP to set up and manage reserved-bandwidth streaming sessions.

IP Multicast enables applications to significantly reduce the load on network resources and to scale to higher levels. For example, an application that broadcasts information to hundreds of recipients in a corporate network can employ reliable multicast services to reduce network load while maintaining reliable delivery.

Reliable services ensure the sender that all packets are received by all of the recipients. Reliable delivery is required by many real-time and non–real-time applications. In the real-time area, data conferencing, Web services, and data broadcast applications use reliable services. Non–real-time applications, such as information and software distribution, and file transfer also need reliable services.

For unicast IP services, error correction and detection in the TCP layer provides reliability. Such traditional techniques for error detection and correction in a large-scale multicast environment might result in an overload of acknowledgments to the sender, which would increase network congestion. Reliable multicast protocols provide error correction schemes, which are designed to overcome the limitations of unreliable multicast datagram delivery without burdening the network. There are many approaches to reducing the number of acknowledgments in a reliable multicast service. Application and network characteristics which may impact the design and operation of reliable multicast protocols include

- Real-time requirements
- Single or multiple senders
- Number of multicast groups and recipients per group
- Scalability as the number of senders and recipients grows
- Ordered or unordered packet delivery
- Delay tolerance
- Average bandwidth requirements
- Continuous or bursty bandwidth usage
- LAN or WAN operation
- Network infrastructure, such as satellite or multihop terrestrial links.

Some protocols are designed to handle asymmetrical data channels, others are not. Applications supporting both simultaneous reliable unicast and reliable multicast transmission can be useful.

RSVP requests defined Quality-of-Service levels over IP networks such as the Internet. The protocol was designed to allow the assignment of priorities to streaming applications, such as audio and video, which generate continuous traffic that requires predictable delivery.

RSVP works by permitting an application transmitting data over a routed network to request and receive a given level of bandwidth. Two classes of reservation are defined: a controlled load reservation provides service approximating *best effort* service under unloaded conditions; a guaranteed service reservation provides service that guarantees both bandwidth and delay.

Replacing Plug-ins New solutions are appearing that use Java to eliminate the need to download and install plug-ins or players. Such an approach will become standard once the Java Media Player AP is being developed by Sun, Silicon Graphics, and Intel. This approach will also ensure client platform independence. Vosaic appears to be one of the few products with a Java replayer that supports H.263.

Nearly all streaming products require users behind a firewall to have a UDP port opened for the video streams to pass through (1558 for StreamWorks, 7000 for VDOLive, 7070 for RealAudio). Rather than punch security holes in the firewall, Xing/StreamWorks has developed a proxy software package you can compile and use, while VDONet/VDOLIve and Progressive Networks/RealPlayer are approaching leading firewall developers to get support for having their streams incorporated into upcoming products. Currently a number of products change from UDP to HTTP or TCP when UDP can't get through firewall restrictions. This reduces the quality of the video. In all cases, it's still a security issue for network managers.

Developing Intelligent Networks

After all the network building above, why is the Internet still so congested?

One major reason is because at the interconnection points between backbone providers, fundamental scaling flaws in the design of the Internet can cause latency and data packet loss.

These scaling flaws include
- Routing inefficiencies
- Lack of adequate network technology upgrades
- Distributed management of public network access points (NAPs)
- Economic settlement conflicts between network providers (peering is free)

The result is unavoidable congestion and poor Internet performance. Internet performance will not improve as long as downloads are constrained at the public exchanges and private peering points of today's Internet.

The public exchange points are the major intersections of the Internet. At these exchange points (MAE-East, MAE-West, PacBell NAP, and so on), the Internet backbones (UUNET, Sprint, and so forth) along with hundreds of local and regional Internet access providers, meet to pass Internet transmissions from one network to another. At these public exchanges enormous amounts of data are sent to and from every connected network. All of this data is transferred from network to network over the same common infrastructure.

With so many users connected to so many different backbones, a vast majority of the data transmissions from Web sites to end users passes from one backbone to another. This arrangement is known as public or private peering. It is the arrangement of traffic exchange between Internet service providers (ISPs). The public NAPs and private peering points are not centrally managed, and no single entity has the economic incentive to facilitate problem resolution, to optimize peering, or to bring about centralized routing administration.

Is anyone doing anything about this that will impact video delivery? Look at *http://www.internap.com/how.htm*. InterNAP bypasses much of the Internet's congestion by directly linking to over 96 percent of the world's Internet connectivity. The direct connections go into major global Internet backbones, including OC3 and DS3 connections. By routing data back through the same carrier from which the request for data was made (called *symmetrical routing*), InterNAP routes data traffic around the public and private exchange points on the Internet.

All of the leading providers of Internet broadcast infrastructure have deployed RealSystem G2's scalable distributed multitiered architecture, pioneered by RealNetworks, to enable the comprehensive distribution of streaming audio, video, and SMIL-based content.

Through the use of RealServer-G2 and RealProxy deployed in operation centers worldwide, RealNetworks and its infrastructure partners have created an integrated network that intelligently bypasses Internet congestion points, distributing content to the edge of the Internet. The result is a higher capacity, more cost effective, and better-quality consumer experience.

Broadcast infrastructure partners supporting Real.com network today include Akamai, Digital Island, Enron Communications, Globix, Inktomi, INTERVU, NextVenue, and Sandpiper Networks.

You can expect the area of intelligent networking to continue to grow exponentially. Just as fast as you can say IPO another innovative company pops up. The following sites are worth watching.

Sycamore (www.sycamorenet.com) focuses on developing the transport, switching, and management products that are required to create a flexible, intelligent optical network. Intelligent Optical Networking offers the promise of transforming the existing fiber-optic transmission core from an inflexible transport medium into an intelligent network foundation for high-speed delivery.

SightPath (www.sightpath.com) provides Intelligent Web content delivery based on the principle that content is best served locally, while being managed centrally. SightPath's content delivery adds intelligence to the network by routing requests to the best source, using bandwidth efficiently, and dynamically adapting to the changing conditions of the network. The result is more reliable delivery of content, easy scalability as needs grow, the ability to use very rich media types, and most importantly, the emergence of new Web services that blur the line between cable television and the Internet.

Burstware (www.burst.com) has pioneered the development of Faster-Than-RealTime video and audio delivery. Burstware Server manages the storage and delivery of video and audio content in Faster-Than-Real-Time.

▣ "Caching-in" on the Edge of the Internet

With bandwidth growing and networks getting "smarter," caching technology innovators are becoming important providers of video on the edge of the Internet.

Inktomi has been a preeminent provider of Internet infrastructure and has provided key software products for caching. One of Inktomi's biggest customers, America Online, receives more than 3.3 billion hits per day through its service.

A firm in the caching arena not using Inktomi's technology is Akamai. Instead, Akamai is using its own proprietary technology and aligning itself to be compatible with other cache technology providers (Cisco Systems, Novell Networks, Network Appliance and CacheFlow).

Akamai is placing several thousand servers on the edge of the Internet. The servers have lots of DRAM and disk storage but are otherwise pretty ordinary. The content gets there because Akamai goes around to content providers and makes a deal. Akamai service modifies the content provider Web so that the Akamai-supported content becomes referenced to Akamai Web servers. Because there are lots of Akamai servers, there is an Akamai server near the requester. Also, the path between requester and server is held to within a single hop, which increases the probability of avoiding network congestion.

Akamai's service needs to know (1) which content is being requested most frequently, (2) where the requests are coming from, (3) what the loads are on their many servers, and

Table 8-4 **Summary of Broadband Access Architecture**

	IDLC	HFC	FTTC/FTTH	LMDS/MMDS	DBS
Transmission Technology	Twisted-pair SONET, TMD	Coaxial fiber MPEG-2, ATM	Fiber-twisted MPEG-2, ATM, TDM, PON, WDM, x-DSL	Wireless-fiber MPEG-2, TDMA, CDMA, FDM, ATM	Satellite MPEG-2, FDM, TDMA, TAM
Problems	Legacy	Upgrade to two-way	Cost to deploy	Expensive	One-way

Note: IDLC—integrated digital loop carrier
     HFC—hybrid fiber coaxial
     FFTH—fiber to the home
     FTTC—fiber to the curb
     LMDS—local multi-point distribution systems
     MMDS—microwave multi-point distribution systems
     DBS—direct broadcast satellite

(4) how the Internet is performing. Having thousands of content servers out in the Internet provides better performance using cheap disks instead of expensive bandwidth. As a result, Akamai is intelligently distributing content on a large scale.

What all this fiber-optic development and new found "intelligence" means to video is that bandwidth over GANs, WANs, MANs, and LANs will soon be ubiquitous and cheap. However, efficient delivery will depend on intelligent software using clusters of local area video servers.

In Table 8-4 access modes and protocols for delivering broadband to homes and businesses are summarized.

Conclusion

Video has very demanding and unique network and software protocol requirements that are only now being adequately addressed. In this chapter, we differentiated three evolutionary steps currently underway in network development.

We provided a brief background on network architecture in order to establish the points of departure between data and voice requirements and the newer video delivery issues. The networks supporting Internet video are critical in delivering high performance and quality for the viewing experience and are an integral part of the Webcasting production process. This chapter described how data is transmitted and controlled over the Internet.

A discussion was included on software used by networks, including network protocol and services. Protocols that have been developed to support real-time multimedia delivery, and Quality-of-Service (QoS) specific for multicast and unicast network services are presented. These include the Real-Time Transport Protocol (RTP), the Real-Time Control Protocol (RTCP) that works in conjunction with RTP, the Resource ReSerVation Protocol (RSVP), and the Real-Time Streaming Protocol (RTSP). Finally, reliable IP multicast protocols are discussed.

We covered the development of intelligent networks and its utilization by existing vendors to deliver video today.

On the basis of this chapter, you should conclude that

- The Internet backbone combination of fiber and DWDM will perform in the 100Tbps range and provide plenty of network bandwidth in the next few years.
- The last mile connectivity will remain twisted-pair, wireless, and coax cable for the next few years, but broadband (1.5Mbps) access will grow to 40 million users in just a few years.
- Intelligent networking software for routing and tracking will lead to general changes in IP networking protocols.

CHAPTER 9

Server Requirements for Video Delivery

Now that you have seen many of the popular streaming software tools, it is appropriate to consider how you will implement your streaming video Web site. Some of the questions you will need to answer include, Do you want a client/server system or a serverless system? Will you use Windows NT or UNIX operating system? Do you need more bandwidth? Will you use IP multicasting? ▶

This chapter ties streaming video standards to protocol server delivery. This includes specifics about RealServer, Microsoft Windows Media Server, and broadband video.

◖◗ Background

A Web server is the server software behind the World Wide Web. It listens for requests from a client, such as a browser like Netscape or Microsoft's Internet Explorer, and then processes it and returns some data. This data usually takes the form of a formatted page with text and graphics. The browser then renders this data to the user.

Web servers communicate with browsers or other clients using the Hypertext Transfer Protocol (HTTP), which is a simple protocol that standardizes the way requests are sent and processed. These HTTP requests are actually plain language text commands.

Most of the documents requested are formatted using Hypertext Markup Language (HTML). HTML is a small subset of another markup language called Standard General Markup Language (SGML), which is in wide use by many organizations and the U.S. government. The Web page is made up of HTML defined text, images, sound, and hyperlinks in the client's Web browser.

◖◗ Serverless or Server-Based Video Streaming

The video server is a program that runs alongside the Web server. The video server for streaming media is similar to a regular Web server—it handles and oversees the distribution and access of streaming files. It runs in the background and monitors access to the streaming files. The actual number of simultaneous users depends on the license associated with the streaming video server software.

Three major approaches are emerging for streaming multimedia content to clients.

▶ The first is the serverless approach, which uses the standard Web server and the associated HTTP protocol to get the multimedia data to the client. Its advantages are that there is one less software piece to learn and manage, and there is no video server to pay for. You simply encode the video in the appropriate format using encoding software and place it on the Web server for URL link similarly to graphics. When a user requests a streaming file, it is sent via HTTP like any other Web data.

▶ The second is the client/server-based approach that uses a separate video server specialized for video streaming. The specialization takes many forms, including optimized routines for reading the huge multimedia files from disk, the flexibility to choose any of UDP/TCP/HTTP/multicast protocols to deliver data, and the option to exploit continuous contact between client and server to dynamically optimize content delivery to the client. The primary advantages of the server-based approach are that it makes more efficient use of the network bandwidth, offers better video quality to the end user, supports advanced features like admission control and multi-stream multimedia content, scales to support large number of end users, and protects content copyright.

▶ The third approach is the clientless solution. It works much like the serverless approach, but here there is no client program to download or install. Instead the video is pushed along to the user with a built-in player, usually written in Java. Once the player is loaded and the movie is buffered into memory, the Java player plays the file. With this method anyone with a Java-enabled browser can play the video.

The tradeoffs clearly indicate that for serious providers of streaming multimedia content, the server-based approach is the superior solution. RealPlayer, StreamWorks, and VDOnet's VDOLive require you to install their audio/video server software on your Web server computer. Other programs, such as Shockwave and VivoActive, are serverless.

▶ Projected Video Server Loading

More than 10 million movies are rented in the United States every day, and a third may be playing at any one time. If these movies were delivered electronically to the home on residential broadband at 1.5Mbps, they would consume 4.5Tbps of aggregate continuous bandwidth. Even if the optical fiber networks with DWDM are targeting that throughput, the most aggressive video server in the next five years would only support 1,000 simultaneous users over a single ATM at 1.5Gbps. Scaling such a server to 3 million simultaneous users would require 3,000 video servers. Long distance transmission is another problem altogether.

Actually on-demand broadband video is not an immediate candidate for Internet transport. But video catalogs and business marketing and conferences would fit the Internet model better, as we discussed in Chapter 2. They are short, accesses can be presumably covered over a larger percentage of the day, and there are many of them suggesting a separate server per company or event. While a single video catalog producer may not justify 1,000 distributed servers, the aggregation of catalog producers would.

The prognosis for broadband usage includes the following.

▶ Broadband Internet will produce traffic causing TCP to be rate-limited. This will give rise to local caching servers.

▶ Transmission costs will be high for video. This will require more local servers.

▶ Video on demand and video catalogs will have many simultaneous visitors. This will require thousands more servers.

▶ Streaming Video Servers

You can publish a simple Web site by renting space on an Internet provider's computer that includes a minimal set of streams for video service. However, a farsighted company will set up its own video server for Intranet as well as Web users. An Intranet video server can be user for corporate announcements and companywide video conferencing. However, how you install, configure, and connect the video server to the intranet and Internet will seriously affect the quality of service. In addition, your company's firewall and security represent important issues to be addressed.

What do you need to set up a video server? Here is a basic shopping list for items that are necessary for setting up a video Web server.

1. Dedicated computer

2. Appropriate operating system

3. Video server software

4. Connection to ISP (consideration of viewer audience requirements leading to the number of simultaneous streams and transfer rates)

5. Database tools

6. Management and monitoring tools

7. Firewall and security

Computer Hardware

Web video servers can run on almost any hardware platform including PCs, MacIntosh, SUN, Alpha, HP, and IBM RISC/600 computers. There are many Web video server software applications installed on Linux, UNIX, and Windows systems. The minimum hardware standards are listed below. Video servers are very disk intensive applications, so it is important to have an optimal drive and controller.

Table 9-1 summarizes the minimum hardware and software requirements for server components and administrators.

Table 9-1   **Recommended and Minimum Server Requirements**

	Recommended	*Minimum for Server*
Processor	Pentium III 500MHz or better	Pentium II 300MHz
Memory	128MB or better	64MB RAM
Bus Architecture	PCI, USB, and AGP	ISA, EISA, MCA
Network Interface Card (NIC)	Ethernet card, Transmission Control Protocol/Internet Protocol (TCP/IP)	Ethernet card, TCP/IP
Disk Controller	Wide SCSI	SCSI

A Web server could be connected to the Internet for public access or through a company's LAN. Any server on the Internet has a unique address and associated domain name normally written as *www.yourcompany.com.*

Platform Operating Systems

The main choices for a platform to run Web servers today include Windows NT/2000, UNIX, and LINUX.

- The Microsoft Windows NT platform is a major competitor for low and mid-range Internet servers. Windows NT has pushed into the Internet arena. The natural NT networking protocol is NetBEUI, which is fine for LANs but not as effective for WANs and the Internet. NT does, however, also support TCP/IP, and thanks to its graphical user interface, GUI, it is very easy to configure and set up. Unfortunately, NT does use up resources for its GUI. In addition, NT can be scaled up, but only on a few multi-processor computers and not with as smooth a path as UNIX. Windows 2000 server is expected to improve Microsoft's competitiveness with UNIX.

- UNIX is the dominate high-end operating system because of its stability and scalability. A number of flavors of UNIX exist including AIX, HP-IX, and the highly popular Solaris. The UNIX operating system has had 25 years as the the most well established and efficient operating system in wide distribution. The operating system uses an open architecture, is easy to configure, and supports TCP/IP. UNIX can run almost any platform, including multiprocessor, mainframe, mins, and workstations. The problem with UNIX is that it currently supports too many different vendor-driven standards.

- In 1991, Linus Torvalds was a computer science student at the University of Helsinki. In his classes, he had a UNIX look-alike operating system that runs on PCs, but wrote something better, called Linux (a combination of his name and UNIX). The result is a first-rate OS that is absolutely free. Today, Linux runs on an estimated 8 million computers, and thousands of programmers are working on improving the OS itself and on developing Linux applications. Microsoft has identified Linux as a major threat to Windows NT.

The following table (Table 9-2) estimates the growth in the major operating systems supporting servers.

The selection of an operating system is important because major cache server farmers are selecting to support a particular operating system (for example CacheFlow primarily uses Linux). As a result, reliability, scalability, and compatibility are affected. It is not clear if one operating system will prove to have a significant advantage in supporting intelligent network development.

Table 9-2   **Server Unit Sales by Operating Systems**

	1999	*2002 est.*
Windows NT/2000	1,900,000	2,300,000
UNIX	478,000	710,000
Linux	173,000	400,000
NetWare	452,000	400,000
Proprietary	160,000	140,000

Video Server Performance

Getting video to display at 30fps (frames per second) at 640 × 480 pixels (near TV resolution) across the Internet isn't a reality at the moment. The reality is that on a typical slow modem connection—such as 28.8Kbps—one can realistically expect about 10fps. On a wider band connection such as a T1 line, 15fps is a realistic, maintainable speed. If the number of people on-line at the same time is high, then more people are trying to share the network, resulting in slower network performance.

Even though the size of the video clip may be very reasonable, running with a bogged down network is going to cause the data that is being sent to be a lower quality. Lower quality is a variable term because it can refer to the quality of the picture itself, whether it's grainy or not, or it could refer to the number of frames being displayed and whether it's jerky or not. If the number of frames expected to be transferred is low, then the picture quality can be higher, and vice versa.

If too many people are hitting your Web site at the same time to see a given video clip, the server's performance could drop dramatically from a lower data transfer rate. Imagine 100 people trying to access the same file, on the same server, at the same time. Network traffic is a big enough problem to contend with, but now imagine the disk drive accessing the video clip at different points in the timeline of that clip, for each of the 100 people. If this is the case, the jerkiness or lower picture or audio quality will be apparent at once.

Video Server Software for RealVideo

RealNetwork's video server software is called RealServer. RealServer uses two main protocols to communicate with clients: RTSP (Real-Time Streaming Protocol) and PNA (Progressive Networks Audio). These protocols work with the two-way TCP connection to send commands from the client such as *start* and *pause,* and RealServer sends information about the clips' titles to the client. Authentication demands from RealServer and passwords supplied by the user are also sent along this connection.

RTSP is a client-server protocol designed specifically for serving multimedia presentations. It is an open standard, one that is very useful for large-scale broadcasting. RTSP delivers RealNetwork's bandwidth control process called *SureStream* with multiple bandwidth encoding.

PNA is the proprietary client-server protocol designed and used by RealNetworks in Real-System versions 5.0 and earlier. The ability to serve via PNA is supported in RealServer G2 for compatibility with older versions of RealPlayer.

In both RTSP and PNM, media clips are streamed over a one-way UDP channel that is separate from the TCP channel.

RealServer can support the following processors: Intel Pentium, Sun Microsystems SPARC, SGI Indy, Hewlett Packard PA-RISC, and the DEC Alpha. It supports the following operating systems: SCO OpenServer, SCO UnixWare Windows 95, Windows NT Server, Linux, FreeBSD, Solaris, Irix, HP/UX, and Digital Unix.

RealServer can deliver a full 60 streams with available RAM of 64MB for dial-up modem streams, 128MB for 100Kbps streams, and 256MB for 300Kbps streams.

Depending upon the level of compression, a single stream of RealAudio requires 10Kbps to 80Kbps of bandwidth and a single stream of RealVideo requires 10Kbps to 500Kbps. The speed and capacity of your network connection should be configured to accommodate the demand you anticipate.

RealServer G2 also supports international standards for streaming media. RealServer and RealPlayer interoperate with RTP-based media servers and clients.

RealServer keeps multiple clips synchronized and uses many advanced features to ensure that clips stream smoothly under adverse network conditions.

Although many Web servers are preconfigured to work with popular tools like RealAudio and RealVideo, if you or others are having problems viewing your streamed video clips, then you'll want to double-check your MIME settings. The MIME types that should be defined so that the HTTP streaming works are: audio/x-pn-realaudio (files with an .rm or .ram file extension), and audio/x-pn-realaudio-plugin (files with an .rpm file extension).

When two clips play side-by-side, for example, RealPlayer uses RTSP to communicate with RealServer about each clip's progress, indicating how much data it needs to keep the presentation synchronized. RealServer can then adjust the data flow, reducing low-priority data if necessary to ensure that crucial data gets through. Communication like this is not possible when a Web server sends clips to RealPlayer.

You don't need to know the specifics of RTSP to create presentations. You just need to ensure that RealServer G2 is available to stream your clips. If only a Web server is available, you can still create multimedia presentations, but you won't be able to use all RealSystem features.

RealServer (see Figure 9-1) streams both live and on-demand material, through unicasting or multicasting. It works with Web servers to stream to clients over networks and the Internet. The process includes the following.

> A visitor browses a Web page and clicks a link to a streaming media presentation served by RealServer.
> RealServer creates a small metafile and sends it to the visitor's Web browser.
> The browser downloads the metafile and sends it to the visitor's RealPlayer. The metafile, called a Ram file, contains the address (or addresses) of the media presentation mentioned in the link.
> RealPlayer reads the link in the metafile and requests the presentation directly from RealServer. RealServer streams the files in the presentation to the RealPlayer.
> Finally, RealPlayer plays the presentation.

As the user clicks a link that points to a RealServer presentation, RealPlayer opens a two-way connection with RealServer. This connection uses TCP to send information back and forth between RealPlayer and RealServer.

Once RealServer approves the request, it sends the requested clip along a one-way UDP channel. As it receives the streamed clip, RealPlayer plays it.

Port settings tell RealServer where it should listen for RTSP, PNA, and HTTP requests. These settings are implied in the URL that points to the content and are assumed by RealPlayer to have certain values. When RealPlayer requests a URL that begins with rtsp://, it sends the request to the RealServer's port 554. RealPlayer directs a URL that begins with pnm:// to port 7070. Requests beginning with http:// are first sent to port 80, and if no response is received, they are redirected to port 8080.

▶ A How-To Example

Our Web site, *www.video-software.com*, provides download links for *free* video players from all the major developers (RealNetworks, Microsoft, Apple, Emblaze, Bitcasting, LZX-MPEG), as well as video encoding tools, editing tools, and server software.

A CD-ROM with example code and streaming video demos is included at the back cover of this book. On the enclosed CD-ROM is an example on a directory called HowTo. It contains a sequential series of examples that takes you through the Internet video production process. Figure 9-1 shows the administration software from RealServer.

Video Server Software for QuickTime

Darwin Streaming Server is server technology that allows you to send streaming QuickTime data to clients across the Internet using the industry standard RTP and RTSP protocols.

The server implements four standard IETF protocols: RTSP (Real-Time Streaming Protocol, RFC 2326), RTP (Real-Time Transport Protocol, RFC 1889), RTCP (Real-Time Transport Control Protocol, RFC 1889), and SDP (Session Description Protocol, RFC 2327).

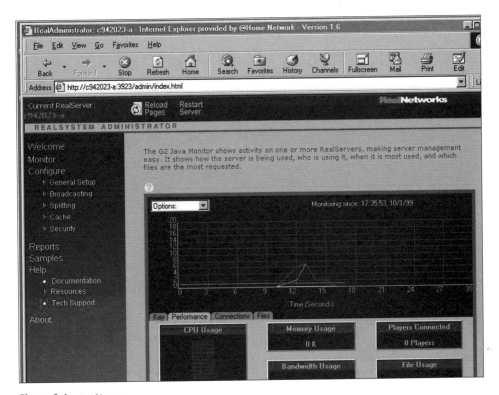

Figure 9-1   **RealServer**

The Server code has three major subsystems: the RTP server, the RTSP server, and common utilities. Each source code file belonging to the RTP subsystem has the prefix RTP. Similarly, each file belonging to the RTSP subsystem has the prefix RTSP. Any other source code file belongs to the Common Utilities subsystem.

Common Utilities is a toolkit of thread management, data structure, networking, and text parsing utilities. The RTP and RTSP servers use these classes pervasively to accomplish the following three goals: (1) reduce repeated code by abstracting similar or identical tasks, (2) make the higher-level code simpler through encapsulation, and (3) separate out any and all platform-specific code. Implementations currently work on MacOS X.

The reflector allows an administrator to deliver live broadcasts to RTSP clients. The reflector is implemented as an RTP module.

When a QuickTime client wants to view a broadcast, it first connects to the Darwin Streaming Server reflector module and directs the module to look for a proper incoming broadcast. If the broadcast is found, the Darwin Streaming Server will then reflect the broadcast to the client.

◖ Video Server Software for Microsoft

Microsoft has a streaming format of its own, called *Active Streaming Format* or *ASF*. To host an ASF file for streamed delivery, you must place the compressed ASF file on either an HTTP server or a Windows Media Services server and link to the file on a Web server.

To post to an HTTP server, simply place both the ASX and ASF files in the same folder as your Web page.

To post to a Windows Media Services server, install Windows Media Services and place the ASF file in an ASF root directory. Place the ASX file in the same folder as the Web page.

The Windows Media server components are a set of services running on Windows NT Server that can unicast and multicast audio, video, and other media to client computers. To deliver live, real-time content, the server works in conjunction with the Windows Media Encoder, which compresses the audio and video feed in real time and passes it to the Windows Media server for delivery to the network. On-demand ASF files must be stored on a server's hard drive and passed to the network by the Windows Media Services server.

Windows Media Services offers bandwidth support delivering live broadcasts or streaming stored multimedia content from as low as 3Kbps of audio to 6Mbps of audio and video. A single server can scale to support over 3,000 simultaneous users.

In either scenario, for people to be able to view your media, they need to have certain settings called MIME types correctly configured. Installation of the Windows Media Player on most browser configurations usually takes care of these settings. However, for some configurations, you may need to manually set client or server MIME associations.

The Windows Media Services allows unicast or multicast live or stored content, or multicast files to users' computers. Microsoft Windows Media Services is built on Windows NT and it is integrated with the operating system's reliability, scalability, performance, and cost.

Windows 2000 will incorporate Quality-of-Service (QoS) features that allow network managers to reserve portions of their network's bandwidth for specific applications like Windows Media Services.

Caching Servers

For many users, speed is dependent on the performance of high performance network server systems. Cost-effective scalable network servers can be built instead of using expensive multiprocessor systems. However, network servers cache files to reduce disk access, and the cluster's physically disjoint memories complicate sharing cached file data.

Caching server appliances store data locally and serve the content most often requested by users, while simultaneously monitoring the source of that content for changes. In doing so, caching servers improve response time for Internet users, deliver fresher content, and more efficiently use existing bandwidth.

Web site owners earmark content such as graphics files, advertising banners, and software downloads to be distributed over a caching server network. This process runs software that makes minor modifications to HTML code. These Web objects offload responsibility for serving the vast majority of bytes while retaining control over serving the initial hit of each page request. This novel method lets e-businesses maintain complete ownership of relationships with users, including counting visitors, placing cookies, and dynamically assembling pages.

Sophisticated algorithms generate a unique map of current Internet traffic conditions, the loads of all servers worldwide, and the locations of Internet users. A global map is constantly updated—as frequently as once per second—ensuring instant responses to Internet outages and congestion.

When a user requests a page containing these objects, his or her browser automatically points to a selected server rather than to the customer's central site. Based on real-time network maps, software directs requests to the specified server best able to satisfy each request, resulting in better performance and reliability than ever before possible. This process, which uses standard Internet protocols, is transparent to all browsers and does not require any plug-ins or user configuration.

An example of the innovative efforts to use clustered caching servers with special ISP access is a recent agreement reached between Digital Island, Sun Microsystems, and Inktomi. It is intended to greatly accelerate Web site performance for consumers and e-business Web sites. Under the agreement, Digital Island will deploy up to 5,000 Sun's Netra carrier-grade servers and Enterprise servers running the Solaris Operating Environment with Inktomi's Traffic Server and Content Delivery. The advanced technology intelligently avoids Internet congestion for all types of Internet traffic, including secure e-business transactions, streaming media, and dynamic content. The Intelligent Network consists of an ATM backbone that connects and is supported by redundant Cisco routers located at four geographically dispersed data centers. Using the ATM backbone, each router on the Digital Island network has a direct connection to all other routers, creating a fully meshed network. Digital Island's distributed data centers permit the Intelligent Network to disseminate information reliably on a global basis and, using its sophisticated data-tracking capability, allows Digital Island to optimize data transmissions internationally, minimizing the use of expensive transoceanic fiber-optic circuits. The build-out is expected to be among the largest deployment of carrier-grade servers at the outer edges of the Internet. Approximately 350 metropolitan areas are expected to be targeted for the deployment of the carrier-grade Sun servers over the next three years, 250 of which are expected to be outside the United States.

These servers will support interactive services over a variety of access methods, including DSL, cable, wireless, and dial-up. The benefits of co-locating the servers include

- Reduced network backbone by keeping content on their network
- Increased performance gains realized through the elimination of network bottlenecks and closer proximity of content to the end users
- Value-added content-delivery services, such as streaming video and secure e-business transactions, and dynamic content efficiently delivered

The Digital Island network does not transmit traffic between continents but rather delivers commercial applications to multiple continents simultaneously. The distributed star architecture used by Digital Island is superior to meshed networks for the distribution of centralized, hybrid, and distributed applications because of its manageability, scalability, and connectivity to local Internet service providers (ISPs) and network service providers (NSPs) through dedicated points-of-presence (POPs).

Digital Island's network peers with ISPs in each country, providing customers with direct access to local markets worldwide. By having direct connections to major ISPs, Digital

Island's customers avoid the oversubscribed U.S. Internet infrastructure. This also allows Digital Island to meet the requirements of the different types of commercial applications that multinational customers need to deploy and update regularly.

Broadband convergence will also result in thousands of Web channels requiring searchable video. Concepts of metadata, indexing, and creating search video are now being developed at innovation companies, such as Virage, Inc. (www.virage.com).

ISPs offering to provide streaming encoding and hosting services are available at the Real-Networks partner groups

> http://partners.real.com/search/index.html?s=xxx&search_keywords=isp&
> displaynum=10&searchtype=a

and Microsoft's partner groups

> http://www.microsoft.com/windows/windowsmedia/en/default.asp.

◖◐ Conclusion

This chapter tied streaming video standards and protocols to bandwidth and server delivery. It included specifics about RealServer, Microsoft Windows Media Server, and broadband video.

On the basis of this chapter you should conclude that

▸ Caching server clusters will lead to new ISP arrangements for rich media providers.
▸ Intelligent networking software for routing and tracking will lead to general changes in IP networking protocols.

CHAPTER **10**

Live
Webcasts

Live Webcasts are in their infancy with respect to their production values. You probably weren't born when Milton Berle
was live on television in the early 1950s, but live Webcasts today often display a similar bravado. ▶

In this chapter, we present live
Webcast applications for existing
narrowband and limited
broadband access. As examples,
we present the basics of
delivering a Webcast with
RealNetworks' RealProducer G2
and Microsoft's Windows Media.

▶ Webcasts

The Internet may someday become the next great broadcast medium. Live Webcast will begin with streaming video narrowband and scale up to MPEG streaming. The modem for products such as Net-TV, can be built in 56Kbps, a cable modem, a satellite connection, or ADSL. The process will be a combination of (1) the scaling up of narrowband streaming providers, such as RealSystem G2 and Windows Media, to streaming MPEG and (2) broadband networking direct delivery of streaming MPEG.

Webcasts must be evaluated in terms of the target audience and the audience size. The flexible interactive nature of the Internet allows Webcasts to use varied strategies of one-to-one, one-to-many, many-to-one, and many-to-many delivery.

Soon there may be streaming MPEG video broadcasts to PCs through digital television (DTV) station affiliates. It will use high-quality, live, streaming video broadcasts directly to the client desktop PCs. Through parallel networking, it will provide users streaming video with two important capabilities: the ability to deliver very high quality streaming video and the ability to reach live audiences of large sizes. And the delivered video will offer large image sizes, not just a small, postage stamp–size frame.

▶ Live Broadcasts

There are a number of ways to broadcast live over the Web with supporting streaming codec, such as RealNetworks' RealProducer or Microsoft's Windows Media. Table 10-1 provides a guide for minimal systems requirements for RealVideo on a Windows PC.

As with a TV broadcast, there are two types of streaming media broadcasts.
  ▸ Live content is broadcast as it occurs. For example, you can broadcast the output of a video camera across the Internet, or an intranet. The video is in real time without writing the content to a clip first.

Table 10-1   **Required Computer Hardware**

	At 15 Frames per Second	*At 5 Frames per Second*
Operating System	Windows 2000	Windows 98
Computer	Dual Pentium III 500MHz, or single CPU, Pentium III, 500MHz	Pentium III 500MHz
Capture Card	Osprey 100, Osprey 1000, Videum AV	Osprey 100, Osprey 1000, ISVR III, Videum AV

▶ Prerecorded content consists of video or audio you record and write to a digitized clip. You can then edit the clip before converting it to a streaming format and broadcasting it across a network. To the viewer, the presentation looks just like a live broadcast.

When a streaming presentation is delivered on demand, it starts from its beginning when the viewer clicks the presentation link in a Web page. Each viewer can receive the presentation at any time and use the player's controls to fast-forward or rewind through the presentation.

In a streaming broadcast, however, the user hosting the broadcast starts the presentation at a certain time. Viewers who click the presentation link join the broadcast in progress. Before the broadcast begins and after it completes, the presentation URL is not valid.

To make an analogy, on-demand content is like a movie on videotape. The viewer can see it at any time, skip forward, rewind, and pause. A streaming broadcast, though, is like a movie shown on a television channel.

The quality of streaming live video varies very widely depending on the following issues:
- ▶ Numerous compatibility issues (such as capture card versus codec)
- ▶ Delivery reliability (server, operating system, ISP, browser)
- ▶ Quality of image issues (compression codec)
- ▶ Image and video/audio feed setting for optimal delivery
- ▶ Frame rate delivered and the number of simultaneous delivery streams

All of these elements should be tested for delivery against your customer's available video players.

▶ RealNetworks' RealProducer Broadcast Example

Figure 10-1 provides a flow diagram of live streaming video over RealNetworks.

To broadcast a RealVideo presentation, the following tools are required:

1. *Source capture equipment.* This equipment captures the broadcast content. It is typically a microphone or video camera connected to an audio or video capture card. For text it could be a live text feed coming in over a network.

2. *Editing equipment.* When broadcasting prerecorded content, first write the source to a digitized file. The editing software is then used to optimize the file for broadcast.

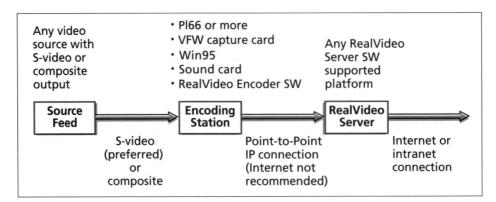

Figure 10-1   RealNetworks' live streaming flow diagram

3. *Broadcast application.* The broadcast application takes the live source and encodes it in the appropriate streaming format, sending the output to RealServer. A RealVideo broadcast application, for example, encodes a camera's video output as RealVideo in real time. A broadcast application typically runs on a separate machine that has a network connection to the RealServer machine. To broadcast prerecorded content, you typically do not need a broadcast application because RealServer can broadcast the clips itself.

4. *RealNetworks encoding tools.* These have live broadcast capability for audio and RGB or YUV video. They guide you through the broadcast process and let you connect to RealServer easily. RealSystem's open architecture also lets you build a broadcast application to send any type of data to RealServer for broadcast.

5. *RealServer.* RealServer streams the broadcast to RealPlayer. The RealServer administrator can give you the broadcast URL and parameters for connecting a broadcast application to RealServer. Because each RealServer has a limit on the number of streams it can produce, verify that the RealServer you intend to use has broadcast capabilities appropriate for your anticipated audience size.

For preparing a live or prerecorded broadcast you can use SureStream with RealSystem G2 codecs (see Figure 10-2). SureStream technology and RealSystem G2 codecs let you broadcast RealAudio or RealVideo at multiple bandwidths. Each viewer's RealPlayer selects an encoding appropriate for its connection speed. RealNetworks encoding tools let you specify SureStream when you begin the broadcast.

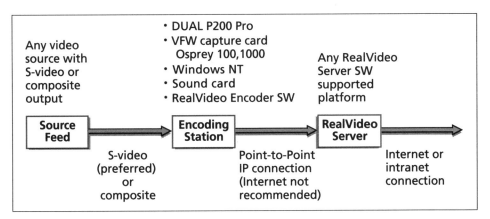

Figure 10-2 **RealProducer flow diagram**

RealServer can archive the broadcast to a file. The RealServer administrator can give you the parameters you need to connect a broadcast application to RealServer.

When you broadcast live content, you don't get a second chance. It's good practice to perform a trial run to ensure that the equipment works properly and the broadcast results are what you expect. Because you can't edit a live broadcast the way you can edit a prerecorded file, it's important to set your audio levels and plan your video shots carefully in advance.

RealServer employs a client/server architecture to provide features such as live broadcasting, interactive stream control (fast-forward and seek options), efficient use of network bandwidth, and scalability that can support large numbers of concurrent users.

Sophisticated compression, buffering, and transmission techniques allow RealServers to stream audio and video animation to players, which continuously decompress and play back the stream in real time. Users can watch or listen to entire programs or navigate on-demand clips to experience what they want when they want it.

Using SMIL, you can embed your broadcast in a multiclip presentation. You might use a SMIL file, for example, to create a video region for your live broadcast and a RealPix region that features rotating ads. The SMIL file then uses the broadcast URL for the video region and a standard URL to the RealPix clip.

However, SMIL does not synchronize on-demand clips with the broadcast. When the SMIL presentation starts, the viewer begins to receive the on-demand clips in the order they are defined by the SMIL grouping and timing tags.

Every piece of equipment in the audio chain—microphone, mixer, and sound card—affects sound quality. It is important to use shielded cables. Unshielded cables increase the chance of introducing line noise and radio frequency interference (RFI) into recordings.

To get the best signal-to-noise ratio, set the input level on each audio device in the signal chain so that it uses its full range of available amplitude without distortion during the program's loudest sections. The signal chain typically includes a microphone, a mixing desk, a compressor, and a sound card. For each piece of equipment, set levels as close as possible to 0 dB without going over.

When broadcasting live audio, it is useful to have a dynamics compressor (gain compression, not data compression), which is a piece of audio equipment that automatically adjusts the volume level. By providing a consistent level, the compressor allows you to set and forget the input levels to the RealAudio encoder. Capture sound with a sampling width of 16 bits.

A How-To Example Delivering Live Unicast with Windows Media

▸ Start the Windows Media Services Administrator. Select **Unicast Publishing Points** on the left tool bar.

▸ Under Broadcast Unicast Publishing Points, check **Use wizard** to create new broadcast publishing point.

▸ Click the **Broadcast** button and select **New.** This will bring up a wizard that will create your Unicast Publishing Point. Click the **Next** button.

▸ Select **Create a broadcast publishing point** and click the **Next** button.

▸ Select Windows Media Encoder as the source of your stream source and click the **Next** button.

▸ Enter a name for your stream in the Alias field and the path to your Windows Media Encoder in the Path field. The path to your Windows Media Encoder should begin with MSBD://. For the port number, enter the number you selected when configuring the Windows Media Encoder. If you accepted the default settings in the encoder, enter **port 7007** and click the **Next** button.

▸ Select **MMS for Protocol** (MMS uses automatic rollover from UDP to TCP and HTTP). Select what you want the wizard to create, and then click the **Next** button.

▸ Review your selections. Click **Next** to accept them or click **Back** to make changes.

▸ Save your ASX file.

▸ Click **Finish** to save your unicast publishing point.

▸ Now you are ready to test your stream. Start the encoder and double-click the ASX file.

▶ A How-To Example Delivering Live Multicast with Windows Media

- Start the Windows Media Services Administrator by going to Start, Programs, Microsoft Windows Media Services, Beta Server Administrator.
- Select **Multicast stations** in the left tool bar.
- Under Stations, select **Use wizard** to create new station.
- Click the **Stations** button and select **New.** This will bring up the wizard to create your multicast station. Click the **Next** button.
- Select **Create a new station** and click the **Next** button.
- Enter a name for your station and a short description. Select your method of distribution.
- Enter a name for the program and a name for the stream. Click the **Next** button.
- Select **Windows Media Encoder** for the source for the stream and click the **Next** button.
- Enter the path to the encoder. You can either use HTTP or MSBD protocol to connect to the encoder. Click the **Next** button.
- If you created a customized setting in the encoder, you will need to save the encoder settings and enter the path to the ASD file. Click the **Next** button.
- Save the NSC file in a location where the client's machine can access it. Click the **Next** button.
- Select how you would like the clients to access the NSC file and the path to the NSC file. Click the **Next** button.
- Select the publishing options you want. Click the **Next** button.
- Review your selections. Click **Finish** to accept them or click **Back** to make changes.
- Save your ASX file and click **Close** to finish creating your multicast station.
- There are a number of ways to broadcast live over the Web with supporting streaming codec, such as RealVideo 5.0 or NetShow 3.0 (beta) at greater than 5fps continuously.
- The streaming live video quality varies very widely depending on the following issues:
  numerous compatibility issues (such as capture card versus codec)
  delivery reliability (server, operating system, ISP, browser)
  quality of image issues (compression MJPEG versus RAW)
  image and video/audio feed setting for optimal delivery
  frame rate delivered and the number of simultaneous delivery streams

▶ Conclusion

In this chapter, we presented the background of producing live video Webcasts.

CHAPTER 11

Future Strategies for Video

We began this book by stating that someday video would be everywhere.

Someday. But not today! ▶

Now it is time for us to weave the big picture together. In this chapter, we will present three concluding issues. First, we provide an update on the status of cable, DSL, and wireless efforts to deliver broadband over the last mile to homes and businesses. Second, we move to the active strategies of codec developers, such as RealNetworks and Microsoft to scale their narrowband compression technologies toward broadband streaming MPEG delivery. And third, we use our crystal ball to describe transmission of HDTV video over the Internet, which will become widely distributed over the next decade or two.

As yet there really is no elegant, cost-effective, and entirely satisfactory appliance that integrates TV, phone, and computer. However, the goal of integrating and standardizing all media is overwhelmingly guiding hardware and software developers' efforts in all three media. From what we have presented in this book, it should be clear that *someday* is coming very soon, and we can already see development toward business-to-customer streaming video.

◗ Cable Leads the Way toward Broadband Delivery

In Chapters 1 and 8, we showed that the combination of fiber infrastructure and DWDM would produce more than adequate backbone network capacity for the multi-Tera bits-per-second future requirements of the Internet. And the promise of fast Internet access for the last mile to the home users has been long anticipated. With more than a million current customers the cable industry is moving fast. But, which last mile high-speed option—cable, DSL, or satellite—is best?

Cable offers the fastest potential download speeds available to home users up to 30Mbps, more than 500 times faster than today's 56Kbps modems. As with cable TV, the provider will send somebody out to install it for you. And once installed, it provides a constant connection, so you never have to dial up for Internet access. The @Home and Road Runner businesses dominate the market.

Actual download speed currently falls far short of the 30Mbps potential, however. Your PC's Ethernet interface brings it down to 4Mbps to start with, and delays on the Internet slow it further. Overall, these structural considerations mean an average download speed of between 1.5Mbps and 3Mbps. Upstream information puts an even worse strain on the infrastructure. @Home has already limited upstream speed to 128Kbps in some markets and is considering this limitation nationwide.

In competition with cable modems, the asymmetric digital subscriber line (ADSL) standard was adopted in 1997, paving the way for the first DSL services. ADSL uses regular phone lines to send information to users at up to 6Mbps. Unlike cable and satellite systems, high-speed phone lines offer high bandwidth upstream at up to 640Kbps. ADSL lets users talk on the same line they are using to access the Internet. In 1999, there were only about 300,000 homes and businesses using DSL.

DSL is clearly superior for buildings in a central business district. Cable will have an advantage in home businesses. However, both cable and telephone operators will have to upgrade their facilities to become regular ISPs. This means they will need routers and high-speed facilities at all central offices. On the other hand, suburban areas will see DSL and cable compete on even terms.

Hughes Electronics introduced the DirecPC satellite dish and box in early 1997. DirecPC promises download speeds of up to 400Kbps, which is slower than cable's usual 1.5Mbps to 3Mbps, but the speed remains constant no matter how many people use the service. Most importantly, DirecPC is available in any U.S. location with an unobstructed view of the southern half of the sky. EchoStar together with Microsoft has created a set-top TV box combining its number-two satellite-TV service, DISH, with WebTV. Net access will come only through a built-in 56Kbps modem, though EchoStar is boasting a data broadcast service at 30Mbps.

The wireless LAN industry has been held back from competing with broadband companies because the existing wireless bandwidth has been significantly less than Ethernet. The wireless IEEE 802.11 standard for 2.4GHz for high rates 11Mbps and may change the competitive landscape.

Future networks may bring cable and telephone closer to ATM, which spans the gap between packet-switching and circuit-switching technology. ATM splits data into small chunks, like a packet serve, but the cells are all equal size. Then instead of routing each cell

Table 11-1   **Bandwidth Requirements**

Application	Required Bandwidth Mbps (after compression)
Video conferencing	0.384
Video games	1.0
Video catalog	1.5
Virtual video mall	1.5
Complex Web pages	1.5
Corporate LAN (10Mbps Ethernet)	1.5
Digital TV (MPEG-2)	
• On demand	1.5
• Live	3
• Sports	6
Entertainment video (HDTV 1080×1920×24-bit color)	19.3 to 38.6
Medical imagery	20
Digital professional photography & stock video	20

individually, ATM sets up a virtual circuit and streams them across the network. ATM is scalable and ultra-fast (622Mbps). It also can allocate bandwidth on demand and prioritize cells streams.

Table 11-1 shows how this new bandwidth access to homes and businesses may be used. Business-to-customer applications, such as video shopping malls and video catalogs are examples.

ID Scaling RealNetworks and Microsoft Codecs for Broadband

Four things need to happen before the broadband industry can take off.

1. Content providers' distribution costs need to drop dramatically.

2. The quality of streamed video, which is limited by the packet loss and other problems that occur in traditional Internet transmission, needs to be improved.

3. Compelling content needs to be developed that gives consumers a reason to invest in a broadband connection.

4. Improved business models need to be created to increase revenues and lower overall costs for the broadband industry.

What is RealNetworks' broadband strategy? RealNetworks is working with broadband providers, such as cable provider @Home. Broadband users tend to use more streaming video product (up to five hours per month) than narrowband customers because they get a better experience.

RealNetworks' broadband codec effort has been to try to develop a MPEG-quality video but at sub-megabit rates in the short term, and over time to deliver true broadband.

As the world moves gradually toward a convergence of the television and PC, people will increasingly use digital set-top boxes to go on-line and watch TV. Because of limited memory, the big set-top makers like General Instrument and Scientific-Atlanta already have their own proprietary compression algorithms.

To get to the point where the set-top box makers will want to bundle them into their product, RealNetworks has to become the de facto compression standard. That means it has to forge as many deals as possible with content providers—as well as with cable, DSL, and satellite companies. But it has to act fast. Unless it is able to lock up proprietary deals now, not only will companies like Microsoft and Apple be likely to become much bigger threats, but set-top makers and studios will probably start devising their own compression technology.

In 1999, RealNetworks announced several broadband-related deals, specifically with *Excite@Home* Liberate, Inktomi, Intel, Enron, and WebTV, a subsidiary of Microsoft. The company is also in talks with a number of cable, DSL, and satellite companies as well as several digital set-top box makers.

Compression and better support of different formats promises to revolutionize on-line video, both at high-speed and low-speed lines.

What is the Windows Media broadband strategy? The Windows Media broadband jump-start initiative is Microsoft's end-to-end strategy for jumpstarting broadband business models and overcoming the barriers to making broadband services a reality.

Microsoft's content delivery strategy includes content delivery through more efficient content distribution systems, such as through land lines or satellite broadcasting, to a cache at the Internet access provider (either xDSL or cable modem), and finally to the end user. These content distribution systems not only increase efficiency but also lower the cost of delivery substantially. The following content distribution systems and Internet access providers have already joined Microsoft's broadband jumpstart initiative:

  ▸ *Content distribution systems.* Akamai Technologies Inc., iBEAM Broadcasting Corp., INTERVU Inc., and Sandpiper Networks
  ▸ *Caching vendors.* InfoLibria, Inktomi Corp., and Network Appliance Inc.
  ▸ *Digital subscriber line (DSL) access providers.* Rhythms NetConnections Inc., North-Point Communications, Covad Communications, Jato Communications Corp., and FirstWorld Communications
  ▸ *Cable access providers.* RoadRunner, which services Time Warner and MediaOne, and High Speed Access Corp.

The content distribution system partners, also known as *edge providers,* move content to the edge of the Internet and as a result, bypass congestion. The edge distribution model circumvents the Internet because content is not subject to the same delivery problems as it is in the standard model. Therefore, the highest quality streamed content is feasible for entertainment, education, and advertising.

◖◗ HDTV over the Internet

By using VDSL lines, traditional telephony service will be able to deliver HDTV signals to customers at the same time that the terrestrial broadcast television industry converts to digital television. VDSL technology has the ability to provide 20Mbps to 50Mbps of digital bandwidth over a single pair of copper wires. This allows high-quality video streams to be transmitted to a user's location without costly rewiring.

Adding multimedia content to static television programs will be easier with the delivery of HDTV over VDSL. By managing disparate data streams from a single source close to the customer, telecommunications companies and other service providers will be able to deliver HDTV in a way that is cost-efficient and easy to install.

The expansion of broadband means there is an opportunity for telecommunications companies to become multimedia service providers. As VDSL and other high-speed access methods become common, subscribers will be able to pick the access method best for them.

Advances in VDSL technology provide a supportive access method for ATM transmission services. HDTV's appetite for bandwidth and the consumer's appetite for picture quality will drive this solution.

The multimedia access switch will aggregate HDTV content, along with Internet data and voice telephony calls, onto a single platform for high-speed delivery, 26 Mbps downstream and 3 Mbps upstream, to each subscriber. The product will then separate the HDTV signal. Lucent Digital Video will provide HDTV encoding and decoding systems. Viewers will be able to see an HDTV display and a standard TV display while receiving regular phone calls, all over the same telephone wire.

◖▷ Building Bridges between the Standards

The future holds a need for an interaction between the TV and the Internet. The Internet Engineering Task Force (IETF) has defined specific types for the Real-Time Transport Protocol (RTP) that can be used to deliver MPEG-2 encoded, TV-quality video over IP networks. AT&T has developed a prototype system that transmits stored or live video using these types, and it works successfully over their intranet.

The video outputs of such systems can be displayed directly on regular TV sets. As the Internet backbone and the residential access bandwidths increase, similar systems can be used to transmit high-quality video over the Internet to residential users. Since this approach requires layer-three functionality at the receivers, it may not be optimal for the transmission of regular TV broadcast channels, a task that requires multi-gigabit-per-second data processing. On the other hand, it opens significant new avenues for video on demand as a part of information on demand and narrowcasting applications to justify its existence along with other means to carry broadcast TV channels.

One problem with the broadcast video is its sequential access. For example, we have to listen to an entire news program although we may not be interested in every news item that it includes. A much better way of viewing news programs can be made possible through a descriptive index to the news provided as a Web page with links for video-on-demand transmission of the news segments. AT&T is developing capability that generates a digital multimedia library of TV programs, automatically using scene change detection and closed captioning information. Together with MPEG-2 over IP, it provides on-demand, nonsequential playback on a regular TV set with video quality.

Both IP-based high quality video-on-demand and narrowcasting applications can be developed based on the existing set of the Internet protocols. In particular, RTP/RTCP can be used for the transport, Session Description Protocol (SDP) can be used for transmitting the session information to the receivers, and Real-Time Streaming Protocol (RTSP) can be used for session control including VCR type control functionality.

Consider the use of the URL information embedded in broadcast TV pictures. Currently, URL references are used in many TV programs, for example providing additional information on the subject matter of the program. Accessing the Web pages pointed to by these requires manual transfer of the displayed URLs from the TV to the Web accessing device, typically a computer. A URL embedded in a picture could be extracted through image analysis and character recognition and transmitted to the Web accessing device, which downloads the indicated page automatically.

There are three main approaches to bridging the gaps between the world's current TV video standards.

The first of these is transcoding. This applies primarily to efforts to replay material from other TV systems using equipment designed with a single particular TV system in mind. Almost all of the solutions based on this technique are replay only and make no provision for the production of material in the *foreign* TV system.

The second approach is that of the true multistandard equipment. With a multistandard video recorder, NTSC tape can be reproduced as a standard NTSC signal, and the same machine if fed with a PAL tape will reproduce it as a standard PAL signal. A multistandard VCR can also be expected to make a perfectly normal NTSC recording of an NTSC input signal and a perfectly normal PAL recording of a PAL input signal.

The third approach is that of standards conversion where the TV signal is converted from one TV system to a standard signal in another.

Standards conversion is the most complex, technically difficult, and degrading of all of the techniques for building bridges between TV standards. It is also the most desirable since the material actually becomes a signal of the destination TV system, which can be recorded and reproduced by equipment of the destination TV system.

Conversion between TV systems with same frame rate is usually reasonably effective. Conversion between TV systems with differing frame rates is extremely difficult. The units that perform these conversions are known as *digital standards converters*.

> What broadband technology convergence needs is meaningful standards. ▶

Without standards, hardware and software developers can't create broad solutions for consumer demand.

Two serious avenues for converging standards include
 ▶ Windows NT-based Media architecture
 ▶ Cisco's architecture for voice, video, and integrated data (AVVID) through network development.

The combination of AT&T's cable broadband strategy with Microsoft's Web-TV software platform within advanced set-top boxes offers an interesting competitive scenario.

Traditionally, standards evolve in three ways.

1. A vendor dominates a market and sets a de facto standard (for example telephony from AT&T or PC operating systems from Microsoft).

2. Standards organizations establish standards (for example, ATM or HDTV).

3. Vendors and market collaboration that cannot be clearly attributed to any one organization (for example, TCP/IP or VCR formats).

Residential broadband networks are moving too fast for a single vendor to dominate or for standards organizations to establish standards. There is no clear architecture or vendor dominating. So how will standards emerge?

The streaming video is at the crossroads of all this technology convergence. It is the bandwidth crisis of delivering video that will prove decisive in the selection of competing technology standards.

▶ Conclusion

This book began by stating that technologies were converging. In each subsequent chapter, the elements of streaming video were presented along with their particular impact on technology convergence. The goal was to show why and where streaming video would play a role as the nexus of technology convergence. The big picture began to emerge in this chapter. Overcoming bandwidth limitations will be a combination of broadband connections and efficient compression algorithms.

The top 10 things you should have learned from this book are:

1. The Internet backbone combination of fiber and DWDM will perform at greater than 10Tbps range and provide plenty of network backbone bandwidth in the next few years.

2. The last mile connectivity will remain twisted pair, wireless, and coax cable for the next few years, but broadband (1.5Mbps) access will grow to 40 million users over that time.

3. Corporate and e-business can make excellent use of the 1.5Mbps access with video product demos, video instructions, and interactive video customer service.

4. The authoring, editing, and Web publishing tools for streaming video are widely available, inexpensive, and easy to use. Your participation and success in building streaming video Web sites and businesses looks great.

5. New codec improvements will emerge rapidly from the numerous competing codec developers.

6. RealNetworks will dominate narrowband streaming for several more years, but Microsoft's Windows Media and Apple's QuickTime will grow rapidly and target the 1.5Mbps and above delivery.

7. Both RealNetworks and Microsoft will scale their codecs to streaming MPEG standards in cooperation with specialized companies like Digital Video and LSX-MPEG, respectively.

8. Caching server clusters will lead to new ISP arrangements for rich media providers.

9. Intelligent networking software for routing and tracking will lead to general changes in IP networking protocols.

10. New standards replacing MPEG-2 will come more quickly than currently anticipated because of the potential demands to achieve benefits to last mile delivery.

APPENDIX A

Our Web Site and CD-ROM

In order to get the full value from this book, it is important for readers to see and hear streaming video on the Web for themselves, as well as explore the most advanced research projects in this field. To support this goal we suggest you visit our associated Web site:

http://www.video-software.com

The Web site (See Figure A-1) provides download links (See Figure A-2) for *free* video players from all the major developers (RealNetworks, Microsoft, Apple, Emblaze, Bitcasting, LZX-MPEG), as well as video encoding tools, editing tools, and server software.

A CD-ROM with example code and streaming video demos is included at the back cover of this book. The CD-ROM provides demos and video examples for the various formats described within the text of the book. In addition, it contains URL links to many of the software and hardware vendors discussed within the book.

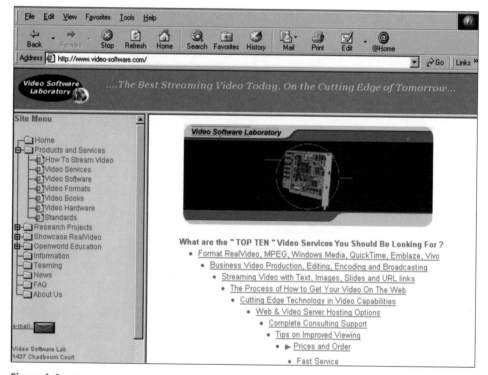

Figure A-1   **Our supporting Web site**

Figure A-2   **Our download page**

The CD-ROM contains two main directories: How To and Video AVI. The How To directory should be copied directly to your C:/ drive by dragging the How To icon from the CD-ROM directory in Windows Explorer to your C:/ directory icon. There is less than 60MB of data to be copied. A few of the examples have location information coded into the example and may not work if copied to a different directory. It is possible, however, to run some of the demos directly from the CD-ROM.

Once the How To directory is copied to your C:/ drive, double-clicking on the file named Index.html will bring the following Web page (Figure A-3) into your browser.

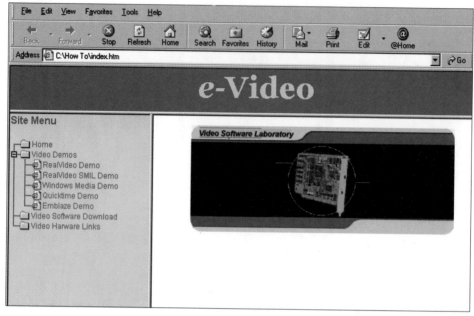

Figure A-3   **On our CD-ROM**

The menu on the left side of the Web page will link to:

- Various demo pages
- Pages with links to download software
- Pages with links to hardware Vendors

It is necessary to be connected by modem to the Internet before linking to URL sites.

Standards Organizations

Throughout this book we have referenced standards and specifications of national and international standards organizations. The following list names and describes the major standards bodies.

American National Standards Institute (ANSI)

The U.S. national organization defining coding standards and signaling. It functions as the U.S. representative to international organizations.

American National Standards Institute
11 West 42nd Street, 13th Floor
New York, NY 10036
(212) 642-4900

International Consultative Committee for Telegraph and Telephone (CCITT)

The CCITT is a committee of the United Nations organization, International Telecommunications Union (ITU).

U.S. Department of Commerce
National Technical Information Service
5285 Port Royal Road
Springfield, VA 22161
(703) 487-4650
www.itu.ch

Institute of Electrical and Electronic Engineers (IEEE)

The IEEE is the U.S. standards organization for electrical and electronics industries. Networking standards are developed in IEEE 802 committees, including:

802.1 Internetworking
802.2 Logic Link Control

802.3 CSMA/CD LANs

802.4 Token Ring LANs

802.5 Token Ring LANs

802.6 Metropolitan Area Networks

802.7 Broadband Technical Advisory Group

802.8 Fiber-Optical Technical Advisory Group

802.9 Integrated Voice and Data

802.10 Network Security

802.11 Wireless Networks

802.12 Demand Priority Access LANs

Institute of Electrical and Electronic Engineers

445 Hoes Lane

P.O. Box 1331

Piscataway, NJ 08855-1331

(908) 981-1393

International Standards Organization (ISO)

The International Standards Organization has representatives from standards organizations around the world.

International Organization for Standardization

1, rue de Varembé

Case pastale 56

CH-1211 Genève 20

SWITZERLAND

41-22-479-0111

www.iso.ch

W3C

The W3C was founded in October 1994 to lead the World Wide Web to developing common protocols that promote interoperability. The international industry consortium is jointly hosted by the *Massachusetts Institute of Technology Laboratory for Computer Science* [MIT/LCS] in the United States; the *Institut National de Recherche en Informatique et en Automatique* [INRIA] in Europe; and the Keio University Shonan Fujisawa Campus in Japan.

The consortium is led by Tim Berners-Lee, director and creator of the World Wide Web, and *Jean-François Abramatic,* chairman. W3C is funded by member organizations and is vendor neutral, working with the global community to produce specifications and reference software that is freely made available throughout the world.

www.w3.org/Consortium
Senior Contract Administrator
Office of Sponsored Programs, E19-750
Massachusetts Institute of Technology
77 Massachusetts Avenue
Cambridge, MA 02139
USA

TV and Tape Standards

Most countries around the world use one of three main television broadcast standards, NTSC, PAL, and SECAM. However, each standard is incompatible with the other. For example, a video recording made in the UK could not be played on U.S. standard VCRs or shown on the TV.

Analog Standards

TV receivers require a source of field timing reference. These signals tell the TV receiver to be ready to receive the next picture. Early set designers decided to use the mains power supply frequency as this source. The older types of power supply would produce rolling hum bars on the TV picture if the mains supply and power source were not at exactly the same frequency. Also TV studios had enormous problems with flicker on their cameras when making programs.

The two mains power frequencies are 50Hz and 60Hz. The issue of field frequency remained sufficiently deep-rooted in both TV standards.

Beyond the initial divide between 50Hz- and 60Hz-based systems, further subdivisions have appeared since the inception of color broadcasting.

The majority of 60Hz-based countries use a technique known as *NTSC,* originally developed in the United States by a committee called the *National Television Systems Committee.* NTSC works perfectly in a video or closed circuit environment but can exhibit problems of varying hue when used in a broadcast environment. This hue change is caused by shifts in the color subcarrier phase of the signal. A modified version of NTSC soon appeared which differed mainly in that the subcarrier phase was reversed on each second line, known as PAL, Phase Alternating Line. PAL has been the most widely adopted where systems are based on 50Hz.

The French designed a system of their own, which is known as *SECAM,* Sequential Couleur Avec Memoire.

In Europe, a few direct satellite broadcasting services use a system called *D-MAC.* There are other MAC-based standards, including B-MAC in Australia and B-MAC60 on some private networks in the United States. There is also a second European variant called *D2-MAC,* which supports additional audio channels, making transmitted signals incompatible.

TV pictures can be transmitted in any of three main frequency ranges, VHF, UHF, and Microwave (Satellite Direct Broadcast). Equipment designed to receive signals in only one of these bands cannot receive transmissions in any of the other bands.

In addition to standard combinations of scan rate, color system, and transmission frequencies, there are further complications when it comes to additional features like stereo sound, subtitling, and information services.

Video Broadcast Standards

The first color TV broadcast system was implemented in the United States in 1953. This was based on the NTSC (**N**ational **T**elevision **S**ystems **C**ommittee) standard. NTSC runs on 525 lines per frame.

System	NTSC
Lines/Field	525/60
Horizontal Frequency	15.734kHz
Vertical Frequency	60Hz
Colour Subcarrier Frequency	3.579545MHz
Video Bandwidth	4.2MHz
Sound Carrier	4.5MHz

The PAL (Phase Alternating Line) standard was introduced in the early 1960s and implemented. The PAL standard uses a wider channel bandwidth than NTSC, which allows for better picture quality. PAL runs on 625 lines per frame.

System	PAL B,G,H	PAL I	PAL D	PAL N	PAL M
Line/Field	625/50	625/50	625/50	625/50	525/60
Horizontal Frequency	15.625kHz	15.625kHz	15.625kHz	15.625kHz	15.750kHz
Vertical Frequency	50Hz	50Hz	50Hz	50Hz	60Hz
Color Subcarrier Frequency	4.433618MHz	4.433618MHz	4.433618MHz	3.582056MHz	3.575611MHz
Video Bandwidth	5.0MHz	5.5MHz	6.0MHz	4.2MHz	4.2MHz
Sound Carrier	5.5MHz	6.0MHz	6.5MHz	4.5MHz	4.5MHz

The SECAM (Sequential Couleur Avec Memoire, or Sequential Color with Memory) standard was introduced in the early 1960s and implemented in France. SECAM uses the same bandwidth as PAL, but transmits the color information sequentially. SECAM runs on 625 lines per frame.

System	SECAM B,G,H	SECAM D,K,K1,L
Line/Field	625/50	625/50
Horizontal Frequency	15.625kHz	15.625kHz
Vertical Frequency	50Hz	50Hz
Video Bandwidth	5.0MHz	6.0MHz
Sound Carrier	5.5MHz	6.5MHz

Video Formats by TV System

Format	Scan Lines/Color
VHS	525/NTSC
	625/PAL
	625/SECAM
S-VHS	525/NTSC
	625/PAL
D-VHS	525/NTSC
DVC	525/NTSC
	625/PAL
Video 8	525/NTSC
	625/PAL
	625/SECAM
Hi 8	525/NTSC
	625/PAL
LaserDisc	525/NTSC
	625/PAL
DVD	525/NTSC
	625/NTSC

Analog Tape Formats
VHS (Video Home System)

This is the format that nearly all home VCRs today use. This format was introduced by JVC in 1976. The VHS format, however, is still very important in terms of distributing taped programs. The problem with the VHS format is that quality of the image on the tape is not really very good. This becomes a problem when you have what appear to be some great shots taken with a professional format machine and then duplicate them onto VHS.

S-VHS (Super VHS)

Super VHS is a marked improvement over VHS. The signals from the camera are handled differently, with color and brightness being split up, resulting in improved color rendition. The tape is similar in size to the VHS tape cassette. S-VHS tape cannot be played in a VHS machine. S-VHS is a common format for use on nonbroadcast video projects and is sometimes used for broadcast video in smaller stations. There are a number of good industrial level camcorders in the S-VHS format, both single piece and two piece for example, the Panasonic Supercam and the JVC VHS-C and S-VHS-C (Compact VHS and S-VHS). These are smaller cassettes than VHS and S-VHS that only hold 30 minutes (sometimes 40 minutes) of tape in regular play. They were created to allow for smaller camcorders. VHS-C tape can be played in regular VHS machines using an adapter. Most camcorders using VHS tape are actually VHS-C machines. There are few S-VHS-C camcorders currently available. A consumer format introduced in 1983, 8 mm uses a much smaller tape size than VHS. The tape is only 8 mm wide and .55 mm to .4 mm thick as compared to the 13 mm wide and .8 mm thick VHS tape. This means that a cassette holding up to 2 hours of tape at regular play is only 2.5 in. by 4 in. (6 cm by 9.5 cm). Compare that to the VHS cassette at 4 in. by 6 in. (10 cm by 16 cm). With miniaturization, however, comes problems. Eight millimeter tape is much more delicate and prone to defects than VHS tape. These defects often take the form of *dropouts,* horizontal streaks on the picture when played back. These defects are caused by physical defects on the tapes or dust. In terms of quality, 8 mm is roughly similar to VHS.

Hi8

Hi8 does for 8 mm what S-VHS does for VHS. There is a marked improvement in picture quality. There have been some good industrial level camcorders in Hi8 format (for example, the Sony EVW100 and the Toshiba TS200), but these have apparently been discontinued by their manufacturers in favor of the more recent digital formats. Used Hi8 industrial-level camcorders are still readily available, and there are many new consumer-level Hi8 camcorders still available (in the $1,000 to $2,000 range). The Canon L1 and L2 line (now discontinued) has been important for nature videographers. These camcorders were the only inexpensive Hi8 camcorders using interchangeable lenses.

3/4" U-Matic

This is an old format introduced in 1971, but it is still used by some videographers who have been using the format for a long time. It can produce good-quality video, and 3/4" decks are still commonly available in duplicating houses. However, there is little reason for somebody just starting into nature videography to get into this format given the technical advantages of some of the other more recent formats.

Betacam and BetacamSP

Betacam is a Sony product first introduced in 1982. It is currently geared for broadcast use, although there have been some less expensive models destined more for industrial use. Betacam, MII, and the digital formats discussed, use a different way of handling color information than the preceding formats. Basically, the color information from the picture is broken into three channels (one each for red, green, and blue information). Formats that handle color in this way are known as component formats in opposition to the composite formats discussed previously. Colors in particular come out looking much more vibrant and objects appear three-dimensional. Also remember that under certain conditions (for example, well lit close-ups), S-VHS and Hi8 shots may be hard to distinguish from Betacam shots. The superiority of Betacam shots comes partly from the technical aspects of the tape format but also in large part because of the use of superior optics and other camcorder and VTR components (and generally better operators!). The difference between Betacam and Betacam SP, introduced in 1986, is in the tape. Betacam SP uses a metal tape and is an improvement over Betacam. Betacam cassettes are large. Ninety-minute cassettes measure 5.5 in. by 10 in. (14 cm by 25 cm). Typically, Betacam field units (camcorders or dockable decks) handle only smaller cassettes with shorter lengths of tape (30 minutes and less). These smaller cassettes are 4 in. by 6 in. (10 cm by 16 cm) in size. Betacam SP is still the de facto standard for professional broadcast videotaping, partly because of the large number of units out in the professional videotape community.

MII

MII, introduced in 1986, is Panasonic's answer to Betacam SP. All MII tape is metal. The 90-minute cassette is 4 in. by 8 in. (11 cm by 19 cm) and is considerably smaller than the 90-minute Betacam SP cassette. However, the dockable decks take only a small 20-minute cassette (3.6 in. by 5 in., or 9 cm by 13 cm). Technically, MII is equal to or superior to Betacam SP, but Panasonic lost out to Sony in terms of public relations, customer support, and the promotion of its product. Panasonic MII field equipment includes several small dockable decks usable with a variety of camera heads and some excellent portable decks.

Digital Tape Formats

Unfortunately, there appears to be somewhat of a proliferation of digital tape formats. Often when neophyte videographers think of digital videotape, they are thinking of DV or DVC, the consumer digital videotape format introduced in 1996. In addition, there are related digital videotape formats using the same cassette size, such as DVCPRO, DVCPRO50, and DVCAM. Then there are other digital tape formats using larger tape such as Digital S, Betacam SX, DS, Digital Betacam, D1, D2, D3, D6, and DCT.

DV and DVC (digital videocassette)

This first consumer digital videotape format was introduced in 1996. The tape used for this format is quite small: 6.35 mm wide and 8.8 microns thick. A cassette with up to approximately 3.5 hours of playing time is only 3.5 in. by 5 in. (9 cm by 12 cm). Smaller cassettes with shorter playing times are also available. Like Betacam SP and MII it is a component format with separate channels for red, green, and blue. The data on the tape is compressed at a 5:1 ratio. This means that four fifths of the data in the original image is thrown away. The quality that can be obtained from this format is close to the quality once expected only in broadcast-quality systems.

DVCPRO

DVCPRO was introduced in 1995 primarily by Panasonic. It is similar in most respects to DV except that the tape speed is twice that of DV, resulting in reduced error rates. DV equipment cannot read DVCPRO tapes or record on DVCPRO tapes. However DVCPRO equipment can play back DV format tapes.

DVCAM

DVCAM was introduced in 1996 by Sony and can be considered as Sony's answer to Panasonic's DVCPRO. DVCAM and DVCPRO are not compatible. DVCAM is partly compatible with DV.

Standards conversion is the most complex, technically difficult and degrading of all of the techniques for building bridges between TV standards. It is also the most desirable since the material actually becomes a signal of the destination TV system, which can be recorded and reproduced by equipment of the destination TV system.

Conversion between TV systems with the same frame rate is usually reasonably effective. Conversion between TV systems with differing frame rates is extremely difficult. The units that perform these conversions are known as digital standards converters.

Telephone Standards

ISO 9000 Series

Founded in 1946, the International Organization for Standardization (ISO) is a federation of 92 member countries that promotes the development of international standards that facilitate world trade. The standards include interface standards, protocol standards, and quality standards. The United States representative to ISO is the American National Standards Institute (ANSI).

The series consists of five related standards, 9000 through 9004.
- ISO 9000 explains fundamental concepts and terms and is a guide to the use of the other standards in the ISO 9000 family.
- ISO 9001 provides quality system requirements in design, development, production, installation, and servicing.
- ISO 9002 provides quality system requirements in production, installation, and servicing.
- ISO 9003 provides quality requirements for product inspection and test.
- ISO 9004 provides guidance on designing and improving quality systems.

In addition, the following standards in the ISO 9000 family serve as guidance documents to support the ISO 9000 series.

CDPD, Digital Cellular, and PCS Networks

Data transmission over wireless networks has received a tremendous amount of attention in the last few years. This is because of the introduction of cellular digital packet data (CDPD), a network technology that provides for wireless transmission of packet data.

Cellular telephones carry voice messages via radio frequency channels rather than traditional telephone lines. It was only a matter of time before this technology would be used for data as well as voice transmission. CDPD is a wireless packet data network based on a specification developed in 1993. The CDPD Forum currently controls the CDPD specification, though it will soon be made into a Telecommunications Industry Association (TIA) standard. In addition to existing wireless data networks, some cellular companies supply a wireless data communication service using one of two approaches. The first approach uses the existing Advanced Mobile Phone Service (AMPS) cellular network and employs analog communications methodologies. The second approach uses digital cellular technology, which is currently being deployed and uses a digital communications methodology to transmit data.

As a result of new digital cellular technology development, two principal digital cellular standards have emerged in the United States. One is called IS-136 Time Division Multiple

Access (TDMA) and the other is called IS-95 Code Division Multiple Access (CDMA). In Europe and a number of other countries, the digital cellular standard is the Global Standard for Mobile Communications (GSM). GSM is also being deployed in some parts of the United States. These digital technologies are being deployed in existing cellular frequencies in the 800MHz band as well as in newly available frequencies in the 1.9GHz band.

Cellular services in the 1.9GHz band are commonly referred to as personal communications services or PCS. The current cellular phone system in the United States is known as AMPS (advanced mobile phone service). AMPS use 50MHz of spectrum in the 800MHz band. The spectrum allocated to AMPS is shared by two cellular carriers in each area or region (that is, geographic market).

Digital Cellular System Standards

The need for digital cellular systems arose as a direct result of the growing popularity of mobile voice services. Digital cellular technology involves digitizing a voice signal and transmitting it over the air as a serial bit stream. Digital cellular is more efficient than analog because it allows multiple transmissions to be carried simultaneously over a single radio channel. Two such techniques, as mentioned above, are TDMA and CDMA.

In the United States, the dominant TDMA standard is IS-136 TDMA and the dominant CDMA standard is IS-95 CDMA. IS-136 TDMA defines how a single 30kHz cellular channel is broken down into smaller increments that can be shared among one or more users.

IS-95 CDMA defines how a single channel can be allocated to support more than one user simultaneously. All mobile users transmit over the same frequency, but each mobile user's signal is combined with a different pseudo-random signal that makes the signal appear to be low-level noise. The original signal can be extracted only by knowing the code.

Global System for Mobile Communications, or GSM, is a digital cellular system standard that has been deployed in much of Europe and a number of other countries. Some PCS carriers are also deploying GSM in the United States. Like IS-136 TDMA, GSM uses time division multiple access, although it is incompatible with IS-136 TDMA.

A CDPD network does not stand alone; it is designed to operate as an extension of existing Transmission Control Protocol/Internet Protocol (TCP/IP) data communication networks.

Most customers connect their corporate networks to CDPD through public data networks. The CDPD network also has a connection to the Internet, providing another possible path between a CDPD-capable mobile device and a corporate network. Mobiles can also connect to servers and services hosted on the Internet using standard Internet applications and protocols, such as HTTP for Web browsing, POP for mail access, FTP for file transfer, and Telnet for terminal sessions.

TCP/IP has emerged in recent years as the wide area networking protocol of choice. By supporting TCP/IP, CDPD allows developers to use existing network applications and tools when designing for the wireless environment. TCP/IP, however, is not unique to CDPD. TCP/IP applications can also operate over circuit-switched analog cellular connections and will be able to operate over future digital PCS connections as well. Given this broad support for TCP/IP, application developers who develop efficient and optimized wireless applications using TCP/IP will be rewarded by multiple wireless transport opportunities.

Industry-standard protocols SLIP (Serial Line Internet Protocol) and PPP (Point-to-Point Protocol) are typically used between the mobile computer and the wireless modem. A number of companies are selling wireless modems for CDPD.

CDPD provides an optimal environment for application development. A large number of TCP/IP-based (and UDP-based) applications that can be used immediately over CDPD exist today. Additionally, development environments and tool sets applicable to TCP/IP also readily support CDPD. For existing applications, some optimization is usually desirable because of the nature of the wireless connection. Nearly all of the tools developed to facilitate TCP/IP application development can be used with CDPD.

As with data transmissions using analog cellular, circuit data over TDMA digital cellular is best suited to applications for which setup time is not an issue and the amount of data exchanged is large. Large file transfers, bulk e-mail, batch operations, and interactive sessions are examples of applications well suited for circuit data over TDMA. TDMA digital PCS systems will also support reliable fax communications. Eventually CDPD itself will operate over TDMA networks. The applications best suited for packet data service will be the same ones well suited for CDPD today. Migrating an application from CDPD today to the TDMA version in the future will be as simple as changing the wireless modem.

Circuit data services for TDMA are defined in TIA standard IS-135. A mobile computer connects to a data-capable digital telephone using a serial cable. The telephone implements the protocols for communicating data over the radio link.

Using the International Standards Organization (ISO) Open Systems Interconnect (OSI) model as a point of comparison, data transmission over the TDMA uses the same industry standard as voice calls (IS-136), but runs a different Link Layer protocol (IS-130). The Link Layer provides services such as data encryption, data compression, and flow control. TDMA data services can support data at 4800bps and 9600bps as well as higher theoretical rates.

The data specifications for TDMA, IS-130, and IS-135 are released standards. Implementation by cellular companies will require software upgrades to TDMA base stations and additional equipment at mobile switching centers. Cellular companies have not disclosed any deployment schedules for data services. But as an increasing number of cellular subscribers use digital service, there will be ample reason to make data service available. The packet data specification for TDMA, which draws on CDPD technology, is currently in development.

TAPI

Your computer network and your phone network were not designed to work together. You can link the two systems at the application level, but first you need a common interface with which to build the applications. The two most significant of these interfaces are Telephony API (TAPI) and Telephony Server API (TSAPI). Both are independent of the method of connection—direct serial link, add-in board, voice server, or switch-to-host link—between computer and phone system.

They attain that independence by abstracting the hardware layer, thus sidestepping the need to write code specific to each proprietary switch (and there are many) while taking advantage of each system's unique capabilities. This pleases developers, but it also allows customers to keep their existing equipment. And both provide a means for extending the specification. Beyond these points, however, each takes a different approach.

Microsoft and Intel were the primary developers of the originally client-based TAPI. TAPI 2.0, however, is built into both the Windows NT Server 4.0 and the Windows NT Workstation 4.0, which allows the OS to function as either a telephony client or server. (Windows 95 currently has built-in support for TAPI 1.4 applications, which are compatible with TAPI 2.0.)

In practice, TAPI 2.0 is focused on the desktop—a PC and a phone. That is, TAPI assumes the desktop to be one end point of each call. It preserves the ability to do third-party call control (calling from one desktop on behalf of another). The *specification allows* for several telephony applications to run simultaneously—over either single or multiple phone lines—on a client or server PC. It provides a means to distinguish different media streams (data, voice, fax) and route calls to the appropriate application or device. Incoming faxes, for example, go to the fax application or machine.

Microsoft has announced several planned enhancements for TAPI 2.0. They include a remote-service provider, intended to speed development of client/server telephony applications; remote administrative tools to aid with client/server configuration issues and reports; and Windows Telephony Service extensions for client access. (The company expects these features to appear in the next beta version of Memphis. At about the same time, Windows 95 will gain TAPI 2.0 support.) TAPI is closed: Microsoft controls it, which makes developers of telephony products nervous. Microsoft claims that since many other companies (more than 40) have contributed to the TAPI specification, it is effectively industry-defined and, therefore, open. However, while dependent organizations define and approve other industry standards, Microsoft remains the final arbiter of what TAPI is.

TSAPI

Server-based TSAPI, developed by Novell and AT&T, is designed to integrate PBX or Centrex phone systems with NetWare networks. The only physical link in the system is between the NetWare file server and the phone network. Applications built with TSAPI have a logical link between the PC and the desktop phone. You can control calls through the applications from either end of the connection or hand off that control to a third party. A server telephony model also eliminates the need for additional hardware to connect desktop PC to phone. This can save a lot of money in a large organization, but there is a trade-off. Because there's no physical connection between the PC and the phone, TSAPI applications cannot identify different media streams as TAPI can. Thus, with TSAPI, you cannot automatically route a fax to a fax application, for example.

Internet Transfer Protocols

One of the most important technical issues necessary for the Internet is TCP/IP, Transmission Control Protocol/Internet Protocol. TCP/IP actually refers to a collection of protocols used for data transfer and is in most UNIX networks. TCP/IP was developed in 1973, but was published as a standard in 1983, as the standard protocol for the ARPAnet wide area network, which was the forerunner of the Internet. It was used for academic networks.

TCP/IP is an open standard that will run a wide range of hardware, including Ethernet, Token Ring, and X.25 on varying computer platforms, such as UNIX, Windows, PDA, Macintosh, and mainframe. It contains a standard method of addressing unique units on a vast network and can route data via a particular route to reduce traffic.

The TCP/IP protocol has five layers as shown in Table E-1.

As a data packet passes through the application layers, each layer adds header and footer information. Once the complete packet is transmitted to the next node, it is passed up the layers with the information headers stripped off one at a time. Finally the packet arrives at the application layer of the destination.

The packets that are passed over the network are called *datagrams*. Each datagram contains a header of relevant information necessary to deliver the datagram correctly. It includes the source and the destination port numbers between computers. There is also a sequence number that allows the destination computer to reconstruct the datagrams in the correct sequence.

Transmission Control Protocol HTTP (Hypertext Transfer Protocol) uses TCP as the protocol for reliable document transfer. If packets are delayed or damaged, TCP will effectively stop traffic until either the original packets or backup packets arrive. Hence it's unsuitable for video and audio.

TCP imposes its own flow control and windowing schemes on the data stream, effectively destroying temporal relations between video frames and audio packets. Reliable message

Table E-1   TCP/IP Layers

Remote File Service		Server Message Block	Network File System	
SMTP		FTP	TELNET	SNMP
Transmission Control Protocol			User Datagram Protocol	
Internet Control Messaging Protocol		Internet Protocol	Address Resolution Protocol	
Media Access				
Transmission Media				

delivery is unnecessary for video and audio—losses are tolerable and TCP retransmission causes further jitter and skew.

UDP (User Datagram Protocol) is the alternative to TCP. RealPlayer, StreamWorks, and VDOLive use this approach. (RealPlayer gives you a choice of UDP or TCP, but the former is preferred.) UDP forsakes TCP's error correction and allows packets to drop out if they are late or damaged. When this happens, you will hear or see a dropout, but the stream will continue. Despite the prospect of dropouts, this approach is arguably better for continuous media delivery. If broadcasting live events, everyone will get the same information simultaneously. One disadvantage to the UDP approach is that many network firewalls block UDP information. While Progressive Networks, Xing, and VDOnet offer work-arounds for client sites (revert to TCP), some users simply may not be able to access UDP files.

RTP, or RealTime Transport Protocol, is the Internet-standard protocol (RFC 1889, 1890) for the transport of real-time data, including audio and video. RTP consists of a data and a control part called *RTCP*. The data part of RTP is a thin protocol providing support for applications with real-time properties such as continuous media (for example, audio and video), including timing reconstruction, loss detection, security, and content identification. RTCP provides support for real-time conferencing of groups of any size within an intranet. This support includes source identification and support for gateways like audio and video bridges as well as multicast-to-unicast translators. It offers quality-of-service feedback from receivers to the multicast group as well as support for the synchronization of different media streams. None of the commercial streaming products uses RTP (Real-Time Transport Protocol), a relatively new standard designed to run over UDP. Initially designed for video at T1 or higher bandwidths, it promises more efficient multimedia streaming than UDP. Streaming vendors are expected to adopt RTP, which is used by the MBone.

In October 1996, Progressive Networks and Netscape Communications Corporation announced that 40 companies proposed an open standard for delivery of real-time media over the Internet. Real Time Streaming Protocol is a communications protocol for control and delivery of real-time media. It defines the connection between streaming media client and server software, and provides a standard way for clients and servers from multiple vendors to stream multimedia content. The first draft of the protocol specification, RTSP 1.0, was submitted to the Internet Engineering Task Force (IETF) on October 9, 1996. RTSP is built on top of Internet standard protocols, including UDP, TCP/IP, RTP, RTCP, SCP, and IP Multicast. Netscape's Media Server and Media Player products use RTSP to stream audio over the Internet.

Vosaic uses VDP, which is an augmented RTP, that is, RTP with demand resend. VDP improves the reliability of the data stream by creating two channels between the client and server. One is a control channel the two machines use to coordinate what information is being sent across the network, and the other channel is for the streaming data. When configured in Java, this protocol, like HTTP, is invisible to the network and can stream through firewalls.

RSVP is an Internet Engineering Task Force (IETF) proposed standard for requesting defined Quality-of-Service levels over IP networks, such as the Internet. The protocol was designed to allow the assignment of priorities to streaming applications, such as audio and video, which generate continuous traffic that requires predictable delivery.

RSVP works by permitting an application transmitting data over a routed network to request and receive a given level of bandwidth. Two classes of reservation are defined: a controlled load reservation provides service approximating "best effort" service under unloaded conditions; a guaranteed service reservation provides service that guarantees both bandwidth and delay.

Compression
Standards

Streaming video across networks faces a diversity in technological infrastructure, such as networks, protocols, and compression standards supported. All the commercial video products are optimized for low bandwidth modem or ISDN connections and are not designed to scale to higher bandwidth networks. The commercial products have their own proprietary standards or have embraced the currently accepted standards (for example, MPEG).

This appendix presents an introduction to the algorithms and architectures that form the underpinnings of the image and video compressions standards, including JPEG (compression of still-images), H.261 and H.263 (video teleconferencing), and MPEG-1 and MPEG-2 (video storage and broadcasting). The next generation of audiovisual coding standards, such as MPEG-4 and MPEG-7, are also briefly described.

The list below outlines the main characteristics of codec standards:

- *H.261.* ITU (International Telecom Union) video coding standard from 1990
- *H.263.* Provisional videoconferencing ITU draft 1996
- *H.310.* Broadband audiovisual communication systems and terminals
- *H.320.* Narrowband visual telephone systems and terminal equipment
- *H.321.* Adaptation of H.320 visual telephone terminals to B-ISDN environments
- *H.322.* Visual telephone systems and terminal equipment for local area networks that provide a guaranteed Quality of Service
- *H.323.* Visual telephone systems and equipment for local area networks that provide a nonguaranteed Quality of Service
- *H.324.* Terminal for low bit rate multimedia communication
- *H.331.* Broadcasting-type audiovisual multipoint systems and terminal equipment
- *MPEG-1.* Targets CD-ROM at 1.5Mbps and includes DirectShow and QuickTime
- *MPEG-2.* For all-digital broadcast TV and DVD-based video at 4Mbps to 9Mbps.
- *MPEG-3.* HDTV 1920Hz × 1080Hz × 30Hz at 20Mbps to 40Mbps. An abandoned standard
- *MPEG-4.* Targets video phone, video mail, remote sensing, and video games
- *MPEG-6.* Wireless transmission
- *MPEG-7.* Content information standard for information searches
- *MPEG-8.* Allows a four-dimensional description of objects

But broadband standards such as MPEG-1 and MPEG-2, which are useful for many types of broadcast and CD-ROM applications, are currently unsuitable for the Internet. Although MPEG-2 has had scalability enhancements, these will not be exploitable until the availability of reasonably priced hardware encoders and decoders. Codecs designed for the Internet require greater bandwidth scalability, lower computational complexity, greater resilience to network losses, and lower encode/decode latency for interactive applications.

DCT-based video delivery, except for MPEG-2, possesses no inherent scalability. To achieve adaptivity, various operations can be applied to the compressed data stream to reduce its bit rate. Among these operations is transcoding, the conversion of one compression standard to another. The DCT-based approach is compatible with current compression standards. Furthermore, it allows reuse of existing audio and video archives without explicitly recoding.

Non-DCT–based compression techniques, for example, layered, subband, and wavelet, are scalable.

The most important video codec standards for streaming video include H.261, H.263, MJPEG, MPEG-1, MPEG-2, and MPEG-4. Compared to video codecs for CD-ROM or TV broadcast, codecs designed for the Internet require greater scalability, lower computational complexity, greater resiliency to network losses, and lower encode/decode latency for videoconferencing. In addition, the codecs must be tightly linked to network delivery software to achieve the highest possible frame rates and picture quality.

H.261 was targeted at teleconferencing applications and is intended for carrying video over ISDN. The actual encoding algorithm is similar to that of MPEG. H.261 needs substantially less CPU power for real-time encoding than MPEG. The algorithm includes a mechanism that optimizes bandwidth usage by trading picture quality against motion, so that a quickly changing picture will have a lower quality than a relatively static picture. H.261 used in this way is thus a constant-bitrate encoding rather than a constant-quality, variable-bitrate encoding.

H.263 is a draft ITU-T standard designed for low bitrate communication. It is expected that the standard will be used for a wide range of bitrates, not just low bitrate applications. H.263 will replace H.261 in many applications. The coding algorithm of H.263 is similar to that used by H.261, however, with some improvements and changes to improve performance and error recovery.

MJPEG for video is a vendor supplied JPEG to individual frames of a video sequence. JPEG is designed for compressing either full-color or gray-scale images of natural, real-world scenes. It works well on photographs, naturalistic artwork, and similar material; not so well on lettering, simple cartoons, or line drawings. JPEG is a lossy compression algorithm that uses DCT-based encoding. JPEG can typically achieve 10:1 to 20:1 compression without visible loss; 30:1 to 50:1 compression is possible with small to moderate defects, while for very-low-quality purposes such as previews or archive indexes, 100:1 compression is quite feasible. Nonlinear video editors are typically used in broadcast TV, commercial postproduction, and high-end corporate media departments. Low bitrate MPEG-1 quality is unacceptable to these customers, and it is difficult to edit video sequences that use interframe compression. Consequently, nonlinear editors will continue to use motion JPEG with low compression factors (for example, 6:1 to 10:1).

MPEG-1, -2, and -4 are currently accepted, and developing standards, for the bandwidth efficient transmission of video and audio. The MPEG-1 codec targets a bandwidth of 1Mbps to 1.5Mbps offering VHS quality video at CIF (352 × 288) resolution and 30fps. MPEG-1 requires expensive hardware for real-time encoding. While decoding can be done in software, most implementations consume a large fraction of a high-end processor. MPEG-1 does not offer resolution scalability, and the video quality is highly susceptible to packet losses, due to the dependencies present in the P (predicted) and B (bidirectionally predicted) frames. The B-frames also introduce latency in the encode process, since encoding frame N needs access to frame N + k, making it less suitable for videoconferencing.

MPEG-2 extends MPEG-1 by including support for higher-resolution video and increased audio capabilities. The targeted bitrate for MPEG-2 is 4Mbps to 15Mbps, providing broadcast quality full-screen video. The MPEG-2 draft standard does cater for scalability. Three (3) types of scalability (signal-to-noise ratio [SNR], spatial and temporal, and one extension [that can be used to implement scalability] data partitioning), have been defined. Compared with MPEG-1, it requires even more expensive hardware to encode and decode. It is also prone to poor video quality in the presence of losses, for the same reasons as MPEG-1. Both MPEG-1 and MPEG-2 are well suited to the purposes for which they were developed. For example, MPEG-1 works very well for playback from CD-ROM, and MPEG-2 is great for high-quality archiving applications and for TV broadcast applications. In the case of satellite broadcasts, MPEG-2 allows > 5 digital channels to be encoded using the same bandwidth as used by a single analog channel today, without sacrificing video quality. Given this major advantage, the large encoding costs are really not a factor. However, for existing computer and Internet infrastructures, MPEG-based solutions are too expensive and require too much bandwidth; they were not designed with the Internet in mind.

The intention of MPEG-4 is to provide a compression scheme suitable for videoconferencing, that is, data rates less than 64Kbps. MPEG-4 is based on the segmentation of audiovisual scenes into AVOs, or audiovisual objects, which can be multiplexed for transmission over heterogeneous networks.

XML and SMIL Standards

◖XML

Computers, of course, are not that smart. They need to be told exactly what and how to do things. The eXtensible Markup Language (XML) is a new language designed to make information self-describing. This simple-sounding change in how computers communicate has the potential to extend the Internet beyond information delivery to many other kinds of activities. XML was completed in early 1998 by the World Wide Web Consortium (W3C), and the standard has spread like wildfire through science and into industries.

The enthusiastic response is fueled by a hope that XML will solve some of the Web's biggest problems: speed and searching.

Both problems arise in large part from the nature of the Web's main language, HTML (Hypertext Markup Language). Although HTML is the most successful electronic-publishing language, it is superficial. It describes how a Web browser should arrange text, images, and push buttons on a page. People and companies want Web sites that take orders, transmit medical records, even run factories and scientific instruments from half a world away. HTML was never designed for such tasks.

So although your doctor may be able to pull up your drug reaction history on his Web browser, he cannot then e-mail it to a specialist and expect her to be able to paste the records directly into her hospital's database. Her computer would not know what to make of the information.

The angle-bracketed labels are called *tags*. HTML has no tag for a drug reaction, which highlights another of its limitations: it is inflexible. Adding a new tag involves a bureaucratic process that can take so long that few attempt it. And yet every application, not just the interchange of medical records, needs its own tags.

The solution, in theory, is very simple: use tags that say what the information is. For example, label the parts of an order for a shirt not as boldface, paragraph, row, and column—what HTML offers—but as price, size, quantity, and color. A program can then recognize this document as a customer order and do whatever it needs to do: display it one way or display it a different way or put it through a bookkeeping system or make a new shirt show up on your doorstep tomorrow.

The Standard Generalized Markup Language, or SGML, describes other languages and has proved useful in many large publishing applications. Indeed, HTML was defined using SGML. The only problem with SGML is that it is too complex for Web browsers.

XML was created by removing frills from SGML to arrive at a more streamlined, digestible metalanguage. XML consists of rules that anyone can follow to create a markup language from scratch. The rules ensure that a single compact program, often called a *parser*, can process all these new languages.

Just as HTML created a way for every computer user to read Internet documents, XML markup makes sense to humans because it consists of nothing more than ordinary text.

The unifying power of XML arises from a few well-chosen rules. One is that tags almost always come in pairs. Like parentheses, they surround the text to which they apply. And like quotation marks, tag pairs can be nested inside one another to multiple levels.

The nesting rule automatically forces a certain simplicity on every XML document, which takes on the structure known in computer science as a *tree*. Another source of XML's unifying strength is its reliance on a new standard called *Unicode,* a character-encoding system that supports intermingling of text in all the world's major languages.

In HTML, a document is generally in one particular language, whether that be English or Japanese. XML enables exchange of information not only between different computer systems but also across national and cultural boundaries. The structural and semantic information that can be added with XML allows these devices to do a great deal of processing on the spot. That not only will take a big load off Web servers but also should reduce network traffic dramatically.

The latest versions of several Web browsers can read an XML document, fetch the appropriate stylesheet, and use it to sort and format the information on the screen. The reader might never know that he is looking at XML rather than HTML—except that XML-based sites run faster and are easier to use.

SMIL

When your multimedia presentation contains multiple clips, such as a slide show and a video played together, you can use Synchronized Multimedia Integration Language (SMIL) to coordinate the parts. Pronounced "smile," SMIL uses a simple but powerful markup language for specifying how and when clips play. SMIL is a special application of XML.

You can create a SMIL file (extension `.smil`) with any text editor or word processor that can save output as plain text. If you are familiar with HTML markup, you will pick up SMIL quickly. In its simplest form, a SMIL file lists multiple media clips played in sequence.

Header Tags

```
<meta.../>
```

The header region's `<meta.../>` tags provide presentation information. A `<meta.../>` tag can also set a base URL for source clips in the SMIL file.

```
<meta.../> Tag Attributes
<layout>...</layout>
```

The `<layout>` and `</layout>` tags define the layout of visual clips, such as video and animation. Within the tags, you define a root-layout region and separate regions for the clips. The layout must be defined with the SMIL header.

```
<root-layout.../>
```

Within `<layout>...</layout>`, `<root-layout>` sets the overall size of the playback area. Clips do not play in the root-layout area.

```
<root-layout.../> Tag Attributes
```

Example

```
<layout>
  <root-layout background-color="maroon" width="250" height="230"/>
  <region .../>
  <region .../>
</layout>
        <region.../>
```

Within `<layout>...</layout>`, `<region>` tags define the size and placement (relative to root-layout) of each region used to play clips.

```
<region.../> Tag Attributes
```

Example

```
<layout>
  <root-layout .../>
  <region id="video" top="5" left="5" width="240" height="180"
    background-color="blue" fit="fill" z-index="3"/>
  <region .../>
</layout>
```

Clip Source Tags

To define locations and timing attributes for clips within a presentation, use a source tag with one of the following clip-type identifiers:

```
<animation .../>

<audio .../>

<image .../>

<ref .../>

<text .../>

<textstream .../>

<video .../>
```

Although a clip-type identifier must start a source tag, the identifier does not affect playback. All clip source tags can use `<ref.../>`, for example.

Clip Source Tag Attributes

Examples

```
<video src="rtsp://realserver.company.com/media/video2.rm" region="video"
begin="40s" clip-begin="5100ms"clip-end="4.5min" fill="freeze"/>

<audio src="rtsp://realserver.company.com/media/music.rm"
dur="10.5s" repeat="5"/>
```

Image Source Tag Options

For a still image, you can include the following options in the image source tag.

A question mark operator ("?") separates image options from the image URL in the clip source tag. Additional options preceded by ampersands ("&") can follow in this format:

```
<image src= "URL?option=value&option=value"/>
```

Note: Image options and values are not in quotation marks because they are part of the quoted src value.

Examples

```
<image src="ad1.gif?bitrate=1000&bgcolor=blue"/>

<image src="ad.gif?url=http://www.company.com&target=_browser" .../>

<image src="stop.gif?url=command:stop()&target=_player" .../>

<image src="seek.gif?url=command:seek(1:35.4)&target=_player" .../>
```

◐ Summary of Graphics Tags

Attribute	Definition	Example
aspect	Default for maintaining aspect ratio of images	aspect='false'
author	Name of author	author='John Smith'
background-color	Initial background color	background-color='#FE3434'
bitrate	Peak bandwidth in bits per second	bitrate='64000'
copyright	Copyright notice	copyright='your company'
duration	Duration of RealPix presentation	duration='50'
height	Height of display window in pixels	height='256'
maxfps	Maximum frames per second for transition effects (Include as last attribute)	maxfps='5'
preroll	Time for which initial data should be buffered	preroll='20'
timeformat	Format for time attributes: dd:hh:mm:ss.xyz or milliseconds	timeformat='dd:hh:mm:ss.xyz'
title	Name of presentation	title='How To'
url	Hyperlink URL for presentation images	url='http://www.video-software.com'
width	Width of display window in pixels	width='256'

Group Tags

```
<par>...</par>
```

The <par> and </par> tags make enclosed clips play in parallel. No attributes are required for a <par> tag.

```
<par> Tag Attributes
```

Examples

```
<par>
 <video src="videos/newsong.rm"/>
 <textstream src="lyrics/newsong.rt"/>
</par>
```

```
   <par endsync="id(text)" repeat="2" begin="4s">
 <video src="videos/newsong.rm"/>
 <textstream id="text" src="lyrics/newsong.rt"/>
</par>
```

```
   <seq>...</seq>
```

The <seq> and </seq> tags group clips that play in sequence. No attributes are required for a <seq> tag.

    <seq> Tag Attributes

Example

```
<seq repeat="3">
 <audio src="rtsp://realserver.company.com/one.rm"/>
 <audio src="rtsp://realserver.company.com/two.rm"/>
</seq>
```

        <switch>...</switch>

The <switch> and </switch> tags contain clips or groups of clips that RealPlayer chooses between, based on its available bandwidth or language preference. Clips or groups that RealPlayer evaluates must include a system-bitrate or system-language attribute.

    <switch> Tag Attributes

Example

```
<switch>
 <audio src="french/seattle.rm" system-language="fr"/>
 <audio src="german/seattle.rm" system-language="de"/>
 <audio src="english/seattle.rm"/>
</switch>
```

Hyperlink Tags

    <a>...</a>

The <a>...</a> tags work like HTML hyperlink tags to connect a media source clip to another clip. But whereas you enclose text between <a> and </a> in HTML, you enclose a media source tag between <a> and </a> in SMIL.

    Tag Attributes

Example

```
<a href="http://www.company.com/index.htm" show="new">
 <video src="video.rm" region="videoregion"/>
</a>
```

An <anchor> tag can define a hot spot hyperlink that can be temporal as well as spatial. It fits within a media source tag.

```
<video ...>
 <anchor .../>
</video>
```

Note that here the <video> source tag does not end with a forward slash as it normally does. Instead, a </video> tag follows it and the <anchor.../> tag.

```
<anchor.../> Tag Attributes
```

Writing Complex SMIL Switch Statements

The SMIL <switch> tag is a powerful feature that lets you specify options that each RealPlayer can choose between, based on its preference settings and available bandwidth. *"Switching Between Alternate Choices"* explains the basics of using the <switch> tag. The following sections give tips on writing complex <switch> statements.

Switching with SureStream Clips

With RealAudio or RealVideo clips encoded for multiple bit rates with SureStream technology, you may or may not need to use the <switch> tag. When the presentation consists solely of a SureStream clip, simply link to that clip within the SMIL file. The clip then streams at the rate appropriate for RealPlayer's connection speed. You do not need to specify bandwidth choices with a <switch> group.

Use the <switch> tag when combining a SureStream clip with other clips encoded for single bandwidths. The SureStream clip is always used, but the <switch> group gives RealPlayer options for other clips. The following example illustrates a RealAudio SureStream clip and a choice between two RealPix presentations built for different bandwidths:

```
<par>
 <audio src="audio/newsong2.rm"/>
 <switch>
  <ref src="image/slideshow1.rp" system-bitrate="47000"/>
  <ref src="image/slideshow2.rp" system-bitrate="20000"/>
 </switch>
</par>
```

Switching with Multiple Test Attributes

You can use multiple <switch> test attributes to have RealPlayer choose clips based on both bandwidth and language. There are two ways to do this. In this first example, each audio clip choice has two test attributes, one for language and one for bandwidth. Both attributes must be viable for RealPlayer to choose the clip.

```
<switch>
 <!-- French language choices -->
 <audio src="sound/audio_fr2.rm" system-language="fr"
system-bitrate="47000"/>
 <audio src="sound/audio_fr1.rm" system-language="fr"
system-bitrate="20000"/>
 <!-- English language choices (default) -->
 <audio src="sound/audio_en2.rm" system-bitrate="47000"/>
 <audio src="sound/audio_en1.rm" system-bitrate="20000"/>
</switch>
```

Because RealPlayer evaluates the `<switch>` choices from top to bottom, selecting the first viable option, the last two choices do not have `system-language` options. This lets all RealPlayers other than those with French as their language preference choose between the two English-language clips.

Streaming a RealAudio or RealVideo Clip

It's simple to add a RealAudio or RealVideo clip to your Web page. Following the instructions below, you can stream the clip from RealServer G2 or download it from a Web server. The clip plays back in RealPlayer.

To create the clip: Prepare your audio or video source file for encoding. This can include normalizing the audio source file or setting the video's window size.

Use a RealNetworks encoding tool to encode the RealAudio or RealVideo clip from your audio or video source file. RealVideo and RealAudio clips use the file extension `.rm`.

To stream the clip from RealServer G2 using Ramgen: Transfer the clip to the RealServer G2 directory prepared by the RealServer administrator.

Link your Web page to the clip with an HTML hyperlink that specifies the RealServer address, the `ramgen` parameter, and the HTTP protocol. You can get this information from the RealServer administrator. In your HTML source file, the link will look like this example:

```
<a href="http://realserver.company.com:8080/ramgen/content/myclip.rm">
Click here</a> to see my RealVideo presentation.
```

In your Web browser, click the link to verify that it works. RealPlayer will launch as a helper application and, after a few seconds of buffering, will play the streaming clip.

To play the clip back from a Web server: With any text editor, open a new file and enter the URL your clip will have on the Web server. For example:

http://www.company.com/media/myclip.rm

Save this file as plain text with the file extension `.ram`. This is your Ram file.

Transfer the media clip and the Ram file to the appropriate directory on the Web server.

Link your Web page to the Ram file (not the media clip) with a standard HTML hyperlink like this:

```
<a href="http://www.company.com/media/myclip.ram">
Click here</a> to see my RealVideo presentation.
```

In your Web browser, click the link to verify that it works. RealPlayer will launch as a helper application and, after a few seconds of buffering, will play the clip.

Embedding a RealVideo Clip in a Web Page

Using RealPlayer's Netscape plug-in, you can embed a RealVideo clip directly in your Web page. The following example assumes that the video is 176 pixels wide by 132 pixels high. It places the video window and the full RealPlayer control panel in your Web page.

To embed the clip in your Web page: In your Web page, add the `<EMBED>` tag with the RealVideo URL, window size, and `ImageWindow` control. The following example assumes RealServer G2 will stream the presentation:

```
<EMBED WIDTH=176 HEIGHT=132
SRC="http://realserver.company.com:8080/
ramgen/content/myclip.rm?embed"
CONTROLS=ImageWindow CONSOLE=one>
```

If you intend to play the clip back from a Web server, use an HTTP URL and link to a Ram file with the extension `.rpm` (see below) as in the following example:

```
<EMBED WIDTH=176 HEIGHT=132
SRC="http://www.company.com/media/myclip.rpm"
CONTROLS=ImageWindow CONSOLE=one>
```

You can then add RealPlayer controls through additional `<EMBED>` tags that all use the same URL for the SRC parameter. The following example embeds the full RealPlayer control panel in the Web page, linking it to the image window through the same console. It assumes RealServer will stream the presentation:

```
<EMBED WIDTH=375 HEIGHT=100
SRC="http://realserver.company.com:8080/
ramgen/content/myclip.rm?embed" CONTROLS=All CONSOLE=one>
```

Use an <EMBED> tag like the following when playing the clip back from a Web server:

```
<EMBED WIDTH=375 HEIGHT=100 SRC="http://www.company.com/media/myclip.rpm"
CONTROLS=All CONSOLE=one>
```

Transfer the clip to the appropriate RealServer G2 or Web server directory. When streaming from G2, you are ready to test the clip because the Web page already contains the link to the RealVideo clip.

To create the Ram file when playing the clip back from a Web server: With any text editor, open a new file and enter the URL your clip will have on the Web server, as in the following example:

http://www.company.com/media/myclip.rm

Save this file as plain text with the file extension .rpm. This is your Ram file. Transfer the Ram file to the appropriate directory on the Web server. In your Web browser, click the link to verify that it works.

URL Reference

As explained throughout this book, URLs to files and clips vary depending on what kind of file or clip you link to and what type of file contains the link.

Bandwidth Preservation

RealText makes a great addition to any SMIL presentation because it takes up so little bandwidth. Streaming technology and compression are advancing, but it's still tough to shove a multimedia presentation down a 33.6Kbps modem—especially since most of those modems only throughput at about 2.2Kbps, despite manufacturers' claims.

You can encode a person's voice at about 1Kbps, and if you are running a slide show with 10KB JPEGs, this means you can download a new graphic every 10 seconds. This leaves you about .2Kbps—more than enough to stream some RealText on the side.

Illustrating Other Page Elements

RealText can be used to illustrate or comment on what's happening in the other media types. For instance, you could run biographical information in one window while video interview streams in another.

Types of Movement

RealText allows a number of familiar, built-in mechanisms for moving type, such as horizontal ticker tape, vertical scrolling news, and TelePrompTer. There is also a generic window type for placing static, unmoving text on the screen.

Generic

Generic text is placed on the screen at a certain position and can appear or disappear over time. You define the height and width of the window as attributes, just as you would for an image.

RealPix is RealNetworks' new format for streaming graphics for RealPlayer G2. RealPix is not a radical departure from standard Web formats. In fact, it is a generic name for graphics optimized for streamed delivery. The main advance is the control over the graphic that the SMIL language gives you in creating a true multimedia presentation. Using SMIL in the G2 player, graphics can transition into one another smoothly and be made to appear and disappear during the presentation.

RealPix is the general classification for graphics supported by RealPlayer. RealPlayer G2 supports GIF, JPEG (slightly modified), and BMP files natively. GIF files can be used in their original format. Animated GIFs are not supported. JPEG files need to be slightly modified in order to be optimized for streaming. This is done using a program called *JPEGTRAN*. JPEGTRAN is a DOS command-line program that only converts one file at a time using the following syntax:

```
jpegtran -restart 1B -outfile output.jpg input.jpg
```

In the example above, output.jpg is the name of the file after it has been converted, and input.jpg is the name before being converted. You cannot overwrite the file with the same name. JPEGTRAN makes changes in the way that a JPEG image displays lost information. If data is lost during streaming, it diffuses it throughout the image so that the empty pixels of lost data are evenly distributed and hard to notice. If this wasn't done and data was lost, you would end up with a black line in the image where data is missing.

RealNetworks provides a tool called the *RealPix Bandwidth Calculator* that helps you calculate how many images can be streamed in a certain time period and also does batch conversion of images using JPEGTRAN.

Wireless Standards

hile a wireless LAN could exist as a sole general-purpose LAN, a wireless LAN is more often seen as an extension to an existing LAN as a means to support mobile users. A wireless LAN is not a metropolitan area network or a wide area network. Unlike those two technologies, wireless LANs have short ranges on the order of meters as opposed to miles.

Standardization of wireless LAN signaling and protocols is 802.11, formed by the Institute of Electrical and Electronics Engineers (IEEE). The IEEE 802.11 standard was finalized in June 1997. The standard defines three different physical implementations:

> ▸ Direct sequence spread spectrum (DSSS) radio
> ▸ Frequency hopping spread spectrum (FHSS) radio
> ▸ Infrared light

The two radio physical implementations operate in the 2.4GHz band and support 1Mbps and 2 Mbps data rates. The range is approximately 100 meters indoors and 1000 meters outdoors. Further work by the IEEE 802.11 group is being done on use of the 5GHz band and 5.5Mbps and 11Mbps data rates.

Within any 802.11 wireless LAN, there are three possible elements:

> ▸ One or more wireless stations
> ▸ One or more wireless access points
> ▸ One portal

Wireless stations are typically portable and usually battery-powered. An access point is used to provide a central coordination function for wireless LANs. In the presence of an access point, the wireless stations no longer communicate with each other directly. All communication is transmitted through the access point. Therefore, wireless stations no longer have to be within range of one another to communicate; they only have to be within range of an access point. The IEEE 802.11 standard doesn't define how access points communicate with each other or with a portal. A portal provides the services necessary to integrate a wireless LAN with a wired LAN.

Cable
Standards

Cable operators have long believed success in the high-speed data business would require that cable modems be interoperable, low-cost, and sold at retail like telephone modems and data network interface cards. This way, MSOs could avoid the capital burden associated with purchasing cable modems and leasing them back to subscribers, and consumers would be able to choose products from a variety of manufacturers.

The Institute of Electronic and Electrical Engineering's (IEEE) 802.14 Cable TV Media Access Control (MAC) and Physical (PHY) Protocol Working Group was formed in May 1994 by a number of vendors to develop international standards for data communications over cable.

Cable operators combined to jump-start the standards process in January 1996 when cable MSOs Comcast, Cox, TCI, and Time Warner, as a limited partnership Multimedia Cable Network System Partners Ltd. (MCNS), issued a request for proposals to publish a set of interface specifications for high-speed cable data. MCNS released its Data Over Cable System Interface Specification (DOCSIS) for cable modem products to vendors in March 1997. To date, more than 20 vendors have announced plans to build products based on the MCNS DOCSIS standard.

The differing cable modem specifications advocated by IEEE 802.14 and MCNS reflect the priorities of each organization. A vendor-driven group, IEEE 802.14 has focused on creating a future-proof standard based on industrial-strength technology. The MSO members of MCNS, on the other hand, are far more concerned with minimizing product costs and time to market. To achieve its objectives, MCNS sought to minimize technical complexity and develop a technology solution that was adequate for its members' needs.

At the physical layer, which defines modulation formats for digital signals, the IEEE and MCNS specifications are similar. The 802.14 specification supports the International Telecommunications Union's (ITU) J.83 Annex A, B, and C standards for 64/256 QAM modulation, providing a maximum 36Mbps of downstream throughput per 6MHz television channel.

The Annex A implementation of 64/256 QAM is the European DVB/DAVIC standard, Annex B is the North American standard supported by MCNS, while Annex C is the Japanese specification.

The proposed 802.14 upstream modulation standard is based on QPSK (quadrature phase shift keying) and 16 QAM, virtually the same as MCNS.

For the media access control (MAC), which sets the rules for network access by users, 802.14 has specified asynchronous transfer mode (ATM) as its default solution from the head-end to the cable modem. MCNS went a different route, using a scheme based on variable-length packets that favors the delivery of Internet Protocol (IP) traffic. Although the MCNS MAC is based on packets and the IEEE specifies fixed ATM cells, both cable modem solutions specify a 10Base-T Ethernet connection from the cable modem to the PC.

IEEE 802.14 committee members say they chose ATM because it best provides the Quality-of-Service (QoS) guarantees required for integrated delivery of video, voice, and data traffic to cable modem units. The group saw ATM as a long-term solution that would provide the flexibility to deliver more than just Internet access.

MCNS members didn't buy the argument. Cable operators are clearly focused on delivering high-speed Internet services to consumers and believed ATM would add unnecessary complexity and cost to cable modem systems. By supporting a variable-length packet implementation, MCNS members plan to capitalize on the favorable pricing associated with Ethernet and IP networking technology.

The standard for cable modems approved by ITU is called V.10, or DOCSIS for data over cable system interface specification. Standardized DOCSIS cable modems started shipping in limited quantities in the third and fourth quarters of 1998. Upstream frequencies are between 5MHz and 42MHz and downstream frequencies are between 50MHz and 750MHz.

Glossary

A

Adaptive Noise Reduction Filter "Intelligent" noise filtering that analyzes each pixel and applies an appropriate filter to remove the noise.

Adaptive Stream Management (ASM) Rules that describe a streamed datatype to RealSystem, helping it make intelligent decisions about how to deliver that datatype's packets efficiently and robustly.

Add/Drop Multiplexer (ADM) A multiplexer capable of extracting or inserting lower-bit-rate signal from a higher-bit-rate multiplexed signal without completely demultiplexing the signal.

All-Optical Network (AON) This term was first used to describe the world's first WDM network test bed that was architected and implemented at MIT's Lincoln Laboratory.

Alternate Datatypes QuickTime data tracks other than video and audio. Includes such datatypes as text and sprites.

Asynchronous The ability to send or receive calls independently and in any order.

Audio Services Device-independent, cross-platform features used by audio rendering plug-ins. The plug-in can use audio services without concern for the specifics of the audio hardware.

Authentication The process that performs password authorization by comparing username/password values sent in by a user against those stored in RealServer's encrypted password file.

B

Backchannel A communications channel from a client to RealServer. To stream data between server and client, RealSystem components use IRMAPacket objects. A file format plug-in, for example, prepares packets that RealServer streams to the client.

Bandwidth The carrying capacity or size of a communications channel; usually expressed in hertz (cycles per second) for analog circuits and in bits per second (bps) for digital circuits.

Basic Authorization A form of password authorization that uses unencrypted usernames and passwords.

Batch List A specific list of movies to be batch compressed.

Bit Rate The rate at which a presentation is streamed, usually expressed in kilobits per second (Kbps).

Blur A form of processing which blurs an image slightly, thereby minimizing subtle frame-to-frame differences and improving compression quality.

Bottlenecks Points in a system slower than the rest of the system, causing overall delays. In the Internet, bottlenecks are often caused by localized problems, such as overloaded switching complexes.

Broadcasting   Streaming the same data source, whether live or prerecorded, to multiple clients.

Buffering   Receiving and storing data before playing it back. The initial buffering time is called preroll. After *preroll,* excessive buffering may stall the presentation.

Burn   Changing a text or sprite track from its alternate datatype into an actual image in the video track.

C

Camcorder   Compact video recording system consisting of a transducer to convert light into electrical signals and a signal that copies the signal to tape.

Channel   A generic term for a communications path on a given medium; multiplexing techniques allow providers to put multiple channels over a single medium.

Cinepak   A commonly used QuickTime codec. Allows temporal and spatial compression, as well as data rate limiting.

Circuit Switching   A switching system that establishes a dedicated physical communications connection between end points, through the network, for the duration of the communications session; this is most often contrasted with packet switching in data communications transmissions.

Client   An application, such as RealPlayer, that receives RealSystem presentations from RealServer.

Clip   A media file within a *presentation.* Clips typically have an internal timeline, as with RealAudio and RealVideo.

CLUT   Abbreviation for color lookup table. See Palette.

Codec   Also called a compressor, a compression/decompression software component which translates video between its uncompressed form and the compressed form in which it is stored on media (disk, for example). The two most

commonly used video codecs for CD-ROM video are Cinepak and Indeo.

The list below outlines the main characteristics of codec standards:

- *H.261.* ITU (International Telecom Union) video coding standard from 1990
- *H.263.* Provisional videoconferencing ITU draft 1996
- *MPEG-1.* Targets CD-ROM at 1.5Mbps and includes DirectShow and QuickTime3
- *MPEG-2.* For all-digital transmission of broadcast TV and DVD—video at 4Mbps to 9Mbps
- *MPEG-3.* An audio standard
- *MPEG-4.* Targets very low bit rate for mobile multimedia, video phone, and video mail
- *MPEG-6.* Wireless transmission
- *MPEG-7.* Content information standard for information searches
- *MPEG-8.* Allows a four-dimensional description of objects

Color Depth   The possible range of colors that can be used in a movie. There are four main choices with video:

- gray scale—black, white, and shades of gray (8-bit)
- 256 colors (8-bit)
- thousands of colors (16-bit)
- millions of colors (24-bit) 256 colors uses a palette; none of the other color depths do.

COM   Component Object Model, a technology used by RealSystem for describing interfaces and exporting objects that implement those interfaces.

Common Class Factory   The IRMACommon-ClassFactory interface used by a component to create objects passed to other RealSystem components.

Container Datatype   A datatype, such as RealMedia File Format (RMFF) or ASF, that can contain other datatypes. Each container datatype is identified by a unique MIME type.

CPU-Intensive   Refers to the tendency of certain processes to use large amounts of processor time. CPU-intensive processes tend to slow the computer down while they are running.

D

Dark Fiber   Fiber-optic cables that have been laid, but have no illuminating signals in them.

Data Rate   The number of bytes per second used to represent a movie. Uncompressed VHS quality video is about 20 megabytes (MB) per second. Single-speed CD-ROM quality is about 100 kilobytes (K) per second, and double-speed CD-ROM quality is about 200K per second.

Data Rate Limited Codec   A codec which allows you to specify the desired target data rate. Cinepak and Indeo are rate-limited codecs.

Data Rate Limiting   The ability of a codec to compress a movie so that it fits within a target data rate.

Datatype   A single datatype, such as RealAudio, RealFlash, or MIDI, that can be rendered by a client. Each datatype is identified by a unique MIME type.

Deinterlace   A filter that removes the interlacing artifacts caused by the two fields-per-frame nature of video.

Delta Frames   Also called *difference frames,* smaller frames which contain only changes, based on key frames containing an entire image. Delta frames are used in temporal compression schemes.

Dense Wave Division Multiplexing (DWDM) An optical (analog) multiplexing technique used to increase the carrying capacity of a fiber network beyond what can currently be accomplished by time division multiplexing (TDM) techniques. Different wavelengths of light are used to transmit multiple streams of information along a single fiber with minimal interference. Dense WDM is a specific type of WDM wherein four or more wavelengths in the 15xx nanometer EDFA gain region are used multiplexed on a fiber. Typical DWDM systems available today for long-distance transmission offer 16 to 40 wavelengths at 2.5Gbps (OC-48 SONET or STM-16 SDH) or 10Gbps (OC-192 SONET or STM-64 SDH) per wavelength. Systems up to 240 wavelengths have been announced. DWDM has been mainly deployed as a point-to-point, static overlay to the optical TDM network to create *virtual fiber.* As such, DWDM is the precursor to optical networking. DWDM has drastically reduced the cost of transport by reducing the number of electrical regenerators required and sharing a single optical amplifier over multiple signals through the use of EDFAs.

DIGEST Authorization   A form of password authorization that uses encrypted usernames and passwords. Communication between RealServer and RealPlayer uses DIGEST Authorization.

Download   to copy a file from a server or network to your machine.

Dry Stream   A stream containing too little data for the RealPlayer to write to an audio device.

E

EMBED Tag   The HTML code that specifies how your movie will be presented within your Web page.

Encoder   An application that converts various types of media files into RealSystem clips ready to be streamed by a RealServer. RealProducer is a standard RealSystem encoder used to create RealVideo and RealAudio files or live streams.

Erbium-Doped Fiber Amplifier (EDFA)   A key enabling technology of DWDM, EDFAs allow the simultaneous amplification of multiple signals in the 15xx nanometer region, for example, multiple 2.5Gbps channels, in the optical domain. EDFAs drastically increase the spacings required between regenerators, which are costly network elements because they (1) require optical/electrical/optical conversion of a signal and (2) operate on a single digital signal, for example, a single SONET or SDH optical signal. DWDM systems using EDFAs can increase regenerator spacings of transmissions to 500–800 km at 2.5Gbps. EDFAs are much less expensive than regenerators and can typically be spaced 80–120 km apart at 2.5Gbps , depending on the quality of the fiber plant and the design goals of the DWDM system.

Event Handling   The process in which programs look for other system activity and respond to it.

Expert System   A computer program which has a deep understanding of a topic and can simulate a human expert, asking and answering questions and making decisions.

F

Fast Start   A feature of QuickTime that allows movies to be viewed inline in QuickTime-compatible browsers before the whole movie has been fully downloaded.

Fiber   The structure that guides light in a fiber-optic system.

"Flat Field" Noise   Slight differences in areas that should be identical, for example, blotchiness in the background behind titles. While often not objectionable to the human eye, *flat field* noise degrades compression and may be removed with the adaptive noise reduction filter.

Flattening   A final pass applied to a compressed movie, which ensures that there are no edits remaining in the movie and that data is laid out in a completely linear fashion. It also ensures that the sound is interleaved properly.

Fps   Frames per second, a measure of the frame rate.

Frame   One single still image among the many that make up a movie.

Frame Duration Data Rate Limiting   A method of limiting data rate by increasing frame duration to meet the desired data rate target.

Frame Rate   The number of frames per second in video. NTSC video (standard American Television) is approximately 30 frames per second (fps). Computers commonly use 12fps to 15fps.

G

G.723   A lossy 8:1 audio codec that works with 16-bit audio. Not available for QuickTime at the time this book was created.

Gamma   The curve that describes how the middle tones of your images appear. Often incorrectly referred to as *"brightness"* and/or *"contrast,"* gamma is a nonlinear function. Changing the value of the gamma affects middle tones while leaving the white and black of the image alone. Used to compensate for differences between Macintosh and PC monitors.

H

H.263   A video codec designed for low data rate videoconferencing.

Header   A chunk of data, delivered from a source to a rendering plug-in when first connecting to a stream, usually used to initialize the stream.

HTML   Hypertext Markup Language. The programming language the World Wide Web uses to display pages, links to other pages, and so on.

HTTP Playback   A reasonable method for sending short clips from a Web server using the HTTP protocol. HTTP streaming does not support all the datatypes of, and is not as robust as, RTSP streaming, however.

Hypernavigation   Occurs when a rendering plug-in directs the client to display a URL at a specified time in a stream. When the plug-in issues a hypernavigation request, the default Web browser opens.

I

IMA   A high-quality audio codec which gives 4 to 1 (4:1) compression. IMA requires 16-bit samples. Based on the standard created by the Interactive Multimedia Association.

Indeo   A codec developed by Intel, which allows temporal and spatial compression as well as data rate limiting. Often produces higher quality video than Cinepak, but doesn't handle some source movies well and is significantly more CPU-intensive.

Inline   Within the browser page, as opposed to needing to be viewed with an external application.

Interface   A collection of related functions exposed by an object and accessed through a unique interface ID.

Interlacing   Horizontal lines in areas of fast movement caused by the fact that a video frame is made up of two separate fields, each 1/60th of a second apart.

Internally Data Rate Limiting Codecs   Codecs such as Cinepak that can limit the data rate of the movies they compress.

Internet   The coolest and biggest time-sink ever invented by humanity.

Intranet   Large private network, often in a corporate environment.

ISDN   A moderately fast connection to the Internet. Theoretical throughput is between 5KBps and12KBps depending on details of the configuration.

K

KBps   Kilobytes per second (often refered to as "Kps"). Specified in this manual as "KBps" to avoid confusion with a different usage of "Kps" or "Kbps" by the telecommunications industry.

Key Frame   In temporal compression, an image which is the basis for determining which changes in sequential difference frames need to be stored.

kHz   Kilohertz, the audio sample rate; a measure of how accurately (frequently) sound is sampled. Higher sample rates yield better sound quality with better high end response but larger files.

Kps   Kilobytes per second, a measure of the data rate. See KBps.

L

Lambda (l)   An optical wavelength.

LAN   Local area network, a network that connects computers within a geographically small region, often within just one building.

Lightpath   Analogous to virtual circuits in the ATM world, a lightpath is a virtual circuit in the optical domain that could consist of multiple spans, each using a different physical wavelength for transmission of information across an optical network.

Local Area Network   See LAN.

M

Mean Filter   Replaces a pixel with the average value of its surroundings. Applying a uniform mean filter blurs the image.

Median Filter   Replaces a pixel with the most typical value of its surroundings, while ignoring extreme values. Applying a uniform median filter tends to remove small details.

MIDI   Musical Instrument Digital Interface. A file format that is used to instruct electronic instruments how to play a piece of music.

MIME Type   Multipurpose Internet mail extension. A datatype specification originally used for mail messages and now generalized to identify datatypes delivered over the Internet.

Modem   An incredibly slow way to drink from the information firehose.

More Info Triangle   The little triangle-shaped buttons that rotate to reveal more information. Similar to the little triangles in the Finder that let you view the contents of a folder without first opening it. Clicking on them once reveals more information; clicking again hides the extra information.

Movie Expert   An expert system which creates and double checks compression settings.

Multimedia   A new art/communication form which merges sound, graphics, and video. Often causes its creators to go insane and/or broke.

N

Network Services   Services that provide cross-platform methods for managing network communications. Any server-side or client-side RealSystem component can use Network Services to create TCP or UDP connections for reading and writing data. Network Services also provides interfaces that let components resolve DNS host names and listen for TCP connections on specified ports.

NMA   Network Monitoring and Analysis (NMA) is a fault management system used by RBOCs to perform network monitoring and surveillance. There are two types of the NMA system, facilities management and switch management. NMA is capable of performing event correlation to determine root cause, create trouble tickets, and track status of outstanding tickets. NMA relies on topology information to perform event correlation. This information can come from TIRKS (via NSDB) or it can be manually entered.

Noise   Any part of a signal which contains unnecessary data. In audio, noise makes the sound harder to hear. In video, it can appear as static or stray pixels. Noise generally interferes with compression.

Noise Reduction   Reducing the variance between pixels with filters, such as blur, mean, or median. Uniform noise reduction applies one filter equally to each pixel. Adaptive noise reduction applies different filters to different kinds of noise.

O

Object   A unique instance of a data structure defined according to the template provided by its class. Each object has its own values for the variables belonging to its class and can respond to the methods defined by its class.

Opaque Optical Networks   The current vision of the optical network whereby conversions from the optical to the electrical and back to the optical domain are required periodically. Such O/E/O conversions are required in order to retime the signal in the digital domain, clean up signal impairments, allow fault isolation, and provide performance monitoring (particularly of signal bit error rate).

Optical Add/Drop Multiplexer (OADM) Also called a wavelength add/drop multiplexer, or WADM. An optical network element that lets specific channels of a multichannel optical transmission system be dropped and/or added without affecting the through signals (the signals that are to be transported through the network node). OADMs, like the electrical ADM counterparts, can simplify networks and lower the cost of network nodes by eliminating unnecessary demultiplexing of through signals.

Optical Amplifier   A device that increases the optical signal strength without an optical to electrical to optical conversion process.

Optical Carrier (OC)   Optical carrier, a designation used as a prefix denoting the optical carrier level of SONET data standards. OC-1/STS-1, OC-3/STS-3, OC-12, OC-48, and OC-192 denote transmission standards for fiber-optic data transmission in SONET frames at data rates of 51.84Mbps, 155.52Mbps, 622.08Mbps, 2.48832Gbps, and 9.95Gbps, respectively.

Optical Carrier (OC-x)   This is base unit found in the SONET hierarchy; the x represents increments of 51.84Mbps (so, OC-1 is 51.84Mbps; OC-3 is 155Mbps, and OC-12 is 622Mbps). See also synchronous optical network.

Optical Cross-Connect (OXC)   Also referred to as OCS. An optical network element that provides for incoming optical signals to be switched to any one of a number of output ports. Some OXCs connect fibers containing multichannel optical signals to the input parts, demultiplex the signals, switch the signals, and recombine/remultiplex the signals to the output ports. Other OXCs connect fibers with single channel optical signals to the input and output ports and simply switch between the two. OXCs can have optical or electrical switch matrices. The differentiator as defined by RHK between OXCs and DCS, Digital Cross-Connect Systems, is one of interface rate and switch fabric granularity. DCS interfaces traditionally have been electrical, and matrix granularity has been less than 50Mbps (DS3 or STS-1). OC-3/STM-1 or OC12/STM-4 interfaces are now available for DCS, but matrix granularity remains at less than 155Mbps. OXCs, in contrast, interconnect at the optical line rate of DWDM and ON elements (for example, OC-48) and have a switch fabric granularity to match (for example, OC-48).

Optical Network   The optical network will provide all basic network requirements in the optical layer; namely, capacity, scalability, reliability, survivability, and manageability. Today, the wavelength is the fundamental object of the optical network. Currently, basic network requirements can be met through a combination of the optical transport layer (DWDM today), that provides scalability and capacity beyond 10Gbps, and the SONET/SDH transport layer, which provides the reliability, survivability, and manageability needed for public networks. The long-term vision of an all-optical network is of a transparent optical network where signals are never converted to the electrical domain between network ingress and egress. The more practical implementation for the near term will be of an opaque optical network, that is, one that works to minimize but still includes optical/electrical/optical conversion. Optical network elements will include terminals, dynamic add/drop multiplexers, and dynamic optical cross-connects.

Optical Networking   The natural evolution of optical transport from a DWDM-based point-to-point transport technology to a more dynamic, intelligent networking technology. Optical networking will use any one of a number of optical multiplexing schemes (for example, WDM, OCDMA, OTDMA) to multiplex multiple channels of information onto a fiber and will add intelligence to the optical transport layer that will provide the reliability, survivability, and manageability today provided by SONET/SDH. Optical networking will enable

the creation, configuration, and management of lightpaths within the optical domain. A key goal of the optical network over today's SONET/SDH-based network is to bring the cost of network nodes down by reducing the number of network elements required and by increasing the granularity of core network operations, such as switching and routing to the wavelength level (for example, to 2.5Gbps OC-48).

Optical Networking Market   The market for optical networking products. This emerging market will grow out of the market for DWDM and SONET/SDH transport, switching, and management equipment.

Optical Network Management Products   An emerging category of optical networking software products that operate at the granularity of a lightpath and that provide provisioning and management of lightpaths in the network at a minimum. These products will be developed both by equipment vendors, as offerings integrated with transport and switching products, and by third-party network management software vendors. This product class will include network and element management systems and will generally be required by service providers to stand alone as well as integrate with existing operations support systems.

Optical Switching Products   An emerging category of optical networking products that operate at the granularity of a lightpath and that provide the following functionality at a minimum: performance monitoring and management, restoration and rerouting enabled by interswitch signaling, wavelength translation, the establishment of end-to-end lightpaths, and delivery of customer services. OXCs are included in this category.

Optical Transport Products   An emerging category of optical networking products that operate at the granularity of a lightpath and that provide the following functionality at a minimum: performance monitoring and management, restoration and rerouting, wavelength translation, and delivery of customer services.

OADMs and DWDM terminals are included in this category.

Output Movie Compressed video ready for playback on the target machine.

P

Packet   A chunk of data delivered from a source to a rendering plug-in at a particular time during the playback of a stream.

Packet Loss   The percentage of packets dropped during a RealSystem streaming presentation.

Palette   The list of colors which are used in an 8-bit color movie. There are several standard palettes, such as the Macintosh System palette. Often referred to as a color lookup table, or simply color table. Often abbreviated CLUT.

Pixel   One dot in a video image. A typical computer screen is 640 pixels wide and 480 pixels tall. Digital video movies are often 320 pixels wide and 240 pixels tall.

Pixelization   When the pixels that make up an image get exaggerated or enlarged. Makes the image look chunky or grainy.

Plug-In   A program or file that adds functionality to another program.

PNA   A proprietary control protocol used by RealServer versions 3.0 through 5.0 to communicate with RealPlayer. RealServer G2 and RealPlayer G2 use the Real-Time Streaming Protocol (RTSP) instead of PNA but support PNA for backward compatibility.

Preroll   The amount of data in milliseconds that a rendering plug-in requests before it receives its first-time synchronization notification. The actual preroll is always equal to or greater than the value requested by the plug-in.

Presentation   One or more clips that are streamed from a server to a client.

Q

QuickTime Alternate Datatypes   See Alternate Datatypes.

QuickTime Music   An alternate datatype that is very similar to MIDI. Allows music to be stored as instructions rather than digitized sounds and then played back with defined instruments within QuickTime. QuickTime Music tracks are much smaller than digitized versions of the same music.

R

RealAudio   A RealSystem datatype for streaming highly compressed audio over a network.

RealFlash   A RealSystem clip-type for streaming Shockwave Flash animation along with a soundtrack.

RealMedia   A blanket term used to refer to RealSystem G2 and the various "real" datatypes that it can stream.

RealMedia Architecture (RMA)   A client/server system developed by RealNetworks that gives content creators the ability to stream any datatype.

RealMedia File Format (RMFF)   A standard tagged file format that uses four-character codes to identify file elements. These codes are 32-bit, represented by a sequence of one to four ASCII alphanumeric characters, padded on the right with space characters. The datatype for four-character codes is FOURCC.

RealPix   A clip-type (file extension .rp) for streaming still images over a network. It uses a mark-up language for creating special effects, such as fades and zooms.

RealPlayer   RealSystem client designed to play multimedia presentations streamed by RealSystem G2 or a Web server.

RealServer G2   Server software developed by RealNetworks and based on the RealSystem G2 architecture. It provides robust streaming of many datatypes to RealSystem clients.

RealSystem   The system for streaming clips such as RealAudio and RealVideo over a network.

RealSystem Client   An application such as RealPlayer that consists of a top-level client and the client core. The top-level client supplies the user interface, communicating to the core and rendering plug-ins. The core handles data transport and provides features such as audio services.

RealText   A clip-type (file extension .rt) for streaming text over a network. It uses a mark-up language for formatting text.

RealVideo   A RealSystem datatype for streaming video.

Registry   The RealServer property registry. This is separate from the Windows registry.

Remote Broadcast Library   A library of methods that ties an encoding application to Real-Server's broadcast plug-in for live broadcast. The encoding application passes encoded data to the library, which then connects to a Real-System broadcast plug-in. The plug-in delivers the stream to RealServer, which broadcasts it.

RSVP   An Internet Engineering Task Force (IETF) proposed standard for requesting defined Quality of Service levels over IP networks such as the Internet. The protocol was designed to allow the assignment of priorities to streaming applications, such as audio and video, which generate continuous traffic that requires predictable delivery. RSVP works by permitting an application transmitting data over a routed network to request and receive a given level of bandwidth. Two classes of reservation are defined: a controlled load reservation provides service approximating "best effort" service under unloaded conditions; a guaranteed service reservation provides service that guarantees both bandwidth and delay.

RTP   Real-Time Protocol (RTP) is the Internet standard protocol (RFC 1889, 1890) for the transport of real-time data, including audio and video. RTP consists of a data and a control part called *RTCP*. The data part of RTP is a thin protocol providing support for applications with real-time properties such as continuous media (for example, audio and video), including timing reconstruction, loss detection, security, and content identification. RTCP provides support for

real-time conferencing of groups of any size within an intranet. This support includes source identification and support for gateways like audio and video bridges as well as multicast-to-unicast translators. It offers Quality of Service feedback from receivers to the multicast group as well as support for the synchronization of different media streams. None of the commercial streaming products uses RTP (Real-Time Transport Protocol), a relatively new standard designed to run over UDP. Initially designed for video at T1 or higher bandwidths, it promises more efficient multimedia streaming than UDP. Streaming vendors are expected to adopt RTP, which is used by the Mbone.

RTSP   Real-Time Streaming Protocol, a protocol jointly developed by RealNetworks and Netscape Communications for streaming multimedia over IP networks. RTSP works with established protocols such as RTP and HTTP and can be implemented on client and server across multiple operating system platforms, including Macintosh, Windows, and UNIX.

Rule   A set of properties and, optionally, an expression that helps RealServer transmit a group of packets intelligently. Each packet is associated with one rule. Rules are part of Adaptive Stream Management (ASM).

S

Sample Rate   The number of samples per second used for audio. A higher sample rate means higher quality audio and handles higher frequency sound better. The two most common sample rates are 11.025kHz and 22.050kHz.

Sample Size   The accuracy with which a sound sample is recorded. Generally, sample size is 8-bit or 16-bit. The latter is more accurate and provides more dynamic range, but takes up more storage space.

SDH   Synchronous Digital Hierarchy (SDH) is the European version of the SONET standard with two major differences: (1) the terminology, (2) the basic line rate in SDH that is equivalent to that of the SONET OC-3/STS-3 rate (that is,

155.52 Mbps). In contrast to the existing Plesiochronous Digital Hierarchy (PDH), SDH allows direct access to tributary signals without demultiplexing the composite signal. As a result, network node costs are reduced because direct multiplexing is cheaper than step-by-step multiplexing. Furthermore, SDH supports advanced operation, administration, and maintenance (OA&M) by dedicating several embedded channels for this purpose. SDH also supports a concatenation mechanism so that lower rate payloads can be combined to form higher rate payloads. The frame in SDH is called the Synchronous Transport Module-1 (STM-1). It consists of 2,430 bytes represented as a 9-row-by-270-column structure similar to the frame in SONET. STM-N frames support line rates of Nx155.52 Mbps. The compatibility between SDH and SONET allows for internetworking at the Administrative Unit-4 (AU-4) level. SDH can support broadband services, such as broadband integrated services digital network (B-ISDN).

Server   A computer that other computers connect to for the purpose of retrieving information. In this book, generally used to mean the computer that hosts your WWW page.

Settings Group   A name for all of the parameters in the Advanced Settings window. Settings Groups can be saved, modified, and deleted.

Site   An object that receives rendered data for display. The client core supplies a site, and the rendering plug-in registers as a site user. The plug-in can then send data without providing platform-specific commands for data display.

SMIL   Synchronized Multimedia Integration Language (SMIL) is a simple, but powerful XML compliant mark-up language that coordinates when and how multimedia files play. A SMIL file (file extension .smi) can be created with any text editor or word processor than saves output as plain text with line breaks. An example of a simple SMIL file that lists multiple media files played in sequence is shown in the template. RealSystem G2 is a whole new media delivery

system with the addition of two new datatypes (RealText and RealPix) in a system that supports SMIL.

Source   A file or live source of data, represented by a single URL, consisting of one or more streams of data.

Source Movie   The original movie to be compressed.

Spatial Compression   Compression of images by elimination of duplicate storage of similar areas within one image. For example, a field of blue in a picture would be stored as one large blue area rather than many individual blue pixels.

Splitter   A device that creates multiple optical signals from a single optical signal.

Sprites   An alternate QuickTime datatype that is made up of small graphic elements (sprites) that have position and time information associated with them. A bouncing ball is a good example of a sprite track.

Stray Pixel Noise   Noise that appears as random pixels which are significantly different from the surrounding pixels. Commonly caused by low-quality sources (such as VHS), multiple duplications, low-light compensation, and so on. May be removed with the adaptive noise reduction filter.

Streaming   Refers to data that is transferred in real time. In this manual, streaming is used to refer to technologies like VDO that match the bandwidth of the video signal to your connection so that you always see the video in real time.

Streamliner   An Apple utility that converts QuickTime files to fast-start QuickTime. Also called Internet Movie Tool.

SureStream   A technology that allows switching to a lower bandwidth encoding in a RealAudio or RealVideo clip to compensate for network congestion. Available only in RealSystem G2.

Synchronous Digital Hierarchy (SDH) The international standard for transmitting digital information over optical networks. Term used by ITU to refer to SONET.

Synchronous Optical Network (SONET)
Standards for transmitting digital information over optical networks. Fiber-optic transmission rates range from 51.84Mbps to 9.95Gbps. It defines a physical interface, optical line rates known as Optical Carrier (OC) signals, frame formats, and an OAM&P (Operations, Administration, Maintenance, and Provisioning) protocol. The base rate is known as OC-1 and runs at 51.84Mbps. Higher rates are a multiple of this, such that OC-12 is equal to 622Mbps (12 times 51.84Mbps).

T

Tbps Terabit per second (1 trillion bits per second), an information carrying capacity measure used for high-speed optical data systems.

TCP HTTP (Hypertext Transfer Protocol) uses Transmission Control Protocol (TCP) as the protocol for reliable document transfer. If packets are delayed or damaged, TCP will effectively stop traffic until either the original packets or backup packets arrive.

Temporal Compression Compression of movies by elimination of duplicate storage of similar areas across sequential images. For example, if several frames in a row have almost identical details, the details need only be stored once.

Temporal Slider An undocumented feature of the compression dialog that may affect some codecs. To access the *Temporal* slider, hold down "option" while leaving the cursor over the *Quality* slider and wait until the preview redraws.

Time Division Multiplexing (TDM) An electrical (digital) multiplexing technique used to allow multiple streams of information to share the same transmission media. For transmission at 155Mbps or above, the electrical TDM signal is typically converted to an optical signal for transport. SONET (Synchronous Optical NETwork) and SDH (Synchronous Digital Hierarchy) standards in North America and the rest of the world, respectively, set the bit rates, frame formats, and other physical and operational characteristics for these optical signals.

TIRKS The Trunks Integrated Record Keeping System (TIRKS) is used by RBOCs to track facility assignments and equipment inventory. TIRKS is used in the circuit order fulfillment process. It helps the RBOC determine if facilities exist to provide service, track order completion, and perform inventory planning. TIRKS interfaces to other systems via the Network and Service Database (NSDB) to provide information to other Telcordia systems to enable flow through automation.

Top-Level Client The part of a RealSystem client that supplies the user interface, communicating to the core and other components such as rendering plug-ins through RealSystem interfaces.

Transparent Optical Networks The original vision of the all-optical network as a network in which a signal is transported from source to destination entirely in the optical domain. After ingress into the network, the signal is never converted to the electrical domain for analog operations, such as amplification and filtering or any other purpose. Signals are amplified, shaped, demultiplexed, remultiplexed, and switched in the optical domain with no regard to the digital content of the signal, for example, bit rate, modulation scheme, or protocol. Digital transparency implies transparency to digital characteristics such as bit rate, format, and protocol. Digital transparency is misleading because analog signal characteristics such as optical power budget are extremely dependent on a digital signal's bit rate and format. Similarly, though modulation transparency implies transparency to whether a signal's modulation is baseband or broadband, amplitude, phase, or frequency, in truth optical power budget will depend strongly on the modulation scheme used. Transparent optical networks are limited in two ways: (1) by analog signal defects (for example, gain tilt, ASE noise, chromatic dispersion, and crosstalk) that accumulate over distance, and (2) by the difficulty of monitoring performance and isolating faults as a signal traverses a network.

U

UDP   User Datagram Protocol (UDP) is the alternative to TCP. RealPlayer, StreamWorks, and VDOLive use this approach. (RealPlayer gives you a choice of UDP or TCP, but the former is preferred.) UDP forsakes TCP's error correction and allows packets to drop out if they are late or damaged. When this happens, you will hear or see a dropout, but the stream will continue. Despite the prospect of dropouts, this approach is arguably better for continuous media delivery. If broadcasting live events, everyone will get the same information simultaneously. One disadvantage to the UDP approach is that many network firewalls block UDP information. While Progressive Networks, Xing, and VDOnet offer work-arounds for client sites (revert to TCP), some users simply may not be able to access UDP files.

Upload   To move a file from your computer to your server.

V

Variable Frame Length Movie   A movie that contains frames that are not all of equal duration.

VDP   RTP with demand resend VDP improves the reliability of the data stream by creating two channels between the client and server. One is a control channel the two machines use to coordinate what information is being sent across the network, and the other channel is for the streaming data. When configured in Java, this protocol, like HTTP, is invisible to the network and can stream through firewalls.

Video Fades   Fades begin a movie with a solid color (such as black) and blend into the beginning of the movie and/or blend the end of a movie back to a solid color.

Volume   A hard disk drive, floppy diskette, CD-ROM, or other storage media.

W

WAN   Wide area network, a data communications facility involving two or more computers with the computers situated at different sites. (See also LAN and Internetwork.)

Wavelength   A measure of the color of the light for which the performance of the fiber has been optimized. It is a length stated in nanometers (nm) or micrometers (um).

Wavelength Division Multiplexer   A passive device that combines light signals with different wavelengths on different fibers onto a single fiber. The wavelength division demultiplexer performs the reverse function.

Wavelength Translation   A function of some OADMs and OXCs whereby a signal entering the network element (NE) on one physical wavelength leaves the network element on a different physical wavelength. This signal could be part of a single lightpath. NEs available today can do fixed wavelength translation, meaning two physical wavelengths used are predetermined and cannot typically be changed without human intervention at the NE.

Web-Ready   A term used to refer to movies that are optimized for distribution on the World Wide Web. Movies must be flattened for cross-platform playback, fast start, and not contain unsupported datatypes. Web-ready movies should also have a low enough data rate that most target users can watch them without unreasonable waiting.

WWW   World Wide Web, the graphical subset of the Internet.

X

XML   EXtensible Markup Language (XML) separates content from format, thus letting the browser decide how and where content gets displayed. XML is not a language, but a system for defining other languages so that they understand their vocabulary.

INDEX

CD-ROM Warranty

Addison Wesley warrants the enclosed disc to be free of defects in materials and faulty workmanship under normal use for a period of ninety days after purchase. If a defect is discovered in the disc during this warranty period, a replacement disc can be obtained at no charge by sending the defective disc, postage prepaid, with proof of purchase to:

Editorial Department
Addison Wesley Professional
75 Arlington Street, Suite 300
Boston, MA 02116

After the ninety-day period, a replacement disc will be sent upon receipt of the defective disc and a check or money order for $10.00, payable to Addison Wesley.

Addison Wesley makes no warranty or representation, either expressed or implied, with respect to this software, its quality, performance, merchantability, or fitness for a particular purpose. In no event will Addison Wesley, its distributors, or dealers be liable for direct, indirect, special, incidental, or consequential damages arising out of the use or inability to use the software. The exclusion of implied warranties is not permitted in some states. Therefore, the above exclusion may not apply to you. This warranty provides you with specific legal rights. There may be other rights that you may have that vary from state to state. The contents of this CD-ROM are intended for personal use only.

More information and updates are available at:
http://www.awl.com/cseng/titles/0-201-70314-9